COMMISSION OF THE EUROPEAN COMMUNIT

Money, economic policy and Europe

Tommaso PADOA-SCHIOPPA

Preface by François-Xavier ORTOLI

THE EUROPEAN PERSPECTIVES SERIES
BRUSSELS

This publication was prepared outside the Commission of the European Communities and is intended as a contribution to public debate on money, economic policy and Europe. It does not necessarily reflect the opinion of the Commission.

This publication is also available in:

DE ISBN 92-825-5145-8
FR ISBN 92-825-4541-5
IT ISBN 92-825-5146-6

Cataloguing data can be found at the end of this publication

Luxembourg: Office for Official Publications of the European Communities, 1985

ISBN 92-825-4410-9

Catalogue number: CB-40-84-286-EN-C

Printed in Greece

Preface

The changing pattern of international economic relations over the last few decades has witnessed three largely interrelated phenomena:

(i) The most important is the global internationalization of economic relations. This trend began with the opening up of our economies following the political changes that took place in the aftermath of the war, and it gathered pace with the efforts, some more methodical, some more ambitious than others, to establish an 'open' economic order – witness GATT and the IMF, the BIS, the OEEC followed by the OECD, the ECSC followed by the EEC, and so on. Although it was accompanied by unprecedented structural changes in our economies, and although with hindsight we can see that it was on a considerable scale, the process was continuous and on the whole painless: helped by a favourable environment of growth, it took place so smoothly that its effects to some extent went unnoticed by governments, business and the general public. Our countries' continuing power to maintain barriers, illusory though they often are, has obscured understanding of the present real degree of economic interdependence and of the resulting limitations on freedom of action. There is no lack of examples of reactions illustrating this kind of misapprehension: exchange controls often continue to be applied as if they had lost none of their effect. Similarly, the protectionist weapon is often wielded regardless of the fact that it has become double-edged and that both specialization at the various stages of production and the internationalization of markets have made our economies, even the largest of them, much more sensitive to the outside world. Lastly, politicians, employers and unions still adopt positions based on a misconception of the room for manoeuvre actually available to each of our countries.

(ii) The second phenomenon is that in the fairly recent past (the last 10 years at the most) the world economy seems to have entered a period of disruptions, which are themselves largely bound up with positions of dominance. Arguments will no doubt continue for a long time on the origins of occurrences whose effects are concentrated in the most sensitive areas of international economic relations. This is true of energy, with changes in relative prices on such a scale as to force our economies to make adjustments of several percentage points of GDP in their use of resources: in the last 10 years, the Community's net energy bill has increased from 1.4% to 3.7% of GDP. The same has been the case in the monetary area, whose day-by-day history has almost reached the point of caricature: the real effective exchange rate of

the US dollar fell by 33% from 1970 to 1975 and has appreciated by more than 35% between 1980 and today. Such fluctuations are irrational in trade terms, but since they pertain to the 'world currency' they heighten its predominance, and nowadays any decision involving interaction between the United States budget, monetary policy and financial market has a very direct influence on short-term decisions and economic calculations.

(iii) *The third phenomenon, which is more recent but full of implications for the future, is the 'shrinking' of the international financial world, its new compactness and homogeneity. The speeding up of financial transactions of whatever amount, lower transaction costs, the very rapid dissemination of information and the ever-increasing sophistication of international communications have brought into being a new, wide and efficient international financial system. This development will undoubtedly continue to grow, and the international network of financial operations will make the independence of each of our economies even more of an illusion and could increase the short-term variability of exchange rates.*

The globalization of economic relations, the multiplicity of disruptions and the growing sophistication of financial transactions are to a large extent at the root of current international monetary problems and the increasing emergence of new sorts of difficulty stemming essentially from the importance of outside influences in the economic management of our countries. They are also to a large extent at the root of European efforts to develop an 'island' of monetary stability in the Community.

The articles appearing in this collection, which were written by Tommaso Padoa-Schioppa during the time when he was the Director-General for Economic and Financial Affairs at the Commission of the European Communities, deal with this set of problems, focusing systematically, through rigorous analysis, on their economic policy aspects.

The first part of the collection deals with the efforts made in recent years to strengthen the Community's monetary integration. For Europe has been particularly vulnerable to the effects of the three phenomena described above, because of its openness to international trade and also because, wanting in financial integration, the Community has seen each Member State trying separately, without any real success, to protect itself against unpredictable external influences. Setting up the European Monetary System in 1979 and devoting every effort to secure and strengthen its operation are a very far-sighted political response as well as a fundamental reaction to preserve the Community as a harmonious economic whole. Padoa-Schioppa's articles on this subject are an important contribution, and they carry a particular stamp of authority, their author having been from the outset associated at the highest level with the establishment of the system. Three particular aspects seem to me to have been quite rightly emphasized:

(i) *The EMS is the embodiment of a determination to preserve all that has been achieved so far in the Community and at the same time an essential pre-condition for any future development; in this respect, as Padoa-Schioppa rightly points out, the benefits of the EMS must be assessed not only in terms of monetary stability, but also bearing in mind that it has allowed the advantages of economic integration in a broader sense to be maintained.*

(ii) The EMS has gradually become a form of collective discipline which its critics frequently disregard: what cannot be emphasized too strongly is how the regular discussions of economic policy and the public statements made (and their consequences), for example on indexation or public finance disequilibria, have developed into a collective economic policy exercise which has played an essential role in the adoption of the economic policy measures made necessary by undue divergences in economic performances.

(iii) The creation of the ECU has led gradually to a form of European monetary identity. Such is certainly the case with the public ECU used between central banks. And it is also the case with the private ECU, which has been favourably received by financial markets in a way that was never imagined.

The second part of the collection deals with international monetary problems. Enlightened future historians looking back on our present-day economic relations will no doubt characterize the first half of the 1980s as being permeated by as it were a quasi-collective attitude (admittedly led by the world's main economic and monetary power) of avoidance or resignation in the face of the importance of exchange rates in the contemporary world economy. The historians will also note that international economic cooperation was being drained of substance during the period and that this trend involved the collective responsibility of the major economic powers. There are disequilibria which, once they have reached a certain point, become difficult to rectify: the movement of the exchange rate for the dollar from 1975 to 1984 is a glaring example. What can be done to correct real maladjustments (distortions in consumption habits, misallocation of productive resources, disproportionate efforts to contain excessive imported inflation, etc.) induced by exchange rates that are out of all touch with reality? All these questions, quite apart from theoretical aspects, basically spring from the fact that the industrialized countries have so far refused to set up the means of ensuring real collective management of present-day economic and monetary interdependence: in this respect, the article which Padoa-Schioppa wrote in 1981 on the problems posed by interdependence in a multipolar world seems to me to be one of the most searching and important contributions written on this subject.

The last part of the collection deals with the general problem which the growing interaction of international economic and monetary relations poses for national policies and institutions. Here, the problem of outside influences which is increasingly confronting our countries, including the larger ones, seems to me to reflect the increasing loss of substance in international economic relations. Padoa-Schioppa shows with particular clarity the limitations of the ***laissez-faire*** *solution in international economic and monetary relations, easy and tempting as it is to do so.*

These clear, elegant, yet densely packed texts will gain a wide readership in universities and among researchers and specialists in international affairs. More than that, they de-

serve to be studied by all those who manage economic and monetary affairs, since it is rare to come across such expert and lucid first-hand accounts.

Padoa-Schioppa's writings bear the mark of a mind that is 'political' in the highest sense of the term: on the basis of a perspicacious analysis of the facts, he draws out their deepest interrelationships, and at the same time, as he identifies the constraints and selects the options, he gives scope to a determination to chart and pursue a course which is ambitious yet prudent.

François-Xavier ORTOLI
Vice-President of the Commission
of the European Communities

Brussels, October 1984

Contents

Introduction

This book brings together papers and articles written between 1979 and 1983, the years during which I served in the Commission of the European Communities in Brussels. The only exception is the article 'Policy cooperation and the EMS experience' which was written in 1984. Minor changes have been made to delete parts relevant only to the occasions on which the papers were first presented and a brief introduction to each helps put them in perspective.

These writings owe much more to the European Communities than just the title of the series ('European Perspectives') under which the Commission has generously decided to publish them. The seam from which the ideas presented in these pages have been extracted has been immensely enriched by contributions that I still recall with gratitude and nostalgia.

First, the institutional environment. The unique feature of the Community, the one that makes it profoundly different from any other system of national or international public institutions, and simultaneously so strong and so weak, is its intrinsically dynamic nature. It is an institutional system that has been designed to develop and that is expected to progress. This may seem a contradiction in terms since institutions are normally considered to be unchanging – but it reflects the true spirit of the Community. This contradiction is a never-ending source of ideas, problems, doubts and insights because it makes one see such familiar realities as money and economic policy from a new angle and in a new light. It makes what we have been trained to consider as given look variable, it continuously provides terms of comparison that sweep away established ideas, it makes the long run appear almost short.

Second, the people. The Community institutions and the city of Brussels play a special role in establishing contacts between persons with similar problems and interests, whose paths would not otherwise cross. This is true for many fields of interest, but it has a special significance in the case of people sharing what is called the 'European fibre'. With them there is not only an intellectual interaction but a conspiracy of beliefs, hopes, wills, and action. It is in this sense that I am especially grateful for the invaluable inspiration and encouragement that I received from N. Andreatta, M. Camdessus, P. Caron, J. Delors, M. Emerson, J.Y. Haberer, L. Gleske, A. Jozzo, M. Kohnstamm, K. McMahon, F.X. Ortoli, F.M. Pandolfi, J.M. Soutou, R. Triffin, M. Wegner, and many other friends and associates.

Rome, January 1985. Tommaso PADOA-SCHIOPPA

PART ONE

European monetary issues

CHAPTER I

The European Monetary Fund: topics for discussion (1979)

This paper was prepared in December 1979 when the EMS had been in existence for about six months. It was presented to the 'Second international seminar on European economic and monetary union' organized by Robert Triffin in Geneva on the theme 'The European Monetary Fund: internal planning and external relations'.

In the charter of the EMS, the so called 'Brussels Resolution', Member States had agreed that a 'final' system would be established within two years and at the time this paper was written there was considerable discussion as to what changes should be made to the initial design.

As it well known, the rendez-vous *with the final phase was not kept and formally the system is still in its provisional format.* De facto, *there have been important developments, as I tried to explain in my later paper, 'The significance of the EMS', which is presented below. I still hold the view, expressed in 1979, that '. . . there are good reasons for thinking that the EMS is not at a stable equilibrium' and therefore believe that institutional changes will eventually be needed. At that point we might go back to the work done during the first two years of the system, when the idea of a definitive design was still politically alive.*

'All too often I have come up against the limits of mere coordination: it makes for discussion, but not decision. In circumstances where union is necessary, it fails to change relations between men and between countries.'

Jean Monnet

1. Introduction

This paper will present little more than what used to be called 'an annotated agenda'. It will do so because many problems need more discussion and clarification and because its purpose is only to introduce a debate.

The main concern of the following pages is thus not so much to offer solutions as to provide the framework for finding them. This, in turn, requires both certainty that the proper headings for a discussion on the Fund have been correctly identified and that the focus is placed at the appropriate level of generality: for instance, a certain number of specific questions that are currently discussed in this area, such as intervention rules, criteria for realignments, etc. do not necessarily need to be finally decided in their content in order to establish the Fund as an institution.

Three main subjects are identified here as constituting the pillars of the next stage of the European Monetary System: credit mechanisms, exchange rate arrangements, and the ECU. The first and the latter are respectively the asset and the liability side of the Fund's balance sheet. The first and the second represent the alternative means by which tensions among member currencies may be relieved within the system. Each of these three pillars has to be built on solid foundations and in such a way as to allow progress from a 'looser' to a 'tighter' system. But the secret of a successful new institution, such as the Fund, will lie perhaps more in the appropriate balance between them than in the perfection of each individually. Discussion should therefore centre first on whether the constituting elements have been identified correctly in the three headings mentioned above, and secondly on the question of the balance among these elements.

A few ideas, that may be worthy of discussion are suggested in the paper. To offer the reader a quick summary, they are listed here:

(i) The conditionality attached to the various credit facilities should be reconsidered and increased;

(ii) The relative roles of the credit facilities and of central rate realignments in the exchange rate mechanism should be re-examined, mainly because it is thought that there is a tendency for the former to be under-utilized and the latter abused;

(iii) The role of the ECU in both the exchange rate and credit mechanism has to be defined in such a way that the EMF becomes the instrument for a coordinated approach to adjustment;

(iv) The system should allow some flexibility in exchange rates even in the next stages. The most important point is not variability *per se* but how changes are made. The Fund should be given the responsibility of managing such a flexibility. Greater stability in exchange rates should be sought initially in an indirect way;

(v) The Fund should be endowed with procedures rather than with specific rules concerning exchange rate arrangements, conditionality, etc.

It is a premise of the paper that the whole system should be organized in such a way as to be an instrument to fight inflation in the Community, and the first meaning to give to the establishment of a 'zone of monetary stability in Europe' should be in the sense of price stability rather than exchange rate stability. No claim for symmetry among high inflation and low inflation countries should be made in this respect. Relatively bold suggestions such as an increased conditionality or a more exclusive role of the ECU are to be discussed in the light of this anti-inflationary goal.

The paper deals with the system very much as a closed economy. For lack of time the section on the 'open system' has not been included but it could be written without too much difficulty, and the second session of this seminar will specifically deal with this question.

The reader may wonder why such favourite chapters in the literature on monetary union, such as intervention rules, convergence to fixed rates, etc., are given little room in this paper. Reasons other than product diversification can be given. The main concern here is with the establishment of a new institution, meaning by that something more steady and stable than case by case coordination, which implies, among other things, that those subjects will be on the agenda of the new institution once it comes into being, rather than on today's agenda. Moreover, too much emphasis has perhaps been given to exchange rate arrangements as the core problem of a monetary union. The Community will have to find its original way in the monetary field as it has done in others, and it is not obvious that the way can be found by immediately focusing on the 'irrevocable fixing of parity rates'; rather, an effort has to be made in an area that could be called the economics of institutions, to which the pages that follow aim to address the reader's thoughts.

2. The credit mechanisms

A. The existing arrangements

Before discussing how the existing credit facilities could be consolidated into the Fund, it is useful to summarize briefly the mechanisms involved and their current use. Basically there are three mechanisms:

(i) the very short-term financing facility;
(ii) the short-term monetary support;
(iii) the medium-term financial assistance.

Apart from the increase in duration and size, these mechanisms were taken over with unchanged operating procedures by the EMS from the previous regime. As we shall see, this poses a problem of integration into the system and one of utilization.

The very short-term financing follows largely from a snake-type[1] intervention mechanism. Compulsory interventions in the currencies of the system make it necessary that the relevant currencies are available to the intervening central bank in theoretically unlimited amounts. The very short-term financing facility allows that the claims and obligations resulting from these interventions are not settled spot, and at the start of the EMS the duration of this unlimited financing was increased from 30 to 45 days after the end of the month during which the intervention took place. This period may be automatically extended for three months subject to the financing not exceeding the debtor quota of the central bank concerned in the short-term monetary support facility; obligations in excess of this limit may be renewed only with the consent of the creditor central banks.

The facility has been used fairly extensively since the start of the EMS.

The short-term support and medium-term assistance were expanded as the table below shows at the start of the EMS. The effect of this expansion was to increase the total credit availability to about 25 000 million ECU. The duration of short-term credits was increased from a maximum of six to nine months, by allowing the possibility of two three-month extensions instead of only one. But neither mechanism has been activated within the EMS and their previous use was very limited.

The short-term monetary support was set up by an agreement between central banks in February 1970 and was extended with the accession of the three new Member States in 1973, but it has only been activated once in 1973 when the Banca d'Italia was granted a dollar credit for the equivalent of 1 600 million units of account. This amount was drawn in March 1974. Under the terms of the STMS the amount would have been available for three months renewable once automatically, giving a total period of six months, but in the event it was renewed both in June and September 1974, and in December was partially converted into medium-term financial assistance. In 1976 Italy was also granted a stand-by facility on the STMS but this was not activated, and in June 1977 the Banca d'Italia renounced its right to do so when Italy received a Community loan.

The medium-term financial assistance has also been used only once, and again by Italy, whose short-term facility was converted into a medium-term one at the end of 1974, as explained above. The dollar equivalent of about 1 200 million units of account

[1] The snake is the name given to the pre-EMS European exchange rate mechanism.

Increase in the short-term monetary support and medium-term financial assistance
(million ECU)

I. Short-term monetary support

	Quotas			
	Debtor		Creditor	
	Old	New	Old	New
Banque Nationale de Belgique	200	580	400	1 160
Danmarks Nationalbank	90	260	180	520
Deutsche Bundesbank	600	1 740	1 200	3 480
Banque de France	600	1 740	1 200	3 480
Central Bank of Ireland	35	100	70	200
Banca d'Italia	400	1 160	800	2 320
Nederlandsche Bank	200	580	400	1 160
Bank of England	600	1 740[1]	1 200	3 480[1]
Total quotas	2 725	7 900	5 450	15 800
Rallonges	3 000	8 800	3 000	8 800

II. Medium-term financial assistance

	Commitment ceilings	
	Old	New
Belgium/Luxembourg	400	1 035
Denmark	180	465
France	1 200	3 105
FR of Germany	1 200	3 105
Ireland	70	180
Italy	800	2 070
Netherlands	400	1 035
United Kingdom	1 200	3 105
Total	5 450	14 100

[1] There is an agreement that the UK will not use its increased quotas until it has become a full participant in the exchange rate mechanism of the EMS.

was lent at an interest rate of 7 9/16% for an average duration of 3 1/2 years, but the repayments were made ahead of schedule and the final tranche was paid off in September 1978. The economic policy conditions attached to the loan were monitored regularly by examinations in the Monetary Committee.

B. Development of the credit mechanisms within the EMS

(a) Consolidation of the credit mechanisms

The resolution of the European Council in Brussels states that the credit mechanisms 'will be consolidated into a single fund in the final phase of the EMS'. To that purpose it is easy to conceive the following alternative formulae:

(i) consolidate the very short and short-term mechanisms;

(ii) consolidate the short- and medium-term mechanisms;

(iii) consolidate all three mechanisms.

In current discussions the choice between these formulae is thought to bear an important relationship to the question of the nature of the Fund. More specifically, it is claimed that the shorter the duration of the mechanism the stronger the 'central bank character' of the institution responsible for it. The rationale of this contention seems to be twofold. First, money, the produce of central banks, is itself of a short-term nature. Second, the existing medium-term mechanism is at present not the responsibility of central banks. However, neither of these points provides, in my view, a strong support to the claim. I will return to that when dealing with the ECU and the institutional aspects of the Fund.

On the relative merits of these three formulae, it is not necessary to summarize here the considerable amount of discussion which has already developed. Rather, it is worth noting that the three mechanisms risk being incorporated in the 'final system' in their existing form in much the same way as they were carried without any qualitative change from the previous regime into the EMS. Before that happens it may be useful to ask whether their present characteristics correspond to the needs of a new system.

(b) Development of the credit mechanisms

At the start of the EMS the most significant change in the credit mechanisms was the change in the amounts available, and it is worth asking whether the amounts available are now appropriate or whether they are too large or too small. The fact that the short and medium-term facilities have remained virtually unused would suggest that the amount available for these is at the moment relatively insignificant and that developments in other directions should be considered first. For the very short-term facility the initial credit is available for an unlimited amount, but the automatic renewal is limited by the debtor quotas in the short-term monetary support arrangement. Although the amount of interventions that may be necessary when the system is under pressure can be very large, there is no clear evidence that increasing the amount of financing available or its duration would be helpful. The main aim of this facility is that of a weapon against speculation, and it is doubtful whether any larger movements over the already extended time span can be considered as being only erratic and likely to be reversed. More fundamental developments of the mechanisms rather than just expanding them in their existing form must therefore be considered.

The connection between credit mechanisms and the definition of the means available to the EMF is at present neither clear nor quite logical. Indeed the credit mechanisms developed historically into a structure that has little to do with the decision to endow the Fund with 20% of member countries' gold and dollar reserves. The existing credit mechanisms have the advantage of making available to each country an amount of reserves greater than its contribution. On the other hand, the endowment of the Fund with deposits of gold, dollars and national currencies has the advantage of clearly defining the asset side of the balance sheet. But the liability side, the ECU, does not correspond at the moment; the amount of resources available to the Fund once the deposits both of reserve assets and possibly national currencies are made does not correspond in quantity or in availability to the amount that countries could receive through the different support mechanisms.

There is also a problem of consistency within the set of the three mechanisms. If there are differences in duration and conditionality, and if the debt contracted under one mechanism can be transformed at maturity into the next-in-length facility (subject to a limit of amount), then one may want to spell out the implicit story of an economy which uses the three mechanisms. Very short-term credit, one can say, is designed to deal with erratic and accidental pressures on the exchange rates, those that are not based on any real disequilibrium in the economy. Inability to repay at maturity, the story goes, may indicate that pressures are perhaps not so accidental and that some kind of disequilibrium is there after all, possibly of a seasonal or even of a cyclical nature. Credit has then to be granted for a longer duration. Similarly, medium-term credit may be interpreted as being granted to deal with even more serious disequilibria, of a cyclical or of a structural character, which can be eliminated only over a longer period of time. This is no doubt only one of the possibilities and it is only meant to show the kind of questions that immediately arise as one tries to rationalize the system of credit facilities. Is the duration of the three mechanisms consistent with the type of source that may cause tensions in the system (the short-term mechanism may be too short, etc.)? More fundamentally: what kind of actions are going to be taken when tensions prove not to be purely erratic and while a currency is supported by one of the facilities? What happens to the central rate while the story goes in the way we have told it? These questions pose the three further points of conditionality, cost, and the balance between credit and realignments as alternative means of relieving tensions, to which we now turn.

There is no element of conditionality in the very short-term facility but it is only automatically available for intervention at the margins. An important difference between the EMS and the snake arrangement is the use of the divergence indicator, which is in general expected to sound an alarm before bilateral margins are reached. Since, in the EMS, interventions should in principle be made in participating currencies, these should perhaps be automatically available for intra-marginal interventions as well, and not only for interventions at the margins. This could be made subject to the understanding, or even the formal condition, that a national currency would only be used by another participant when that currency is on the opposite side of its central rate as compared to the currency of the intervening central bank, so that the action would have the effect of bringing it closer to its central rate. The practice under the present arrangements is that a central bank requiring another currency in the system for intra-marginal intervention has to ask permission and there could be instances where this is not granted, in which case the only alternative would be to intervene in dollars. The short-term facility, like the very short-term, has no elements of conditionality initially, but there can be some conditionality in granting an extension. The medium-term financing in contrast has a strong element of conditionality, involving non-monetary aspects of policy, such as budgetary policy, etc. The introduction of new elements of conditionality is conceivable and perhaps desirable at least for the short-term mechanism. It should aim at variables such as interest rates, growth in monetary aggregates, exchange rates, etc., i.e. variables that are within the strictly monetary horizon and the responsibility of central banks.

As to the cost of credits to a debtor, in the short-term and medium-term mechanisms this is decided at the time the credit is granted. In the very short-term facility, the interest rate is calculated as the weighted average of the official discount rates of all EEC central banks, with the weights corresponding to those in the ECU; and whereas this has an element of generosity in that the discount rates are frequently lower than other rates, it could be questioned whether there is not a case for the interest cost being borne more widely than only by the country whose currency has arrived at its lower intervention limit, especially if its currency is not divergent while others are. It may be that it is at that position because of the general characteristics of the whole system *vis-à-vis* the outside world and not only because of its own internal policies. If it has already made efforts to adapt those policies, there is an argument in favour of the fact that the cost of supplying some credit should be borne more widely. However, it should also be remembered that the general acceptability of an asset can be adversely affected if it bears an artificially low interest rate.

The third point is that of having the appropriate balance between the use of credit and parity adjustments in the exchange rate mechanism. Although it is clear that, given the potential size of international capital movements, no volume of credit is sufficient to hold an exchange rate at a non-equilibrium level for long, it seems that adjustment of central rates has been resorted to more and more frequently and that credit facilities have been used very little. Indeed, it must be asked whether the realignment option is not being abused. I shall return to this later.

These brief remarks suggest a paradox and two conclusions. The paradox is that although it is suggested here that there should be a greater use of the credit facilities, it is also suggested that there should be increased conditionality, which in itself may be thought to discourage such use. This will be returned to below. The two conclusions that are going to emerge again in the following discussion of the other aspects are, first, that the key of the system is not so much on the perfection of each of its building blocks as on the balance between them; second, that the essence of the Fund is not so much in the specific rules that may be chosen at the outset as in the procedures that will be established to adopt the rules.

3. The exchange rate arrangements

Exchange rate arrangements, i.e. both intervention rules and realignment procedures, and the credit mechanisms are the two instruments by which tensions among currencies can be relieved. Within one country, where exchange rates are irreversibly fixed, only credit (or transfer) mechanisms are at work. Within the EMS as it is now exchange rate adjustments are limited by (a) exchange rate agreements (intervention rules, etc.) and (b) realignment procedures. These are also the two subjects on which we have to express ourselves, after briefly reviewing the existing arrangements.

A. The existing arrangements

To classify an exchange rate mechanism with words like 'fixed', 'floating' or 'crawling' is more difficult in practice than in theory. However, for any construction that, like the EMS, carries the ambitious name of a 'system' in the area of exchange rate relationships, some place has to be found in the fixed-floating spectrum.

It is perhaps too early to say in which direction the EMS is developing. As far as the currencies outside the system are concerned, it seems as a whole to be towards the floating end of the spectrum, although there is agreement that the unlimited fluctuations of currencies like the dollar may cause problems within the system. As far as the currencies within the system are concerned, the experience of the September 1979 realignment would suggest that we are moving towards the direction, taken by the snake since 1976, of a crawling peg without formal decision rules about the size or frequency of the crawl.

During its history, the snake moved substantially towards increased flexibility: so much so that it adopted for at least some of its realignments one of the main characteristics of a crawling peg system,[1] i.e. that changes in central rates were accomplished within the margins and so did not cause a discontinuity in market rates. Over the period 1973-78 two distinct phases may be identified. In the first phase, between September 1973 and October 1976, there were no changes in central rates in the snake amongst those members which remained in the system to the end; in the second phase starting with the adjustment of October 1976 and ending with the final snake realignment two years later, there were four changes in central rates. In contrast, the following table, which shows the balance-of-payments positions and inflation rates of the countries concerned, shows no marked changes between the two time periods.

As far as the balance of payments is concerned, it can be seen that there was a substantial worsening in the position of all countries but an improvement in the relative position of Denmark. On the inflation side the position of Denmark remained very unfavourable relative to that of Germany throughout the period, whereas that of Belgium and the Netherlands relative to Germany was nearly at Danish levels over the period 1974-77 but has since improved. Table 2 shows that, despite the fact that there was substantial evidence at the beginning of the period that some shift in real exchange rates between Germany and the other members was needed, there was no realignment between September 1973 and October 1976.

[1] See Niels Thygesen: 'The European Monetary System – An approximal implementation of the crawling peg?', Rio de Janeiro Conference, October 1979.

Table 1

Balance of payments (1) and inflation rates (2) in snake countries 1973-79

Year	Fr of Germany		Netherlands		Belgium		Denmark	
	(1)	(2)	(1)	(2)	(1)	(2)	(1)	(2)
1973	1.3	7.6	4.0	8.9	3.3	5.8	-1.7	10.1
1974	2.6	7.1	3.2	9.6	2.1	12.2	-3.0	12.4
1975	1.0	6.1	2.5	9.8	1.2	12.2	-1.5	9.7
1976	0.8	4.5	3.2	8.8	0.9	7.7	-4.8	10.1
1977	0.9	3.8	0.9	6.1	-1.5	6.8	-3.7	10.9
1978	1.5	2.6	-0.7	4.4	-1.5	4.5	-2.6	9.4
1979[1]	-0.2	4.3	-0.3	4.8	-1.8	4.5	-3.7	9.7

(1) Balance of payments: current balance in GDP, percentage shares.
(2) Consumer prices, percentage changes.
[1] Forecast.
Source: European Economy, No 4, November 1979.

Table 2

Changes in central rates in the snake
(against the EMUA)

(%)

Date	DM	HFL	BFR/LFR	DKR
March 1973	+3	–	–	–
June 1973	+5 1/2	–	–	–
September 1973	–	+5	–	–
October 1976	+2	–	–	-4
April 1977	–	–	–	-3
August 1977	–	–	–	-5
October 1978	+4	+2	+2	–

The above tables therefore show that initially exchange rate changes were resisted, but that a policy was later followed of trying to adjust through nominal rate changes.

The Danish krone moved down by a cumulative amount of 18% against the German mark whereas the Belgian and Luxembourg francs moved by just under 9% and the florin by only a total of 4%. In the latter group of countries, tight domestic monetary policies achieved a substantial reduction in the rate of inflation, but in Denmark the inflation rate was allowed to at least match that of its trading partners with matching shifts in the exchange rate. The realignment mechanism shifted from being used only in response to fundamental disequilibrium to accommodating differing inflation rates and monetary policies.

The initial period of the EMS shows that the new system could be moving in the same direction, with rather frequent use being made of the realignment mechanism.

B. Less flexibility?

It is often claimed that the system should move towards the fixed end of the spectrum. Tensions ought to be resolved to a larger extent through policy changes, backed up if necessary by credit from the Fund. Exchange rate changes would still be necessary while the economic performance of the participating countries is so different, but a major objective should be to achieve conditions which will make exchange rate changes as infrequent as possible and eventually unnecessary. And the relevant policies will be much more likely to be successful if the markets know that the authorities are determined to avoid an exchange rate change.

Prior to generalized floating it was argued that national authorities would be much better able to control prices, interest rates and output in their economy if the external constraint was removed by freeing the exchange rate. Experience has cast serious doubts on this argument.[1] Great and increasing interdependence of the economies, capital mobility, widespread indexation, and the role of expectations in exchange rate determination have led to a weakening of the effectiveness of exchange rate policy to complement domestic stabilization policy.

In a relatively independent reality with low capital mobility, exchange rate flexibility may no doubt enhance the effectiveness of domestic monetary and fiscal policy, as either a monetary expansion or a fiscal stimulus will lower the exchange rate by increasing imports and reducing exports. However, with high capital mobility the direction of the exchange rate movement, following a fiscal stimulus, becomes uncertain. Such a stimulus will, with an unchanged money supply, raise the domestic rate of interest and give rise to capital inflows; if capital is very mobile, the effect on the capital account of the balance of payments could outweigh that on the trade deficit and the exchange rate would appreciate, offsetting the effects of the stimulus. Expectations would speed up this process even if there were some stickiness in capital movements.

While it may be difficult to give a full empirical justification for a move towards more stable exchange rates within the Community, two main propositions seem to be increasingly accepted.

First, the type of exchange rate flexibility that has been prevailing over the past few years has been disappointing in that, despite what was predicted by theory about the stabilizing effects of speculation, exchange rates turned out to display much greater volatility than expected. The volatility in terms of short and medium-term fluctuations was often such as to serve no useful purpose as regards balance of payments adjust-

---

[1] See Stanley W. Black: *Floating Exchange Rates and National Economy Policy*, Yale University Press, New Haven and London, 1977.

ments. Instead it had the undesirable effects of both distorting resource allocation between tradeables and non-tradeables through large swings in their relative prices, and of discouraging investment and trade and hence reducing growth and employment through increasing risks.

Second, it seems to be increasingly accepted, although not empirically proved,[1] that flexible exchange rates may entail inflationary ratchet effects. The case can most clearly be argued for Italy and the UK. The 'overshooting' of exchange rates in Italy in 1976 and in the UK in 1974 seemed to contribute substantially to inflation. The evidence is that causation between exchange and inflation rates works in both directions and that in the short-run the most important direction is from exchange rate movements to prices, rather that the reverse, which seems to be the most important relationship for the long term equilibrium rate of exchange in accordance with purchasing power parity theories.

Current discussions about future developments of the EMS in the area of exchange rates are often based on discomfort with the present 'excessive' flexibility. They tend thus to focus on the two following points: (a) the appropriate intervention rules (including a common dollar policy, intra-marginal intervention, and the like) that could reduce tension within the system and (b) the possible evolution through which the existing margins could gradually narrow to approach a fixed rate system, itself taken as the final stage of monetary union.

The experience of the first months of the EMS has shown that while credit mechanisms have remained largely unused, a tendency may be developing to use, and perhaps to abuse of, 'realignments'. A paradoxical situation is thus emerging: that of a system that, while created to increase the role of domestic policy (monetary and fiscal) relative to exchange rate policy to adjust for external disequilibria, ends up providing the ideal structure for a more frequent recourse to central parity changes. A comparison between intra-EMS and EMS-dollar relationships might perhaps show that the role of credit compared to exchange rate adjustment has been relatively more important for the latter than for the former. One of the causes of the breakdown of the Bretton Woods system was the lack of a non-crisis way of adjustment, and the early years of the snake agreement showed the same problem, with adjustments often being accomplished by currencies leaving the system. More recent experience with the snake and the early experience of the EMS suggest the danger of a complete reversal of this situation.

C. Possible developments

To depart from this path of very frequent realignments is no doubt a necessity. But for various reasons it may be questioned whether the adoption of new intervention rules and the narrowing of the margins are steps in the right direction and whether these are

[1] See M. Goldstein: 'Downward price inflexibility, ratchet effects and the inflationary impact of import price changes: some empirical evidence', IMF Staff Papers, November 1977.

relevant problems for defining the Fund. For one thing, new intervention rules, though certainly important, can be adopted outside and without the Fund. As an institution, the Fund will only play a role if it itself will be enabled to set rules and if it will do so in a new way and with a new perspective. More fundamentally, an evolution towards narrower margins has to be considered with great caution, since it will be a progress to a tighter monetary union only if appropriate conditions are met. Without such conditions the system risks either a breakdown (exit of the franc and the lira from the snake) or an even greater abuse of parity adjustments.

We are accustomed to associate progress towards monetary union with a reduction in the variability of exchange rates because of the historical experiences at national levels, where it may be difficult to imagine a central bank endowed with the power of varying exchange rates between regions. But in this area, as in others, the Community may well find its own original path. And it may be 'a quite mistaken form of monetary supranationalism to start by fixing rigidly the exchange rates between national currencies as a first step towards a supranational currency. We are at the very early confederal stage in our affairs'.[1]

There is no reason why a change in rates between member currencies should not remain possible, at least for a certain time, even within the union. The crucial point is not variability, but how the relevant decisions are made.

These considerations suggest that the following criteria are relevant for defining the role of the Fund in the exchange rate mechanism:

(i) Procedures, rather than specific rules, should be defined for the Fund in the area of exchange rate arrangements. It is neither realistic nor necessary to endow the Fund with predetermined rules. These are typically necessary as long as an institution like the Fund does not exist. Instead, the Fund should be endowed with decisional procedures, to be utilized, in circumstances that are inevitably changing and impossible to forecast, to create a 'zone of monetary stability'. This holds both for interventions and realignments. If central rate adjustments are to take place only in response to fundamental disequilibrium, then it follows that the economic fundamentals within the Member States in relationship to their exchange rates (amongst themselves) should be continuously monitored by the Fund.

(ii) The degree of exchange rate variability should not necessarily be reduced, although some reduction would result from limiting adjustments to those (but not necessarily all) that are based on diverging 'fundamentals'. More importantly, variability should not be reduced directly, i.e. by applying more restrictive intervention and realignment rules. Rather, it should be reduced indirectly, i.e. by creating conditions for both the conduct of domestic monetary policies and the use of conditional credit facilities to play a gradually greater role relative to parity changes.

(iii) An appropriate balance has to be found between the use of credit mechanisms and exchange rate changes, and this in turn requires a clearly established role for the ECU. A balanced role of these three aspects of the system can only be ensured by jointly managing them within the same institution.

[1] J. Meade: *The Various Forms of Exchange Rate Flexibility,* American Enterprise Institute for Public Policy Research, 1966.

4. The ECU

It has been argued above that the three parts of the system in its present form have largely been taken over from the previous arrangements and that they are neither complete nor fit together in a satisfactory way. They are also more characterized by a series of bilateral relationships than by a coherent multilateral system. The goal of a Fund is to both coordinate the workings of the three main parts of the system so as to ensure a correct balance between them, and to multilateralize each part. To assess the extent of the problem as far as the ECU is concerned, it is necessary to consider the ECU's present position and some of the implications of making it the true centre of the system consistent with the developments discussed above. This can be done by considering two aspects of the ECU: the way it is created and the way it is used.

A. The existing arrangements

With the current system of three-month revolving swaps, the vast majority of ECU reserves do not have an existence of their own. They simply represent, under a different name, the particular gold and dollars belonging to the central bank concerned. Hence one 'Bank of France ECU' does not equal one 'Bank of Ireland ECU', as each gives the bank concerned the right to a different proportion of other reserve assets, gold and dollars. This can be expressed in another way by saying that the previous exchange risk position has remained unchanged by the creation of these ECU. Only the ECU that are used have an existence which is in any way different from the gold and dollars by which they are backed. But this is true only within the total period of the swap agreements. For at the end of that period if the swaps are unwound, so that all the participants reclaim their original amount of gold and dollars, these ECU also lose their existence.

Parallel to this precarious and largely bilateral way of coming into existence, are the numerous limitations that surround the use of the ECU as *numéraire,* means of settlement, reserve asset and its position in the credit mechanisms.

In the exchange rate mechanism the ECU is used for defining the central rates and so it is formally the *numéraire,* although the practical consequences of this are very limited as in everyday dealings on the exchange markets the *numéraire* used is the dollar. Also, the ECU is not used in practice as the *numéraire* when there is a realignment of central rates. The consequences for the ECU are deduced from the desired bilateral rate changes rather than vice versa, clearly demonstrating the strong bilateral nature of the system. The ECU is also used as a basis for the calculation of the divergence indicator, but this potentially important function is somewhat marred by the complicated, and not altogether satisfactory, adjustments that have to be made because of the non-participation of sterling and the adoption by the lira of wider margins.

As to settlements, those for compulsory interventions can be made in ECU, although even on this very limited class of settlements there are a number of restrictions. The procedure is that when a financing operation falls due, settlement is carried out in the creditor's currency if possible, i.e. if there has been some shift in the market positions;

and only if this is not the case, is the settlement carried out in ECU, and even then the creditor is not obliged to accept settlement in ECU for an amount exceeding 50% of the claim being settled.

Looking at the ECU as a reserve asset, all the central banks hold 20% of their gold and dollar reserves in ECU, but the system by which this is done means that the practical effects are extremely limited. Each bank has entered into a separate three-month swap agreement with the European Fund for Monetary Cooperation (EMCF) for 20% of its gold and dollar reserves. It then manages these reserves on behalf of the EMCF and so, although it formally has ECU as reserves on its books, there is no real transfer to the EMCF. The exchange risk position remains completely unchanged and the EMCF has no control over the assets. It is agreed that these three-month swaps will continue for a period of two years from the beginning of the system.

Finally, credit under the very short-term facility is by nature given in a Community currency but it is accounted for in ECU and settled in ECU subject to the conditions given above. There is a provision that short-term credit can be granted in ECU and medium-term assistance is granted in ECU, but, as seen above, these facilities have not so far been used.

Thus, while the creation of ECU is now linked to the specific and temporary swap mechanism, its use is restricted to the official Community circuit and even in that circuit its use is very limited.

B. Possible developments

An easy way of dealing with the establishment of the ECU is to analyse how the arrangements could develop beyond today's swap system. It seems clear that if the ECU are to have a permanent existence of their own, the temporary arrangements have to become permanent, i.e. the swaps made to continue for ever with an independent exchange risk. It is less clear, however, that this should require a transfer of property of gold and dollar reserves. What has to be conferred to the Fund is not necessarily the property of non-ECU reserves (gold and dollars), but their management. And, rather than approaching the problem from that highly controversial and relatively 'static' side, it may be perhaps more fruitful to approach it from the functional side of the uses of the ECU.

The use of the ECU could be conceivably extended in various directions. Firstly, in the Community official circuit. It seems obvious that a 'full utilization' of the ECU should entail the elimination of the existing 50% limit of acceptability in intra-Community settlements. Secondly, the ECU could be used outside the Community official circuit, both on private markets and with third countries.

The question of the use of the ECU outside the Community will be returned to later and that of its use by the private sector is not within the scope of the paper. But it is worth observing that though it may seem to be the most ambitious, this latter development may well be spontaneous. It should be remembered that what is probably the most important monetary and financial development of the last 20 years, the growth of Eurocurrency markets, has largely been a spontaneous phenomenon. In this area, if official institutions have a role to play, it will not so much be a functional or operational role, as a regulatory and supervisory one, namely the role of permitting banks to open ECU-denominated accounts.

Within the general area of responsibility of a monetary authority, we are dealing here with the function of bank supervision, which is twin, but not identical, to the function of central banking. Current discussions about controlling Euromarkets suggest here that the parallel with ECU deposits can be pursued further.

The establishment of the ECU as the reserve asset and settlement instrument within the Community, depends upon its ability to satisfy the two major interrelated criteria of (i) leading to stability within the system, and (ii) being easily controllable in the interest of trade growth.

The international monetary system was stable when gold was the only reserve asset, but there were liquidity problems as the supply of gold was not linked to need, and was physically more restricted than the growth of world trade. For a time the dollar provided a stable system but then it produced problems of both stability and liquidity. At first liquidity growth was too restricted but then with growing American deficits, which had the desired result of expanding liquidity, the stability was affected as Triffin had forecast that it would be.[1] A confidence problem developed and reserve holders tried to substitute one reserve asset for another, thereby creating unbearable strains within the system both for the reserve centre and for the others who are forced to hold a non-optimal portfolio of reserves.

The existing preoccupations and reservations about the possible consequences of fully promoting the ECU can largely be interpreted as doubts about the ability of the new system to satisfy the two criteria mentioned above. This in turn leads to the problem of the 'monetary quality' of the ECU and of the inflationary pressures that might arise because of its establishment. A distinction should be made here.

The ECU is the liability of the Fund while the various forms of credit are its asset, in much the same way as the national currency is the liability of the central bank 'backed' by credits *vis-à-vis* the private sector, the Treasury and the rest of the world. It follows that any change in volume of total assets, for example due to a change of total credit extended through the various facilities, would result in a change of total supply of ECU. That would be true regardless of the type of asset created or destroyed by the Fund, whether short-term credit, medium-term credit, dollar or other.

A separate and independent question is that of determining the monetary nature of the ECU thus created. And here it may be useful to distinguish the ECU as a *numéraire* from the ECU as a medium of exchange. EMF liabilities should all be denominated in ECU but do not need to be all sight-liabilities, i.e. money. It would be technically con-

[1] See R. Triffin: *Gold and the Dollar Crisis,* Yale University Press, New Haven 1960.

ceivable, and it may indeed be advisable, to enable the Fund to create, against its assets, ECU liabilities with longer maturities, e.g. when the amount of assets held goes beyond the desired amount of Community-currency creation. In this respect the Fund would operate like a substitution account, or like a central bank empowered to sterilize Treasury-created or balance-of-payment-created liquidity by issuing its own securities.

Concern with price stability is at the origin of a reluctance to promote the establishment of the ECU by conferring full 'moneyness' to it. One more currency, it is felt, equals more money, hence more inflation. And the maintenance of limited acceptability of the ECU is seen as the way to avoid the danger.

This preoccupation with the inflationary consequences of the ECU is particularly deep where inflation has been fought more successfully in the last years, and it has to be considered most seriously. Indeed to create 'a zone of monetary stability in Europe' must be interpreted primarily in the sense of price stability, exchange rate stability being simply an aspect of this.

Trying to think of an ECU strongly oriented in an anti-inflationary sense, leads back to the two aspects that were mentioned at the beginning of this section: the way the ECU is created, and the way it is used. It also leads to a link between the ECU and the credit mechanisms. In this light, three possibilities should be considered:

(a) a more exclusive role of the ECU as a means for intra-Community settlement;
(b) a system of severe conditions surrounding ECU creation; and
(c) the endowment of the Fund with the power to create ECU-denominated, non-monetary assets.

The last point was mentioned above and does not need to be expanded further. The significance of the other two can be caught intuitively, but a few words of comment may be useful.

As to exclusivity, it has first to be recalled that at the national level exclusivity is as essential a feature of money as is full acceptability: the production of money is a monopoly. At a world level, it is clear that the stability problem can be solved by having only one reserve asset. A scheme of this sort was proposed by Triffin as early as 1959, when he suggested that dollar and sterling balances should be converted into claims on the IMF. The substitution account and suggestions for an international monetary system based on the SDR have similarities. It must also be asked whether such a system could run on a Community scale and if so whether this would have the desired quality of stability.

In such a system there is of course no place for any acceptance limits on ECU. Also it should be noted that in this case the ECU would not be exchangeable by members of the system into other reserve assets simply because they wanted to change the composition of their reserves, as this would just re-create the confidence problem in another form. Its gold and dollar backing, although still possible and desirable for other reasons, would not be necessary unless all non-ECU reserves were conferred to the Fund, i.e. unless exclusivity were extended to reserve holdings. The main question about such a scheme is how far it would add to total stability when Member States only hold a proportion of their reserves in ECU. The confidence problem would not exist for the Fund as the reserve centre of the system itself, but member central banks would still feel the effects of the problem in the rest of the international system to the extent that they hold the remaining part of their reserves in other reserve assets.

Finally severe conditions should be established for the creation of ECU. One could think of quantitative rules such as the fixation of a maximum growth rate linked to growth of intra-Community trade. But alternatively, and no doubt more rationally, such severity could be linked to the new elements of conditionality that would accompany the consolidation of the credit mechanisms.

5. Concluding remarks

A. Institutional and organizational aspects

The considerations above have not attempted to provide a blueprint for the Fund and they have concentrated exclusively on some of its possible characteristics from a functional point of view. Nothing has been said about the organizational structure of the Fund, or the so-called institutional aspects. It seemed preferable to concentrate on the functional side, which lends itself more easily to a technical analysis. However, it is often felt that no clear description of the functions of the Fund can be made without spelling out its organizational and institutional aspects. And it is certainly true that functional, institutional and organizational aspects have to be treated consistently. The concept of institution, however, should not be used in too narrow a sense. Indeed it should include all the elements that are susceptible of becoming the permanent, and somewhat non-reversible, characteristics of the system, such as reinforced conditionality, joint management of reserves, power to set rules for the management of exchange rates, exclusive role of the ECU, etc. Thus what is sometimes called the institutional aspect of the EMF is perhaps only a part of what deserves the name of institution: the organizational, legal part of it.

With this clarification, and without aiming at completeness, it may be useful to stress a few points for a discussion on the so-called institutional aspects.

First, a distinction should be made between different aspects of the EMF problem, i.e. (i) the definition of the functions of the Fund; (ii) the definition of the organic structure of the Fund; and (iii) the link between the Fund, national monetary authorities (treasury and central banks), and Community institutions. The three aspects are related, but different.

Second, it should be borne in mind that today there is no unique formula valid in all member countries for the distribution of roles between the treasury and the central bank. The same function (setting official rates, changing reserve rates, fixing monetary targets, etc.) lies in the hands of the treasury in one country and in those of the central bank in another. This fact by itself suggests that the chosen functional solution has no obvious implication as to the 'central bank vs treasury' nature of the Fund as an institution. Central banks are highly pragmatic inventions and Community pragmatism is most likely to find its new, original pattern.

Third, the choices that have to be made as to the powers and functions of the Fund should not be confused with the choices about the selection of the national institutions from which national representatives in the Fund will be appointed. Similarly, the members of the executive board of the IMF carry specific powers and responsibilities, independently of where they come from.

With these clarifications, four points for the debate can be mentioned:

(i) The organic structure of the Fund. The IMF-EIB formula that distinguishes a technical from a political decision level and has some way of weighting votes is particularly interesting in this respect. The example of the Federal Reserve System is of course also interesting.

(ii) The need for a 'permanent' structure, both with some powers to make technical decisions and with the function of supplying information and leading the decision process.

(iii) The problem of voting rules within the Fund.

(iv) The scope of responsibilities of the Fund. This is also the problem of placing the Fund in the context of other Community institutions.

B. Why have a Fund?

The naughty question has been left for the end. However, to ask whether there is any reason to set up the Fund other than compliance with a resolution of the European Council is quite legitimate. Only two brief remarks drawn from the preceding pages will be offered as elements for an answer: they relate to the present state of the EMS, and to the role of a new institution.

Some judgment has to be made on the system in its present form. If it is considered that it is not at a stable equilibrium, then some evolution must be envisaged if a move backwards is not to become inevitable. There are good reasons for thinking that the EMS is not at a stable equilibrium. Firstly, there is a tendency for internal tensions to be dealt with by recourse to central rate realignments rather than policy adjustments and/or credit facilities. This polarization is likely to be self-destructive as the system will abuse the realignment option to such an extent that it will no longer provide the external discipline for which it was designed. Secondly, there is no clear way of dealing with tensions produced from the exterior. This topic has not been discussed in the paper as it is the subject of the discussion in the following session of this seminar, but it forms an integral part of the whole and there must be a well-balanced way of dealing with these tensions if the system is to survive.

If progress towards a 'zone of monetary stability in Europe' requires a 'tighter' system and a better balance between the various elements, then the problem of creating an appropriate institutional framework arises inevitably. Indeed, only by dealing with credit mechanisms, exchange rate arrangements, and the use of the ECU within one single body and one set of formal established procedures will it be possible to proceed along an intermediate path between the simple registration of existing divergencies and a too ambitious programme of instantaneous convergence. After all money is an institutional reality by its very nature and the ECU needs for its establishment to be the liability of a vital institution.

Historical experience suggests that periods of profound change in economic, social and political order often open 'institutional breaches' to inflationary processes. It is of the utmost importance to be aware of these dangers in considering the development of a new monetary institution. But dangers do not always come from where they are expected. And one may question whether the best way to avoid more inflation is to limit the role of the EMF and the ECU. Recent experience shows that the 'existing order' does not prevent monetary disorder prevailing in certain countries and, from there, to threaten the Community as a whole. Thus one is entitled to ask whether the monetary anarchy, that some fear may be increased by creating a new system, is not with us already, whether institutional and social breaches are not already wide open and whether the establishment of the Fund, properly conceived, could not be a way to close them.

Brussels, November 1979

CHAPTER II

The ECU and the European Monetary System (1981)

This paper on 'The ECU and the European Monetary System' was presented in March 1981 in Trieste at the conference on 'Un Mercato Finanziario Italiano in Euroscudi' organized by the Istituto per gli Studi Assicurativi and by the Italian section of the European Federalist Movement. It was written when the EMS was two years old and the second phase appeared to have been only postponed.

While in the previous essay I described the three pillars of the system, stressing the need for a balance between them, here I dealt at greater length with the ECU. The importance of the progress made by the ECU can be checked by reading 'The ECU: exploring the map', which was written two years later and is presented below.

1. The ECU is a 'basket' currency of a special kind, not only because, like the special drawing right (SDR), it is backed by an official institution set up in the public and not in the private interest but also for a host of other reasons that distinguish it clearly from the SDR. Let me briefly review these reasons, which economists and the financial community alike often tend to overlook.

First, the currencies making up the ECU are linked to one another through an exchange rate mechanism: their inclusion in the basket is not therefore the only bond uniting them. Direct ties also exist in that there are rules governing their exchange rate relationships and rules governing the procedures to be followed in cases where these relationships come under pressure.

The second reason is that the ECU is the monetary expression of an integrated economic area, of a genuine common market and of economies that, in many respects, have already been unified. Even in its present simplified composition, the special drawing right is still made up of five very loosely related currencies that embrace an economic area with much looser internal links; previously, the special drawing right had an even more heterogeneous composition.

A third reason is that the ECU is the monetary expression of an institutional reality that differs a great deal from that of international organizations such as the International Monetary Fund and the OECD. This reality flows from a body of Community law, an elected parliament, a variety of common policies and a budget, i.e. from an entity which, in an embryonic state in some fields and more developed in others, has virtually all the powers of government. If it is true that currency needs to be backed by the infrastructure of a public authority, this fact is of great importance.

What is more, the ECU already has a qualitatively wide range of applications even though, quantitatively speaking, this range is very limited. The ECU is used primarily in connection with the European Monetary System, which I will discuss in a few moments. It has a wide variety of other applications in the Community set-up. The Community budget, for instance, is denominated in ECU and, although it involves relatively modest sums of money, is the product of an intense political and institutional decision-making process. The budget is negotiated between Member States, with figures expressed in ECU. The ECU is also used in the common agricultural policy, about which I will say more later, as farm prices are fixed in ECU. In addition, it is beginning to be used in dealings with the rest of the world since, under the European Development Fund, the Community's financial links with the countries that have signed the Lomé Convention are expressed in ECU.

The ECU also has non-official, or private, uses. Certain bank accounts are denominated in ECU as are various bond issues. Contracts are also concluded in ECU. I shall not deal with them here. I know full well that these uses are still very limited and am aware of the obstacles to their extension.

Lastly, the ECU is a 'basket' currency of a particular type because the European Monetary System confers a monetary power, albeit an embryonic one. A nucleus of monetary organization has, therefore, been added to all existing powers, institutions and Community decision-making procedures in the different sectors I have mentioned. I shall particularly dwell on the European Monetary System because, as I stated earlier, it seems to me that its further development provides the link between the Community's own development and the need for financial transactors to be given a framework which affords them broader scope for action and opens up wider prospects and without which private transactions loose their appeal.

2. There are two facets to the European Monetary System: it is both an achievement and a promise.

The achievement is the European Monetary System in its present form, in which the ECU performs a number of functions: it is used for defining currency parities, for determining each member country's divergence from the other currencies and hence for identifying the currency that 'deviates' in either direction, and it serves as a means of settlement between central banks. When ECU are created against dollars, one *numéraire* is simply substituted for another but when ECU are created against gold, there is genuine money creation either because gold has ceased to be a means of payment or because the rules for converting gold into ECU permit a revaluation of gold that many central banks did not undertake prior to establishment of the European Monetary System.

3. I should also like to speak to you about the European Monetary System as a promise, a promise which determines most of the scope for developing the ECU and a promise of a system that evolves, reaches its definitive form and then moves on to what is nowadays referred to as its 'institutional stage'; all in all, a system that expands and strengthens over time. The Heads of State or Government in the Community have made several points about the characteristics the European Monetary System should display in its second stage. Two points stand out: a European Monetary Fund will be set up, with the various aspects of the system to be adapted and the credit mechanisms between countries reinforced as part of the process; at the centre of the system, once it has entered its institutional stage, will be the ECU, which will then have to play its full role as a reserve instrument and a means of settlement.

In the eyes of the public authorities and the private sector, further development of the European Monetary System is essential if there is to be widespread and final acceptance of the ECU. Where the authorities are concerned, the EMS has been, and still is, a sort of 'catalyst for political resolve' without which there would not be the necessary stimulus to overcome the numerous minor difficulties that are always discovered in protracted and arduous Community negotiations. For private sector, this 'promise' seems to be the basis for its hope that the system will be strengthened; without such hope it will be difficult – particularly in the financial field where it is necessary to take a long view – to take private decisions on the use of the ECU. It is therefore the strength of the promise made by the public authorities that may at this stage already induce some change in attitudes in the private sector.

4. But why should the European Monetary System be developed further? One answer springs immediately to mind: because this has been promised. Yet this reason alone would probably not be sufficient. As we well know, it has happened all too often that promises were not kept. However, there are other, deeper-rooted reasons.

The first is that, without closer monetary organization, the Community's achievements to date would be placed in jeopardy. This becomes evident when we re-read, for example, what was written about agricultural policy and the common market in the 1970s, that the Community's achievements have come under increasing threat because of the absence of any monetary order, while such an order had existed 20 years earlier when the policies were launched. In the first place, therefore, it is the need to defend its achievements that is obliging the Community to reinforce its monetary organization.

The second reason is the need for monetary stability. In all the countries of the Community, and this now even includes those with a strong currency, achieving monetary stability where prices are concerned requires monetary organization that goes beyond the national framework. For many years, a number of countries have apparently been able to do without this. They were in a strong monetary position, had a powerful central bank, enjoyed a consensus among the various social groups and applied consistent policies. As far as they were concerned, the European Monetary System seemed to shield them from inflation elsewhere by periodically revaluing their currencies. Witness the German experience between 1974 and 1979. It is in the very countries that enjoyed the greatest monetary stability that the limitations of such a policy are now apparent. More so than in the past, Italian inflation, French inflation and British inflation pose a problem for the strong currencies, and the need for monetary organization going beyond the confines of the national economy is now more pressing.

The third reason has to do with the development of the international monetary system. Now that the dollar has ceased to play a central role the international monetary system has gradually broken up into a multipolar system, with several currencies alternately playing the role of an international currency. Yet there is no currency beside the dollar that is strong enough to perform this function fully without running serious risks itself. And the dollar no longer has the strength necessary to continue the universal function it performed in the two decades following the Second World War. What is needed, therefore, is reliance on a combination of currencies in order that, in its present inevitable multipolar phase, the international monetary system is able to operate in a sufficiently orderly manner, allowing further integration of world trade or at least safeguarding what has already been achieved without undue risk.

To my mind, these are the fundamental elements of the pressure for further development of the European Monetary System. They are neither monetary in the strict sense nor financial but they are crucial from the angle of what the public authorities can do to develop the EMS further.

5. The question that now arises is how the European Monetary System should or could be further developed and consolidated. The first point to be made is that a monetary set-up is not good just because there has been a move from national to Community level. Community-level monetary arrangements may be unsatisfactory. The mere desire to move from one level to another is not therefore sufficient. It is, in fact, essential that the Community's monetary constitution should rest on foundations that guarantee its smooth working.

For any currency, the first need is stability and it is with this in mind that the choice between the various technical solutions available will have to be made. For any group of countries, monetary stability becomes a problem when the external position of one of them deteriorates. In other words, the difficulty being experienced by a particular country, firm or region affects the entire system only once it spreads beyond the relevant confines. In the case of a country, this happens when the problem transcends national boundaries. The external difficulty is a balance-of-payments difficulty. It can be resolved by using one of three instruments: the exchange rate, financing of the deficit, or domestic economic adjustment. A country in difficulties must operate within the triangle formed by these instruments. Consequently, any form of monetary organization at Community level must somehow embrace all three of them.

The exchange rate instrument is already used within the European Monetary System since the decisions on central rates are Community decisions. No country participating in the system may adjust the parity of its currency without following a Community procedure.

The second instrument, financing of the external deficit, is less clearly integrated in the system's procedures, for two reasons. First, because the facilities under the system operate too automatically. The quantity of ECU created is a function of the amount of gold or dollar contributions, i.e. it is largely dependent on the market price of gold. It so happens that the market price of gold has risen sharply since the inception of the European Monetary System; this has led to the creation of a large quantity of ECU and has allowed a number of countries to finance their external deficits perhaps too easily, and hence to postpone more radical adjustments to their economies. Moreover, Member States find it unduly easy to borrow on private international markets. There is no reason for any of them to draw on 'conditional' credit, that is to say credit tied to economic policy conditions, as funds can be raised on the international market at much the same financial cost and at no 'political cost'. Generally speaking, Member States' credit worthiness is higher than the size of their balance-of-payments deficits because their share of the resources flowing back from the oil-producing countries tends to be greater than their share of the total deficit of the oil-importing countries. Credit is not a sufficiently stringent economic policy condition.

The third means of remedying an external imbalance, namely domestic economic adjustment, is even less subject to Community disciplines since decisions on money creation and interest-rate levels are currently taken under coordination procedures that are not very strict. These procedures are important and make for better decisions than would be taken if there were no coordination at all, but they do not significantly affect conduct that 'deviates from the Community line'. Countries with stable currencies for example have very few instruments with which to influence the monetary policies of countries with high inflation.

6. Two principles should govern application of the three instruments of exchange rate, financing of the deficit and economic adjustment, as they are used to achieve stability within the European Monetary System of tomorrow.

First, they should be incorporated in a single decision-making procedure. In other words, they should be fitted into a balanced Community structure in which their use would be subject to some fair combination of constraints. Failing this, the system will tend to take the line of least resistance, according preference to a particular measure not because of its intrinsic value but because of the ease with which it can be taken.

Second, this single procedural arrangement must also permit the adoption of discretionary measures and must not be based solely on compulsory compliance with automatic rules. At present, the mechanism for creating ECU is automatic and thus involves no evolution, assessment or judgment and is confined to recording in the books what happens on the gold market. In other fields, including the Community procedure for currency realignments, decisions are discretionary and, for this very reason, difficult to take. In currency management there is always the problem of choosing between mechanical rules and discretionary decisions, even at national level. Generally speaking, in the Community and internationally, the tendency to prefer rigid rules is, in essence, reinforced by the fact that such rules make negotiations that much less difficult. Any negotiations to secure a consensus take a long time, in some cases too long a time for the decision that needs to be taken. In addition, the adoption of rigid rules may give the impression that less decision-making power has been handed over or that this power has been handed over to a neutral entity and not to other persons or institutions. But the monetary sphere is a sphere in which it must be possible to take discretionary decisions. Effective currency management requires a minimum of discretionary power.

7. The two principles I have just mentioned (single procedural arrangement, possibility of discretionary decisions), indicate, to my mind, the direction in which the European Monetary System can be further developed. It is probably no coincidence that they also correspond to the two points which the European Council specifically mentioned when setting up the system, namely the ECU and the European Monetary Fund. From this angle, the ECU can be seen as the factor joining together the different measures that can be taken to rectify an external imbalance, while the European Monetary Fund can be viewed as the institution invested with discretionary decision-making powers and not simply as a body recording the results of application of predetermined rigid rules.

Even in its embryonic state, the ECU already performs this unifying role. It serves as the bench mark for fixing exchange rates. It is used for denominating loans and in this way is connected with the second instrument I mentioned earlier, financing of the external deficit. However, it has virtually no link with the third instrument, which comprises domestic adjustment, money creation and interest rate policies. For this reason, guidelines are needed that would enable the ECU to join together the different measures for restoring equilibrium. Technically speaking, this means that we need to examine and define the different ways in which the ECU can be used and created. For example, if a member country's external financing needs could be met solely in ECU, a number of easy solutions, such as borrowing on private markets, could be ruled out or restricted. Community currency would be needed in order to finance an imbalance, in the same way as the central bank in any country will nowadays perform a monetary control function when the needs of a particular bank or sector of the economy generate demand for central-bank money. The role of the ECU could conceivably be reinforced along similar lines, for example by linking a country's domestic money creation to the quantity of ECU it possesses.

There is no doubt that, if measures of this kind were taken, decision-making would become more difficult and any decisions taken would be more clearly perceived as economic policy decisions. It would then be necessary to devise a structure within which such decisions could be taken. The European Monetary Fund could be this structure and the current discussions on details of its organization are reminiscent of those in the past on the role, institutional status and decision-making mechanism of a country's central bank.

8. To wind up, I should like to ask two questions. I said earlier that the European Monetary System should be further developed but I did not say that this was a foregone conclusion. Hence my first question: will it in fact happen? And my second question: when will the ECU become a genuine currency?

The first question is difficult to answer. I would be inclined to say that we do not know whether the system will be strengthened but that we are aware of the dangers we will face if this does not happen, just as we do not know whether world peace will be preserved but we do know the dangers we will face if it is broken. It is a fact that the Community is at differing stages of development in the wide variety of fields it encompasses and is thus lacking in cohesion. The fundamental question is whether it will move ahead or slip back. The best way to approach the problem where the ECU is concerned is to look at the most closely integrated Community policy, the common agricultural policy. For it to work effectively, this policy requires virtually full monetary integration, and it is experiencing very serious difficulties at the moment because such a degree of monetary integration does not, in practice, exist. We need only look at what happens during farm price negotiations or at events between 1969, when parities began to slide, and 1979, when the European Monetary System was set up. For a decade now a system of multiple exchange rates has gradually developed that runs counter to a common market in agricultural products, even if it has helped for a number of years to preserve some of its achievements. The degree of monetary organization is altogether insufficient at this advanced stage of the common organization of agricultural markets and will remain so as long as inflation rates diverge so widely between Member States.

On the question of when the ECU will become a genuine currency, I believe that the ECU will become a fully-fledged currency once it has ceased to be a basket of currencies and has become a basket of goods and services, in other words once the prices of a number of goods and services are expressed first in ECU, prices in other currencies then being derived prices. Allow me to illustrate my point with two examples involving goods that, to my mind, are important here. The first example is once again taken from the common agricultural policy. In the farm sector, prices are already fixed in ECU: for 8 000 000 farmers in Europe, the prices of their produce are expressed in ECU. The makings of a non-currency basket thus already exist in the Community. The second example concerns use of the ECU as the currency denomination for financial instruments. A financial instrument is in the final analysis a basket of future goods, and planning today to denominate credit instruments in ECU means assuming that the promise I referred to earlier will be kept. It means acting in the belief that there will ultimately be a sufficient quantity of goods and services denominated in ECU, in other words that the ECU and the European Monetary System will have advanced sufficiently to warrant this anticipatory behaviour.

CHAPTER III

What contribution has the EMS made and can it now make in an unsettled period? (1981)

The third chapter, 'What contribution has the EMS made and can it now make in an unsettled period?' was written in December 1981 and presented in Rome at the 'European business forum: finance, investment & trade'.

The main thrust of the argument is that a unified approach is needed to exchange rate management, balance-of-payments financing and domestic adjustment, and that only such an approach can achieve 'the twin objective of giving the Community its own monetary organization and fostering monetary stability'.

In a few days, exactly 10 years will have elapsed since the last world-wide attempt to organize international monetary relationships around a parity system took place at the Smithsonian Institute in Washington. That attempt soon failed, and was never resumed.

In the 10 years that have followed, two opposite and yet complementary developments have dominated world monetary relationships. These developments involve the private and the government area respectively. The first, in the private area, has been an extraordinary and almost unprecedented rate of financial innovation throughout the world, both domestically and internationally. The second, in the government area, has been such a decline in the degree of the public authorities' involvement in international monetary and financial matters, that we would be tempted to say these matters have now become an area of almost pure *laissez faire,* did we not know that the world of *laissez faire* was in reality a highly organized, highly governed and highly supervised world.

These two developments have jointly contributed to, as well as been determined by, an almost unprecedented degree of instability and uncertainty about monetary standards, i.e. about the value of currencies both in terms of other currencies and in terms of their power to buy goods and services. But what is interesting is that they have been to some extent complementary. Increasing financial sophistication has helped economic agents to relieve some of the pain coming from monetary uncertainty, but in the meantime, by making money increasingly endogenous, it has made it possible for private operators to evade the monetary discipline sought by public authorities.

The European Monetary System is in many ways an unorthodox event in the second area, that is the area of government. As all heretical movements, it has many enemies and few passionate defenders. The latter sometimes think that today's heresy will be tomorrow's orthodoxy. The EMS is unorthodox for many reasons. It is an act of government, in a period in which governments tend not to act. It is a departure from monetary *laissez faire,* in a period dominated by floating rates and private financial intermediation. It constitutes institutional change, in a period of institutional immobility. Finally, it has touched, albeit very gently, the sensitive nerve of sovereignty, in a period in which sovereignty has become an intellectual and political taboo, that only the violence of arms or the ingenuity of business seem to be allowed to violate.

The title of my remarks speaks of an 'unsettled period' and asks what contribution the EMS has made and can make in the future – I suppose essentially to make it less unsettled. I shall not, of course, explore in what way and for which reasons our period is an unsettled one. Let me, however, just state my conviction that what makes it unsettled is much more a decline in the ability to govern than a decline in economic welfare as such. Indeed, the generation living in these very years of distress and pessimism, enjoys levels of welfare that have never been attained before and that it may be daring to take as granted for the future. The widespread and very deep sense of uncertainty and insecurity that marks these years is, I think, due to the fact that we have lost most of the confidence we had in our ability to govern our economies.

The EMS must be seen in this light. It concerns only one of the two dramatic problems of our day, namely monetary stability. It would be preposterous to present it as a cure for the other, namely unemployment. But it is also true that we no longer believe in a fundamental conflict between high employment and price stability.

+

+ +

I shall consider the two questions contained in my title, the past and the future, separately, and thus start with a brief account of the way the system has functioned since its establishment.

Currency management within the EMS has not, generally speaking, given rise to major conflicts. The divergence indicator, which provides a systematic signal of the extent to which each EMS currency diverges from the group as a whole, has fulfilled the role expected of it.

The maximum permissible spread between two currencies at any time has frequently been taken up.

In spite of the central rate adjustments made in 1979 and in March 1981, there has been very little movement in the effective exchange rates of the currencies participating in the EMS exchange rate mechanism. Trade between EMS countries has not therefore been affected by the wide fluctuations in exchange rates internationally. This development contrasts with the widely divergent exchange rate movements recorded within the Community in the period 1973-78, and is an important factor for an area in which some 46% of trade (in 1979, for the EMS countries) is effected between member countries. However, in view of the persistent inflation differentials between member countries, this development also means that countries having less stable prices have imported stability through the mechanism of direct price interdependence, while countries having more stable prices have gained from the slower rise in their costs.

The relative stability of effective exchange rates within the system has so far not been matched by a greater convergence of costs and prices. When expressed in national currencies, average annual divergences in cost and price trends between EMS partners were, in many cases, quite substantial. For the years 1979-81, aggregate variations in the relative levels of unit labour costs in national currency have ranged from –14.5% in Germany to +32.7% in Italy. The accumulation of such deviations in a relatively short period may be primarily ascribed to two factors: a monetary and interest rate policy tailored to maintaining nominal exchange rates, and the existence of deviations in the reverse direction accumulated during the preceding period.

A shift from a low to a high relative cost and price level should serve to exert pressure in favour of increased domestic stability if backed up by appropriate policies. This is often the only way in which the real problems of domestic adjustment are forced into the open (Belgium is one example). These problems would otherwise be obscured by the spiral of devaluation and inflation; and devaluations would do nothing to resolve the basic problems (this was the experience in the United Kingdom and in Italy between 1973 and 1978). It is important that the EMS stabilization mechanism should be allowed to operate in countries where inflation or the level of relative costs is still too high; this not only means that monetary policy must defend the exchange rate but also that domestic adjustment, notably in the areas of incomes and public finances, must be facilitated and speeded up through other appropriate measures. Quite independently from the existence of the EMS, such internal adjustment is necessary in order to open up possibilities of economic growth in conditions of stability and to increase employment. The EMS simply highlights the need for adjustment and helps its realization along.

This account of the functioning of the system in its first three years of existence can be summarized in one sentence and two qualifications. The sentence is: 'the system has greatly improved intra-Community exchange rate relationships, but has failed to produce the desirable degree of convergence towards price stability'. This would be my answer to the question on the past.

The first qualification concerns exchange rates. One should not interpret the sentence as asserting that exchange rate stability is always desirable, regardless of underlying economic conditions. Contrary to the Bretton Woods system, the EMS should avoid excessive rigidity, it should resist both full or over-accommodation of cost and price trends, and any stubborn defence of unrealistic exchange rates. Exchange rate management is an art, and the system performed it well in the last three years.

The second qualification regards price stability and concerns those who, in countries with a good record on this core, sometimes accuse the EMS of being a source of inflation. This charge is totally unjustified and derives from some confusion as to the implicit term of comparison. When one says that the system has failed to produce price stability, the term of comparison cannot be 1978, a year in which inflation rates were indeed lower and less divergent than today, because since then the second oil shock and the extraordinary appreciation of the dollar are the true new causes of the deteriorating price performance. On the other hand, nobody would dare to say that, had the EMS not existed, price trends would be more stable and less divergent than they are: most observers in fact believe precisely the opposite. The relevant term of comparison is neither a pre-EMS nor a non-EMS situation, but rather what we consider to be our best price stability objective. I would thus conclude in this regard that the system needs to be improved.

+

\+ +

This leads straight into the second, more challenging question: what contribution can the system make in the future?

The answer I would suggest to this question is the following: 'A stronger EMS could become a more effective instrument to foster price stability and it could contribute to a better handling of two major problems that trouble our countries: the maintenance of the common market and the organization of world monetary relationships'.

This answer derives from two different lines of reasoning that I shall now briefly illustrate. One, of a more technical nature, relates to the functioning of the system, its imperfections and the necessary improvements. The other, more general, relates to the profound historical and economic problems that are, and will presumably be, at work in our economic systems.

\+ + +

Taking the technical aspects first: what are the main imperfections of the system as it is today? One should here avoid two types of simplistic, and therefore popular answers.

The first of these is that the system is too rigid (others say it is too flexible). It is a simplistic answer because it considers the EMS as a mere exchange rate mechanism, and because, even from this narrow point of view, it disregards its fundamental feature, which is precisely that of providing a certain combination of rules and discretion. I believe that this combination has been fundamentally balanced, that it is sound and consistent with the present state of our economies and financial markets. It has avoided the absurd exchange rate movements experienced throughout most of the 1970s and that we still experience between major world currencies today. In a system which provides for discretionary management, there may of course be instances in which the best decision is not taken or is not taken at the most timely moment. So far, I do not think there have been any significant instances of this sort, but even if this had been the case, it would not constitute an instrinsic defect of the system, any more than the fact that in a particular case the discount rate may be changed a few weeks too late or a few weeks too early is an intrinsic defect of the charter of a central bank.

The second simplistic answer consists in saying that the lack of success in achieving greater price stability is due to external, non-monetary factors: the oil shock, the strong dollar, lax fiscal policies, excessive wage increases. This again is a simplistic answer because, although it is obviously true that such factors have worked against price stability, it is equally true that in discussing the imperfections and the possible improvements of the EMS one must look at the system internally to see how its mechanisms and its structure might better contribute to greater monetary stability. It is of course evident that if all surrounding factors were behaving so well as to assure low and uniform inflation rates in all our countries, a monetary union would be possible. I dare say that in that case it would not only be possible, it would also be superfluous.

If we reject these simplistic answers, we need a slightly more elaborate one, that can be stated as follows: 'the system has failed to achieve a better degree of price stability because it has not produced sufficient monetary discipline in the Community'. Here 'the system' means that we must consider discipline induced by the system rather than by other external factors, which are of course extremely important, but that cannot be used as an alibi when talking about the system itself; 'monetary discipline' means that we have to consider monetary policy in all its aspects, and not only in terms of exchange rates; 'in the Community' means in all countries of the Community. In short, the European Monetary System has failed to produce greater price stability in the Community because it does not envelop all the dimensions of monetary policy into a unique set of common decisions directed towards monetary discipline.

Monetary relationships between member countries involve three policy dimensions: exchange rate variations, balance of payments financing, and domestic adjustment. Only a unified approach to these three dimensions will eventually allow (allow, not ensure) achievement of the twin objective of giving the Community its own monetary organization and of fostering monetary stability. Only discretionary policy decisions taken in common will enable the Community to pursue price stability through changing internal and external conditions.

In the present system neither the unity of approach nor the possibility of discretionary decisions are realized to a sufficient degree. The unity of approach is impaired both by the large and unregulated access to extra-Community financing of intra-Community imbalances, and by the overly loose constraints on domestic policies. The constraint on the third dimension, i.e. on the exchange rate, is insufficient to globally orient policies towards monetary stability. The lack of adjustment thus leads either to a ratification through exchange rate variations, or to an excessively protracted recourse to uncontrolled and unconditional international credit as an artificial way to support the parity. The need for discretionary decisions is frustrated by the extremely automatic nature of the existing rules governing the creation of ECU, the interest rates, the quantity, the cost and availability of Community credit.

In summary, the technical line of reasoning suggests that there are indeed shortcomings within the EMS as it is. These do not lie in an 'excess of ambition' or in an excess of discipline as some say; on the contrary, they consist in an insufficient discipline and in an imbalance in the way the various aspects of monetary policy are dealt with.

+

+ +

Technical considerations would in themselves justify an evolution of the present system as a step towards both greater monetary integration and greater monetary stability. Technical solutions, into which I shall not enter here, are in fact available. But it seems unlikely that progress will be induced by purely technical considerations.

The decision to promote the evolution of the EMS will be an important political decision.As such, it will be provoked by deep historical and economic forces rather than by merely technical requirements. What are these deep forces? I think they are related to at least two problems that trouble all our countries at present and that will continue to trouble them in the years to come. The evolution of the EMS has to be seen in the light of the contribution it can give to a better handling of these problems.

The first problem is the future of the common market. The Treaty of Rome created a system which, for its proper functioning, requires some form of monetary organization. When the Treaty was drawn up this framework was provided by the Bretton Woods system and it was provided in such a solid and convincing way that monetary matters were almost ignored in the Treaty. The common market cannot survive for long in a state of monetary anarchy. This is something which is not always fully perceived by monetary authorities, but is evident to businessmen, to farmers and – from time to time – becomes clear to politicians. If one reads what was written in the mid-1970s before the creation of the EMS, one finds a surprisingly strong feeling that the whole construction of a common market for agricultural and industrial products risked being undermined by the lack of a satisfactory form of monetary organization.

Seen in this light, it is not surprising that the issue of European monetary integration was first raised in coincidence with the unmistakable signs of decline of the Bretton Woods system in the late 1960s. The repeated efforts that have been made since then show the necessity for our countries to sustain European trade and agricultural arrangements with an adequate monetary organization.

The second problem is related to the evolution of international economic and monetary relationships. In the last 20 years the relative position of the United States in the world economy has profoundly changed and a tripolar system has emerged. Not only in terms of industry, agriculture and total and per capita income, but also as a trade partner and as a holder of international reserves, the Community has become one of the three great areas of the industrialized world. It is against the background of this development that one has to place the evolution of the EMS.

Some may think that the regained strength of the US dollar in 1980 and 1981 will lead back to a system based exclusively on the American currency. I do not share this view. It may well be that the dollar will never return to its 1978 weakness, but monetary phenomena have evolved in the last years in accordance with the other magnitudes that I have just mentioned, and a reversal of the trend seems unlikely. Too many things have changed.

The international monetary system will thus probably continue for some years to be based on more than one reserve currency. This will have two consequences. First, an international monetary world based on several currencies will need more, not less, management than one based on a single currency. Secondly, Europe will inevitably, in one form or another, be one of the reserve issuing centres.

An appropriately developed EMS could be the optimal way to organize the European pole of the international monetary system. By giving the Community a unique and simple monetary expression, it would help the orderly evolution of the multi-currency reserve system. It would increase the effectiveness of the Euro-American monetary dialogue. It would spread over several European shoulders the burden of an international currency role. Finally, it would protect intra-Community monetary and trade arrangements from potentially disruptive shocks coming from the outside.

In 1978, when the EMS was established, there was an almost unique constellation of favourable stars. A weak and weakening dollar raised with increasing urgency the problem of the possible international role of the German mark, and the German authorities were reluctant to let their currency carry a burden that had proved too heavy even for politically and economically much larger powers. Europe was shaken by one of its recurrent moods of dissatisfaction with the so-called American leadership. Two eminent political leaders like Chancellor Schmidt and President Giscard d'Estaing were at the height of their political power and prestige, and their ambitions were not cooled by imminent electoral deadlines. The European Commission had shown political courage and vision in raising the issue of monetary integration at a time in which, though urgent and relevant, it was considered with almost universal scepticism. The explosion of policy and economic divergencies in European countries that had followed the first oil shock seemed to be dampening and leaving the place to greater convergence. In Germany there was a conviction that the basic economic policy philosophy in France was moving strongly to a free-market type of conception. This was indeed an exceptional constellation. And even so, the birth of the system required strong political will, surprise-action, and strict confidentiality in its early stages. And even so, it has caused deep contrasts and conflicts in some countries, and it could not start with the full participation of all member countries.

At the end of 1981 the stars seem less favourable. But is this really so, or is it not that we have lost the ability to see the stars? The history of this century in Europe should be a warning: we have been often blind, and blind in the moment of the greatest danger.

CHAPTER IV

Memorandum on the European Monetary System (1983)

In early 1983 I had the great honour of being invited by the House of Lords to give evidence on the European Monetary System. I testified before the Subcommittee on the Finance, Economic and Regional Policy of the European Communities on my last day as Director-General for Economic and Financial Affairs of the Commission of the European Communities.

It is often said that scientific progress is a matter of good questions, not of good answers. This also applies to economic policy. The fact of being asked straightforward, fundamental questions by such a distinguished group of men helped to clarify my own ideas. I was pleased to see some of these ideas in the final report in which the House of Lords recommended that sterling should join the EMS.

QUESTION 1. *What are the principal objectives of the EMS? To what extent is it simply a practical arrangement for helping to stabilize European currencies rather than a stage towards full European monetary union?*

The EMS serves two principal purposes. The first is to preserve the *acquis communautaire* in trade and agriculture. It provides an organization which limits the scope for exchange rate manipulation and prevents the currencies of member countries from fluctuating excessively in relation to each other. A certain stability of exchange rates is essential if the free movement of goods and services within the Community is not to be threatened by demands for protection as a result of costs and prices in different member countries getting 'out of line', even if only temporarily. In the agricultural sector a particular problem arises because, under the Community's common agricultural policy, farm prices are fixed in ECU, their level in national money is determined by the rate of exchange between the national currency and the ECU. In principle, this rate should correspond to the actual rate of exchange on the currency market or to the parity fixed in the EMS, but in practice a different rate ('green rate') may be applied as a temporary measure to protect agricultural producers or consumers from the immediate consequences of an exchange rate adjustment. This leads, at least temporarily, to agricultural prices that are higher, or lower, than those that would result from the application of the ECU central rate. The corresponding difficulties to be overcome in annual price negotiations, which are further enhanced by the divergence of inflation in member countries, are a consequence of the fact that the present degree of monetary integration is lagging behind the level of integration achieved in the organization of the Community agricultural market.

The second purpose is to foster monetary stability in the sense of allowing countries to pursue their stabilization policies in a way which maximizes the advantage which can be drawn from exchange rate policies.

A distinction between a 'practical arrangement for helping stabilize European currencies' and 'a stage towards full European monetary union' is difficult to make. Both elements are there. The EMS certainly has a political ambition that goes beyond the existing arrangements and that derives from the general objectives of the Treaties and from the subsequent Council decisions concerning economic convergence and the creation of economic and monetary union, as well as from the resolution which has created the EMS. To the extent to which such an ambition creates expectations, and because it is linked to many other arrangements and policies of the Community, the EMS as it is now derives part of its strength from being conceived as a stage towards full European monetary union.

QUESTION 2. *Why are exchange rate fluctuations undesirable? Is there evidence that they discourage international trade and investment between countries in an undesirable way? If so, are completely fixed exchange rates required to avoid these effects, or can they be mitigated by an adjustable-peg system such as the EMS?*

Not all forms of exchange rate variability are damaging. Very short-term volatility (i.e. daily movements around a stable trend) is not particularly damaging to price stability, trade or investment. By contrast, medium to long-term volatility or overshooting (i.e. cycles developing over several quarters or years) is more likely to do real harm.

It is difficult to prove that exchange rate variability discourages trade and investment. In particular it must be admitted that the econometric evidence is by no means conclusive. However, it is clear that medium-term exchange rate volatility does increase uncertainty and costs, which cannot be avoided entirely by use of forward markets, since these do not as a rule provide cover for periods much beyond a year and do not exist for all currencies. This being so, it would be very surprising if it did not discourage trade and investment at least to some extent. In a multi-country economy, whether its coverage is regional, like that of the European Community, or much wider, like that of the OECD, trade arrangements and monetary arrangements are complementary. It is doubtful whether free trade can survive for very long in the absence of some effective monetary organization, meaning by this arrangements which oblige countries to have at least some regard for the consequences of monetary and exchange rate developments on their trading partners. The increasing clamour for protectionism in those countries whose currencies have become over-valued as a result of the somewhat anarchic exchange rate conditions that have prevailed in recent years is a constant reminder of this danger. Without wishing to be complacent we think it is fair to claim that the erosion of free trade and the pressure to erect protectionist barriers has been rather more successfully resisted within the European Community than it has within the world trading community as a whole (at least so far as trade relations between member countries are concerned). There are various reasons for this, but an extremely important one, in our view, is that the Community has a monetary system, which, however imperfect it may be, does nevertheless oblige the participants to pay due regard to the effects of their monetary and exchange rate policies upon their partners and does considerably reduce the likelihood of member currencies becoming badly misaligned with each other.

Exchange rates should remain adjustable. Economic and institutional conditions make a system of 'completely fixed exchange rates' quite unrealistic today. What is essential is not that rates should be irrevocably fixed, but that changes in exchange rates, if and when they occur, should be a matter for collective rather than unilateral decision and that they should be accompanied by programmes that promote greater economic convergence in the future. This has been the main achievement of the EMS.

QUESTION 3. *How successful has the EMS been in reducing the fluctuations in European exchange rates since its inception? What degree of intervention by the authorities has been required to achieve this? In your judgment, has the amount of speculation in foreign exchange markets increased or decreased as a result of the operation of the EMS?*

We do not know what would have happened if the EMS had not existed.

The EMS has been rather successful in reducing exchange rate variability between participating currencies. If one compares the experience during the four years that the EMS has been in operation with that during the previous four years the variability of EMS currencies against each other has been some 35% less in the post-EMS period. Similarly, if one compares the experience of EMS currencies with other major currencies during the 1979-82 period, the average variability of the latter against all currencies has been about 70% greater than the average variability of EMS currencies. Variability is measured here by the average bilateral percentage change of each currency against the currencies of the industrial countries.

Floating was 'managed' before March 1979 and would no doubt have continued to be managed even if there had been no EMS, so it is difficult to say how much intervention would have taken place without the EMS. On the other hand, even with the EMS in operation intervention should not be and is not the only, or even the most important, instrument for maintaining exchange rate stability. It is a useful means of resisting pressures on the exchange rate which are not consistent with the fundamental conditions of the economy; it is also useful as a kind of 'bridging measure' to support an exchange rate until the economic, financial, and political conditions necessary to bring about an effective adjustment – and which may include a change in the exchange rate – have been created.

As regards speculation – meaning by that decisions motivated essentially by the prospect of making short-term gains as a result of exchange rate movements – it is difficult to state with confidence whether speculation has increased or decreased as a result of the existence of the EMS. There are times when the known commitment of the authorities to defend an exchange rate discourages speculation. But there are other times when the prospects for gain arising from a sizeable one-step change in the exchange rate may encourage speculation. In the first two years of the EMS's existence there was very little speculation – perhaps less than might have been expected in the light of the economic fundamentals. In the third year there was more speculation, but it could be argued that this was justified by the existence of greater divergence, both in policies and in economic performance, between the member countries. In the fourth and most recent year the level of speculation has remained high – higher perhaps than was justified in view of the fact that policies have shown a considerable convergence during this most recent period, even if this has not yet been reflected in a convergence of economic performance.

QUESTION 4. *Why was the snake unsuccessful in achieving exchange rate stability in the period of its operation? In what way does the EMS differ from the snake? Do these differences enhance its prospects of success?*

Measured against the objectives of economic and monetary union put forward in the Werner report, out of which the snake arrangements arose in April 1972, the snake's success was rather limited. The snake was unable to keep together the major European currencies; one after the other sterling, the lira and the French franc all dropped out. There are various reasons for this lack of cohesion. Most of them relate to the difficulties inherent to the effort to tie together under an exchange rate link countries differing in their economic situation, in the capacity of their policies to maintain internal and external equilibria and in the measures adopted in the pursuit of those policies. Less common commitment to monetary stability than today, less political commitment to monetary cooperation in Europe and greater hopes in the working of a floating rate system were the background against which the snake had to cope with the monetary consequences of the first oil price crisis.

There are differences in the mechanisms between the snake and the EMS and differences between the political commitments, with the latter reflected in the former, at least in some cases. A much stronger element of Community monetary solidarity in the EMS is incorporated in the very definition of the ECU as a basket currency compared with the former European monetary unit of account (EMUA) which was defined in terms of gold. The basket definition of the ECU implies that exchange rate changes of one currency entail changes of all other currencies with respect to the ECU as well. This and the decision to put the ECU at the centre of the EMS has far-reaching consequences, in particular in making adjustments of central rates subject to mutual agreement by a common procedure, whereas in the snake, parity adjustments *vis-à-vis* the EMUA had no impact on partner currencies' EMUA rates and could be made after consultation by the respective monetary authorities. The divergence indicator which, however imperfectly, acts as a warning device, hinting at severe strains within the EMS exchange rate system and leading to an examination of the underlying conditions and a presumption that the authorities of the country concerned will adopt adequate measures to correct the situation, is another feature of the EMS directly related to the basket definition of the ECU. A third example is the impact of central rate changes on the CAP through their effect on monetary compensatory amounts and, in a second stage, on the setting of agricultural prices in ECU. The pooling of member central banks' reserves at the EMCF and the upgrading of the amounts available under the credit mechanisms and the modifications of their terms all reflect the increased significance of Community solidarity within the EMS compared to the functioning of the snake.

It can fairly be claimed that the EMS has already proved more successful than the snake. Thus, while sterling, the lira and the French franc had all dropped out of the snake within two years, the EMS has managed to hold together three of the Community's four major currencies over a period of four years, despite conditions which were just as unfavourable as those prevailing in the 1970s. It has also, despite the lack of progress in creating a formal institutional framework, been much more successful in achieving convergence of economic policies in member countries. At the risk of some oversimplification it might be said that, during the snake period, each major member country pursued its own economic objectives without much regard for whether they were compatible with those of its partners and, when this produced strains on the exchange rate, the deficit countries, one by one, dropped out of the system. Since the inception of the EMS attitudes have changed. Policies have not, of course, always been mutually compatible, but, in contrast to what happened previously, when such incompatibility produced payments imbalances and strains in the foreign exchange market, the major countries have been prepared to modify their internal policies in order to correct these imbalances and stay within the system, rather than stick with their policies and drop out. The EMS constraint has been an important factor in furthering the process of de-indexation in countries such as Belgium, Denmark and Italy and we are firmly convinced that this will improve the performance of these countries in achieving greater price stability in the future. Finally the EMS has established the Community's monetary identity in a way in which the snake never did. The most obvious expression of this identity is the ECU, which, in contrast to the EMUA, is widely used as a unit of account, plays a useful role as a reserve asset and instrument of settlement between member countries and is now developing rapidly as a financial instrument in the private sector.

QUESTION 5. *What constraints does participation in the EMS place on domestic monetary and fiscal policy? Has participation proved to be inconsistent with strict adherence to domestic monetary targets?*

The objective of the EMS is not just to achieve stability of exchange rates between participating currencies, but to achieve monetary stability in a wider sense that includes prices as well as exchange rates. This is why the commitment to maintain fixed rates has been more of a constraint on the higher-inflation participants than on the low-inflation ones. It is the former rather than the latter which have more often had to modify their internal policies in order to remain within the system. Belgium, Denmark, France and Italy have made substantial and far-reaching changes in their domestic economic policies, because these policies were leading to an unacceptable loss of foreign exchange.

Experience has shown that, whatever the theoreticians might have expected, participation in the system has not in practice proved inconsistent with adherence to domestic monetary targets. From the point of view of deficit countries, participation in the EMS has probably strengthened the hand of the authorities in adhering to their targets. Surplus countries have been able to avoid intervention on a scale that would have produced large, unwanted increases in the money supply by revaluing their currencies from time to time.

In general, constraints on domestic monetary policy arise much more as a result of the openness of the economy of the country concerned than from its participation in the EMS. Small open economies with floating exchange rates have not found that the absence of a formal obligation to intervene in support of the exchange rate has enabled them to pursue domestic economic objectives regardless of the external consequences. Switzerland and some of the Scandinavian countries are examples which spring to mind.

QUESTION 6. *To what extent is the long-run success of the EMS dependent on convergence in economic performance between the participating countries?*

Are there discernable signs of such convergence in the period since its inception?

The EMS was established with the explicit objective of furthering economic convergence among the Member States. So obviously it cannot really be considered a complete 'success' until substantial progress towards that objective has been made. On the other hand its achievement in avoiding unnecessary variability of exchange rates and in ensuring the orderly adjustment of parities when the need arises, which is essential for the efficient functioning of the common market, is clear for all to see. In this respect the EMS is already a complete success, despite the fact that it has had to operate in conditions that have been made particularly difficult by the long recession and the excessive exchange rate variability of the dollar and the yen.

It is true that if you look at inflation rates and the balance of payments performance of member countries in 1978 – the year immediately before the EMS was launched – and compare the figures with those for the years since EMS was launched it appears that rates of inflation among Community countries were more divergent in 1982 than in 1978. But this is not the appropriate comparison to make, because 1978 was a year of relative economic stability, whereas during the following four years the Community's economy has been subjected to serious shocks from outside, in particular the oil crisis of 1979-80 and its aftermath. The appropriate question to ask is whether economic performance within the Community would have been more or less divergent during this period if there had been no EMS than it has been with EMS. Of course it is impossible to give a straightforward factual answer to this question. But it is our firm view, as close observers of the policy-making process in member countries, that membership of the EMS has been an important and influential factor shaping individual countries' policies in such a way as to prevent them from getting too far out of line with those of their partners. It has produced greater efforts to bring down inflation than might otherwise have been made in countries where the inflation rate was high and has had some marginal moderating influence in countries where it was low.

QUESTION 7. *What criteria are and should be used for central parity adjustments within the EMS? How frequent and how large can such adjustments be permitted to be? If the system permits flexibility, how does it differ from a 'crawling-peg' mechanism for the exchange rate?*

Setting exchange rates at an appropriate level requires judgment and discretion. It is not something which can be done by the mechanical application of some predetermined formula, however complex and ingenious this may be. It is an art and not a science.

Obviously in arriving at a judgment as to the appropriate exchange rate for a currency, policy-makers should pay due attention to a certain number of fundamental economic variables. They should look at the country's basic balance of payments and try to form a judgment as to whether it is in equilibrium and, if not, how big a change and in what direction is required. They should look at the cyclical position of the economy in order to determine whether and to what extent any disequilibrium which does exist is the result of productive capacity in that country being more or less fully utilized than in its trading partners. They should look at competitiveness to see whether it has improved or deteriorated in comparison with some normative level. And they should look at the structure of the country's trade, in case there have been changes which may have implications for the exchange rate – for example the development or exhaustion of indigenous sources of energy.

As a general rule one might advance the proposition that to the extent that an external imbalance is cyclical it should either be financed or adjusted by acting on relative income levels through changes in internal economic policy. To the extent that the imbalance results from changes in competitiveness or trade structure a change in the exchange rate designed to alter relative cost and price levels is more likely to be appropriate. In practice, however, it is often very difficult to judge to what extent an imbalance is cyglical and to what extent it is structural, so that the appropriate remedy may not be obvious.

Moreover adjustment of the exchange rate interacts with economic policy. It not only reflects the past development of the 'fundamentals' but also influences their future behaviour. For example, the more a country's costs and prices have risen in relation to those of its competitors the larger will be the devaluation required to correct for this loss of competitiveness. But the larger the devaluation the greater will be the additional inflationary cost-push imparted to the economy and hence the greater the risk that the divergence between its rate of inflation and that of its competitors will increase rather than diminish in future. Thus the optimal exchange rate adjustment in certain circumstances may be one which does not fully compensate for the inflation differential and this has generally been the criterion followed in the EMS. The frequency and size of adjustments have to be decided in such a way as not only to entail broad consistency with the fundamentals, but also to optimize the effect of stabilization policies.

The difference between the EMS and a 'crawling-peg' regime is precisely that in the latter this element of discretion is lacking. A crawling peg does not permit the choice of an exchange rate change which is optimal from the policy-maker's point of view. Of course, greater discretion carries with it an increased possibility of error.

QUESTION 8. *How robust is the EMS to fluctuations in the US dollar relative to European currencies, bearing in mind the differing influences of the dollar exchange rate on European economies? Is a concerted policy towards the dollar required? If so, what form might it take?*

In principle, the EMS can be considered as a block floating against outside currencies, with the internal cohesion of its components being independent of relationships with third currencies. In practice, there is a relationship between intra-EMS cohesion and movements *vis-à-vis* the outside and in particular the evolution of the dollar. There are two main reasons for this. First, the dollar exposure varies from one EMS currency to another, according to the share of the dollar in foreign trade: for example, this share is about 50% for Italy and less than 30% for Germany. Secondly, to the extent to which fluctuations in the US dollar are associated with changes in the currency composition of private and official portfolios, intra-EMS tensions may be aggravated or alleviated by the fact that EMS currencies do not participate in the process of currency diversification in proportions equal to their weights in the system. In particular, the DM represents about 35% of the ECU but it takes much more than 35%, if not the totality, of changes in currency compositions between the dollar and the Community currencies. As a consequence, a weakening of the dollar *vis-à-vis* the EMS block produces a strengthening of the position of the German mark relative to the other EMS currencies; a strengthening of the dollar *vis-à-vis* the EMS produces the opposite effect. As the DM tends to be a strong currency in the system, intra-EMS tensions tend to be greater with a weak than with a strong dollar.

A concerted policy towards the dollar is necessary not only because of the diversified degree of dollar exposure or the differing influences mentioned above, but simply because eight currencies tied by a system of agreed parities cannot conduct eight independent policies *vis-à-vis* the dollar.

The (short-term) need for most EMS currencies to follow the movements of the DM against the dollar and the subsequent parallelism in the development of interest rate policies by member countries can be regarded as a form of *de facto* coordination of dollar policies. The coordination of intervention policies against the dollar and in a broader sense the establishment of target zones for the exchange rates between the US dollar and the EMS currencies lay out a wide field of activity, not only for intra-European but also for transatlantic concertation and cooperation towards a better organization of the international monetary system.

QUESTION 9. *It was originally envisaged that central bank intervention would occur when the agreed margins away from the central parity are reached and the intervention would be in participating currencies. In practice, substantial intramarginal intervention has occurred and intervention has often been in dollars. Is this desirable, or does it create problems for the operation of the EMS?*

Only interventions at the margins are compulsory, but the possibility of intramarginal interventions has always been allowed for. Intramarginal interventions have been practiced and the technique is recognized as useful and efficient at times. The main reason is that when a currency is close to one or other of its intervention limits, speculation, based upon expectations of a parity change, increases and the maintenance of the exchange rate may then require more intervention than would have been necessary if the rate had not moved into the 'danger zone'. On the other hand, it is true that the necessary consensus for certain adjustment policies may be easier to obtain when there is a visible threat to the exchange rate than when a currency gives the impression of staying comfortably within its margins, even if this happens at the price of substantial interventions.

Another issue is the choice of currency for intramarginal interventions. Basic EMS regulations state that 'interventions shall in principle be effected in currencies of the participating central banks'. This should be applied to all interventions, not only to those at the margins. On the other hand, explicit provisions enabling member countries to dispose of Community currencies only exist when such currencies are needed to intervene at the margins. There is a gap here in the EMS provisions. It is to fill such a gap that in March 1982 the Commission proposed, in forms that do not jeopardize the control of member monetary authorities over their own currencies, to open access to Community currencies for intramarginal interventions.

QUESTION 10. *How symmetrical are the obligations for adjustment within the EMS as between strong and weak currencies? How is this influenced by the dual operation of the parity grid system and the divergence criterion?*

An element of symmetry in the obligations for adjustment is provided through the functioning of the divergence indicator. When a currency – whether strong or weak – crosses its 'threshold of divergence' it creates a presumption that the authorities concerned will correct this situation by adequate measures (intervention in the foreign exchange market, changes in interest rates, other changes in internal economic policy, or adjustment of the exchange rate). If no measures are taken by the authorities of the divergent currency, the latter are expected to justify their inaction.

However, given the commitment to monetary stability in the wider sense, and in particular to price stability, 'symmetry' in this context should be interpreted to mean that the measures taken by a divergent currency should ideally be such as to contribute to rather than militate against the achievement of this objective. Thus, for example, in the inflationary conditions which have been characteristic of the last four years it would not have been appropriate for a surplus country which found itself in a position of 'upward divergence' to take measures that would have brought its price level close to the Community average, even though such action might have led to greater exchange rate stability within the system. The appropriate action by the authorities of a strong but divergent currency in these circumstances is to revalue and this is the rule which has in fact been followed by those member currencies which have been persistently strong.

By contrast, in the case of a currency which is diverging downwards, the emphasis should rather be placed on measures designed to correct the external balance by restraining internal demand. Only if it is clear that costs and prices have got so badly out of line with those in other member countries that there is no real prospect of restoring competitiveness in this way, should recourse be had to devaluation. If devaluation is inevitable, it is essential that it should be accompanied by vigorous measures to control domestic demand. Otherwise it will simply aggravate existing inflationary pressures and the initial competitive advantage gained will be swiftly eroded.

These principles have gradually gained general acceptance, beginning with the first 'snake-type' realignment of September 1979, followed by the almost unilateral devaluations of the Danish krone and the Italian lira in November 1979 and March 1981 and then the three realignments of October 1981, February 1982 and June 1982 when increasingly important changes in internal economic policy have accompanied and reinforced the parity changes that were decided in common.

QUESTION 11. *What is the role of the ECU? Has it become more than an accounting unit? Must it do so if the ideals of EMU and a European Monetary Fund are to be achieved? What problems arise from the inclusion of non-participating currencies in the ECU?*

Originally, the role of the ECU, dating back to a period well before the establishment of the EMS, was that of a unit of account.

From 1975 to 1978, the European unit of account, as it was then called, was used by various institutions (the EIB from 18 March 1975; the EDF – under the Lomé Convention – from 21 April 1975; the ECSC from 24 April 1975) and for a variety of purposes (the general budget from 21 April 1978; in customs matters from 23 November 1978). With effect from April 1979, the ECU was introduced into the common agricultural policy, but with specific conversion rates ('green rates'). Finally, in January 1981, the ECU replaced the EUA in all the sectors in which the latter had been used and has thus become the sole unit of account used by the Community authorities.

With the inception of the EMS, the official use of the ECU and its field of application have become much larger. In particular, the ECU has become a key reserve asset created by the European Monetary Cooperation Fund for the EEC central banks against the transfer, by these banks, in the form of three-month revolving swaps, of 20% of their gold assets and 20% of their dollar reserves. A debtor central bank may use ECU to repay debts incurred under the very short-term financing arrangements of the EMS when such debts fall due for settlement. However, the creditor central bank is not obliged to accept settlement in ECU of more than 50% of its claim. In other cases ECU may be used by central banks by mutual agreement.

Apart from its role as a reserve asset, the ECU also serves as *numéraire* for the exchange rate mechanism, as the basis for calculating the indicator of divergence and as the denominator for operations in both the intervention and credit mechanisms.

However, it is the use of the ECU in the private sector which has recently proved the most dynamic field of activity.

It was in 1982 that the ECU may be said to have 'taken off' in the private sector, with the creation of the complete banking infrastructure which was necessary once issues were to be not only denominated, but also settled, in ECU. Official recognition of the ECU as a currency by Italy, Belgium and France, together with a favourable or, at any rate, neutral official attitude in most other member countries have enabled those banks which wish to do so to offer a wide range of services in ECU.

There has been considerable diversity in these developments between member countries, depending upon the scope provided by differing national legislation. Thus Belgium, which is the seat of the Community's institutions, which are substantial borrowers in ECU, has become the centre for banking and lending operations in ECU; in Italy the ECU is used above all for export and import finance; while in France there have been a number of interesting cases of the ECU being used for commercial purposes.

Precise figures are available only for public note and bond issues in ECU, but according to unofficial estimates from the banking sector the situation as of February 1983 is that:

(i) ECU deposits now amount to around 3 000 million ECU, divided equally between sight and time deposits;

(ii) short-term trade credit outstanding, covering foreign transactions, exceeds 1 000 million ECU in Italy alone;

(iii) the total of syndicated bank credits amounts to 650 million ECU;

(iv) there have been over 30 note and bond issues since April 1981 for a total of 2 500 million ECU.

In the second half of 1982 the ECU was the fourth most widely used currency in the Eurocurrency and Eurobond markets. In January this year it had risen to third place, after the dollar and the German mark, with 4% of the market.

On the whole, the ECU seems to have overtaken the other basket-type currency, the SDR, in popularity, less two years after the composition of the latter was simplified to include only five currencies. The differences between the SDR and the ECU help to explain the greater success of the ECU in private markets. First of all, the ECU basket is much more homogeneous, its component currencies being officially linked in the exchange rate arrangement. Secondly, the ECU is the monetary expression of a highly integrated economic area and of a true common market, whereas, even in its streamlined form, the SDR basket is composed of currencies of countries whose economic ties are much looser. Thirdly, the ECU provides a more complete alternative to the dollar as an asset than does the SDR in which the dollar is the largest single component. Fourthly, as already indicated, the ECU is used for operational purposes by Community institutions (e.g. the Community budget, Community borrowing and lending operations, etc.). Finally, the institutional organization of the European Communities, which comprises Community law, several Community policies, a Community budget and an elected parliament, makes the ECU the expression of a political reality that is much more developed than that of other international organizations such as the IMF, and provides it with the core of the infrastructure of a monetary authority.

It should be added that the virtues of a basket, considered from the point of view of currency diversification are different from those of a basket considered as the embryo of a common currency: from the first point of view, the more heterogeneous are the components, the better; from the second point of view, the opposite may be true.

At present, except for the definition and the use of identical exchange rates – the latter being determined by the foreign exchange market – there is no connection between the use of the ECU within the official framework of the EMS and its use by the private sector; in the former case, I am referring to an agreement between the authorities of the Member States and to Community decisions; in the latter, each operation gives rise to a contract under private law. Nevertheless, the ECU is not completely lacking a 'lender of last resort', since each of its components does have a lender of last resort. Thus the lender of last resort exists in a sort of two-stage procedure. Technically, it would not be difficult to establish a point of contact between the two different circuits of the official and the private ECU. At that point, all the ingredients of a fully fledged monetary system would be there.

Practical experience with the EMS has shown that certain disadvantages flow from the fact that the ECU includes currencies which do not participate in the exchange rate mechanism. These are not simply of a technical nature (such as the corrections which have to be made to the divergence indicator), but concern also the determination of the value of assets and liabilities in ECU *vis-à-vis* the EMCF which arise from very short-term financing operations, and the value of ECU reserves acquired by swaps against gold and dollars. Moreover, the technical need to assign a fictitious ECU central rate to such currencies can have unforeseeable effects on the determination of the monetary compensatory amounts in the context of the common agricultural policy which uses ECU central rates as the main point of reference. Finally, progress in the private use of the ECU could be hampered by the fluctuation of component currencies which were not participating in the EMS exchange rate arrangements. This would reflect unfavourably upon the status of the ECU as the unit of a zone of monetary stability.

QUESTION 12. *In what ways do you see the EMS developing? How is this influenced by the recent and prospective enlargement of the EEC?*

It is possible to conceive of three forms, by no means mutually exclusive, which the future development of the EMS might take:

(i) development *within* the existing legal framework;

(ii) development *of* the existing legal framework;

(iii) development *outside* the existing legal framework.

So far as development within the existing legal framework is concerned, it is fair to say that the process of exchange rate determination within the EMS has been fully 'communitized' – i.e. the decision-making process is a common one in which all members have a say. It is worth noting in passing that in this respect the EMS has progressed further than the wider international community ever did under the Bretton Woods regime, where exchange rate adjustments were, to a large extent, made unilaterally by the country concerned.

In contrast, decisions regarding adjustment and financing are still left very much to individual member countries and there is undoubtedly scope for further 'communitization' of these. There are grounds for optimism here. As regard adjustment, it is now much more widely recognized than it was a few years ago that, with or without exchange rate changes, action to control the domestic price level and internal demand is an essential condition for the maintenance of external balance. All members accept that their domestic policies will be scrutinized critically by their partners for their external implications. Similarly with financing, where, however, less progress has been made. Although the decision whether to finance or adjust rests ultimately with the country concerned, all members should accept a degree of surveillance, within the Monetary Committee, over their foreign borrowing activities and external indebtedness and should not unduly postpone recourse to financing through official lending institutions.

So far as development of the existing legal framework is concerned we must guarantee that the EMS is established on a sound and orthodox basis and that its development is conducive to the attainment of its final objectives. The Community dimension represents a more favourable environment for monetary orthodoxy. A European monetary institution would enjoy a greater degree of freedom from short-term political pressures (financing public deficits, reducing interest rates, etc.). It would not be totally exempted from political control, but it would, by its very nature, follow longer-term economic targets. However, so long as the political commitment to innovation is lacking, development of the existing legal framework cannot be expected to comprise dramatic initiatives such as the creation of a European Monetary Fund. It is much more likely, if it occurs at all, to consist of small and detailed changes to the working of the existing mechanisms – for example, the introduction of new regulations governing the use of Community currencies for intramarginal intervention of the kind proposed last year by the Commission.

So far as development outside the existing legal framework is concerned, the main element here is the private use of the ECU. As already mentioned, this is at present the most dynamic feature of European monetary development, as the figures given in reply to Question 11 amply demonstrate. We may be approaching a situation in which the ECU grows in importance in private markets without any corresponding growth of the official authority which should control it. We must remember that, after all, money developed long before the setting up of central banks.

As to the implications of enlargement of the Community for the EMS, we believe that, if the decision-making mechanisms are efficient and work smoothly, an increased number of currencies and countries participating in the EMS should not constitute a major problem. Given the existing degree of interdependence amongst European currencies, the national monetary authorities must engage in a fairly close concertation effort whether they participate in the EMS or not. It is conceivable that participation in the EMS might facilitate their task.

QUESTION 13. *In view of the large movements of sterling against the European currencies in the last three years, would UK participation in the EMS have been feasible? If so, what adjustments to policy would have been necessary and what would have been the consequences for economic policy?*

If sterling had been participating in the EMS exchange rate arrangements during 1979-83 it would probably have had to be revalued fairly substantially against the other member currencies during the period from 1979 to early1981 when it was particularly strong. Depending upon how large the revaluation had been, it might later, when its status as a petro-currency ceased to be a factor making for strength on the foreign exchange markets, have had to be devalued. However, it is doubtful whether it would have experienced such extreme movements as it did in fact when floating independently. One of the main objectives of a fixed-but-adjustable rate regime such as the EMS is precisely to avoid this type of 'overshooting'. The EMS has been rather successful in avoiding overshooting so far as those currencies which have participated in the system are concerned and there is no *a priori* reason to suppose that it would not have had a positive effect on the sterling exchange rate in this respect.

The corollary of this, of course, is that the Bank of England would almost certainly have had to intervene more than it has in fact intervened, buying more foreign currency during the period up to early 1981 when sterling was strong, and selling more foreign currency over the last two years during which sterling has weakened. Whether, at the end of the day, net official intervention over the whole four-year period would have been any greater than it has in fact been is impossible to say. But gross intervention would certainly have been much heavier.

A policy of this kind, combining occasional adjustment of sterling's pivot rate against EMS currencies with fairly active central bank intervention, would not have been incompatible with the United Kingdom's internal economic objectives. If, as it seems plausible to suppose, it would have avoided the extreme over-valuation of sterling which actually occurred during 1980-81 the downward pressure on prices might have been rather less severe and the rate of inflation might not have slowed down so sharply as it did in fact during 1981-82. At the same time the United Kingdom's competitive position would not have been so badly damaged and the impact on real output and employment would have been less serious.

QUESTION 14. *Would you regard UK participation in the EMS as desirable? What modifications (if any) to the EMS might make participation more feasible and attractive? If the UK does not participate, what alternative arrangements for achieving a greater degree of exchange rate stability might be considered?*

The full participation of the UK in the EMS is desirable. It would be beneficial to the UK itself, in that it would help (for reasons which have been set out in the reply to the preceding question) to dampen the extreme volatility of the exchange rate which has been a characteristic of UK experience during recent years and which has had unfortunate consequences for the economy. It would be beneficial to the Community as a whole in that it would further the process of economic integration.

It is unlikely that minor modifications to the system would make it more attractive to the UK. The original reluctance of the UK authorities to join appears to have been motivated by a belief that the rules of the system were unduly weighted in favour of surplus countries. In fact the UK has turned out to be a surplus country itself, but the UK authorities have still preferred to stay out of the system, apparently in the belief, firstly, that commitment to a fixed exchange rate would make it more difficult to achieve their domestic monetary targets and, secondly, that sterling's status as a petro-currency makes for inherent instability *vis-à-vis* the currencies of the EMS countries, most of which are substantial net importers of energy products. In these conditions, they believe, a policy of independent, albeit managed, floating is the one which best suits the UK's requirements.

We are not convinced by these arguments. We believe, for the reasons given in our reply to Question 5 that EMS membership is perfectly compatible with commitment to internal monetary targets, and the experience of member countries, most notably the Federal Republic of Germany, provides convincing evidence of this. We also believe that the petro-currency argument should not be overdone. The United Kingdom's position in this respect is not so very different from that of the Netherlands. Both countries are largely self-sufficient in energy production, the UK being at present a small net exporter while the Netherlands is a small net importer. (In 1980-81 net energy exports averaged 0.5% of GDP in the UK, while net energy imports averaged just over 1% of GDP in the Netherlands. For the rest of the Community net energy imports averaged 5% of GDP.) This means that the UK and Netherlands current accounts tend to improve relatively to those of other EMS countries when energy prices rise and to deteriorate relatively to those of other EMS countries when energy prices fall. In fact the Netherlands current balance has registered an even more spectacular relative improvement over the last three years than the United Kingdom's. But this has not proved a serious obstacle to Netherlands participation in the EMS exchange rate arrangements.

If the UK prefers not to join the EMS exchange rate arrangements, there are of course other ways of achieving a greater degree of exchange rate stability. One possibility would be to peg sterling informally to the ECU. Another would be to peg to a representative 'basket' of currencies, weighted according to their importance to UK trade. Such a basket would of course include major non-Community currencies such as the dollar and yen. In recent years this practice has been followed with some success by several Scandinavian countries. However, compared with full membership of the EMS, neither of these options appears to have any great technical advantages, whereas from a political point of view they would undoubtedly be a poor substitute.

CHAPTER V

The ECU: exploring the map (1983)

This short paper was written for the ECU Newsletter, *a bulletin published by the Istituto Bancario San Paolo with news and comments about the ECU.*

The EMS has generated greater impetus in the field of spontaneous market developments than in that of official and institutional initiatives. The paper explores the much debated question of the extent to which existing institutional arrangements limit such spontaneous evolution as regards the determination of the ECU exchange rate. It argues that, contrary to common opinion, there is no logical impediment to the ECU developing an 'independent' exchange rate on the market.

Cities, mountains, and rivers can be easily indentified on a map even when they are small. It is more difficult to read the name of an entire region whose widely spaced letters cross several countries and cover the small print of specific towns or rivers. Who has not wasted his time searching on a map for a place he was staring at without seeing it? A similar thing happens with the European Communities. We have to get used to 'seeing' it at a glance as it covers areas we have been taught to consider as separate entities.

This can be done for information. The systematic presentation of figures relating to the ECU transactions of individuals or countries using a variety of techniques can help to form a picture that, because of its being so widespread and recent, is not easily seen by businessmen, journalists and policy-makers who are accustomed to operating day to day on a more localized scale. In recent months I have often had to explain to some incredulous listener who should have known the facts better than me, that with the dollar and the German mark, the ECU is now the world's third major currency on the Euro-bond market! Indeed those who are closely in touch with the ECU market are more concerned about over-rapid growth than any failure of the market to take off.

In operating terms, a similar exercise could be the setting up of a clearing system of the kind recently mentioned in the international press. By facilitating contacts between ECU dealers looking for a counterpart, such a system would help putting off the moment when any one ECU ceases to exist because it has been unbundled into its component parts in order to hedge against the exchange risk. Here too, the linking of separate and mutually unrecognized operations transforms reality.

One may object that the ECU is no reality at all, that it's just a basket of currencies, and that it will remain a mere reflection of the 'real' currencies which are its component parts until an organization has been set up to control its issue and the way it works. Is it not true that the healthiest and most orthodox EC country bans and ignores the ECU, considering it a mere indexation clause?

Let us take the risk of reading from the time rather than the space map, and briefly investigate the logical and practical process by which the ECU could become a 'true' money. In doing so, let us not face the question whether this process is likely or desirable. We might then consider three different stages.

The first stage is 'definition'. The ECU does not exist in any form or for any function. Only its definition exists. 'Someone' declares that the ECU is worth DM 0.828, plus HFL 0.286, etc. Such a declaration has no practical market effect. We have had this stage already. The 'someone' was the EC Council in its decision of 18 December 1978.

The second stage is 'free floating'. On the basis of the declared definition, some operators begin to bundle ECU and to deal in them. This adds a new line and a new column to the exchange rate matrix. If exchange arbitrage produces consistent values, the figures in the ECU line and column will probably, at least initially, be a mere reflection of the movement of the other currencies. The ECU will be influenced, but will exert no influence of its own. Behind the other lines and columns of the matrix, there lie whole systems of productions, trade, income, prices expressed in those currencies; and behind them, States, armies, central banks. In contrast, the ECU is backed by little more than the EC agricultural prices denominated in ECU but in fact administered in national currencies and controlled by a 'green rate' system. Not an army, nor a central bank, merely an EC Council decision and the idea, once expressed even by De Gaulle, that 'cette Europe, un jour il faudra bien la faire'.

However, the fact that exchange rate impulses run only 'one way' from national currencies to the ECU, is not a logical necessity, it is only a practical probability. Rather than the consequence of the will of legislators and official authorities, it is only the result of behavioural choices made by operators. Indeed, nothing prevents a businessman from quoting the price of a newspaper or a service or a bond in ECU rather than in another currency and deal in them as such. This is already happening for some types of asset, as the statictics in this *ECU Newsletter* show.

If ECU trading were to outstrip trading in other currencies, it could well happen that the ECU would become something different from a mere sum of other currencies: it would become a currency on its own, with an identified supply and demand. It could even be conceived that impulses in the exchange rates would flow from the ECU rather than only towards it. Obviously arbitrage would continue to make sure that currency rates in the matrix are consistent, but there is nothing that forces the ECU market rate to be always identical to the one declared. In a sense, the definition of the ECU as a basket would become a relic of the past as the gold definition of paper currencies. The ECU would be a free floating currency. This would bring us to the height of the second stage. In a different scenario, Hayek has explored this process in his essay on 'The Denationalization of Money'.

The third stage is 'governed exchange'. 'Somebody' buys or sells ECU in order to regulate the price. To do so efficiently he has to be able to create ECU and to offer something attractive in return, if he wants to buy them. This may be another currency, financial assets, gold, etc. If his aim is not profit but stabilization or, more generally, the offer to the public of a high quality monetary standard, he will in fact be acting like a 'government'.

The process described here is only partly a chronological sequence. Each of the three stages may exist in part, or coexist with parts of the other two. Today we find elements of the first stage together with seeds of the second and third. Some of these seeds have grown and multiplied at impressive speed. There's no certitude that we will ever see the complete picture. But no reason to assert that we never shall.

CHAPTER VI

Policy cooperation and the EMS experience (1984)[1]

This paper, the only one in the collection to have been prepared after I left the Commission, was presented in June 1984 at the NBER-CEPR Conference on 'The international coordination of economic policy' in London, and will be included in a forthcoming publication by the Cambridge University Press.

The starting point for this paper was stimulated by the consideration that, despite the widespread scepticism surrounding the launch of the EMS, the system is now fine and in good health.

After outlining the issues of multi-country coordination and placing the EMS in this framework, the paper evaluates its effects on exchange rate variability, monetary and real convergence and the implementation of a common policy towards the US dollar. In an analysis of the system at work, anecdotal evidence is used to assess the influence it has had on the behaviour of institutions and markets and how it has changed the cooperative game among member countries.

The paper concludes that the EMS is something of a success story in that it strikes a good balance between 'rules' and 'discretion'.

1 The author is indebted to S. Rebecchini for valuable help in the preparation of this paper. He retains full responsibility both for any errors and the opinions contained in these pages.

1. Introduction

To many academic observers the European Monetary System is a somewhat mysterious animal. It cannot be classified as a fixed rate regime since it has allowed much more flexibility than the Bretton Woods system. It is even less a floating rate regime since it is based on the commitment of member countries to defend agreed parities. The effects and consequences of the EMS are also difficult to define precisely. If scepticism was the prevailing attitude five years ago, surprise at what is often recognized as the 'success' of the system is the attitude today.

The purpose of this paper is to assess the significance and performance of the EMS by drawing on the author's involvement with economic policy-making rather than economic analysis. While the two professions of economic policy-making and economic analysis have much in common, since they deal essentially with the same problems, important differences in perspectives, objectives and tools make the dialogue between them difficult at times. Factors which are central to policy-making seem difficult to incorporate into rigorous analysis, to the point that academic economists sometimes prefer to ignore them altogether. Policy-makers, on the other hand, are hard pressed to catch the relevant messages generated by increasingly sophisticated techniques of formal analysis.

Most of the academic literature on exchange rate relationships in the last 10 years or so has, perhaps not surprisingly, usually concluded that better results can be obtained if the exchange rate is allowed to move, or at least if a fixed rate constraint can be switched on and off at will. The policy-maker, however, emerges with the disturbing feeling that this fails to capture the essence of a system like the EMS. To him the basic reason for adopting such a system is the structural change it brings in the interplay between the exchange rate and other areas of policy. After the adoption of a system like the EMS, the policy-making structure of a group of interdependent countries is not simply the previous one *plus* an exchange rate constraint – it is a new structure, in which policy behaviour, the ranking of objectives, and the procedures for coordination between sovereign countries are profoundly affected by the new regime, although they have not been formally reformed.

The policy-maker is well aware of the limits of his analysis and will want to check his conclusions with those obtained by professional economists. However, he is only likely to accept the results of this check if it incorporates the elements he deems essential, or if it convincingly argues that they are of negligible importance.

This paper presents three aspects of the European Monetary System. It first discusses (Section II) systemic issues which in the view of the author are at the heart of the policy process of multi-country economies, that is economies that embrace several sovereign countries. It is argued that the crucial question in the process of policy cooperation is to combine the necessary degree of discretion with the need to take action at the multi-country rather than at the individual country level. The members of a multi-country economy are unlikely to opt for a cooperative game unless an appropriate institutional framework is established. The collapse of the Bretton Woods fixed exchange rate system can be explained in the light of the double alternative 'rules versus discretion' and '*ad hoc* versus institutionalized cooperation'. The European Monetary System can be seen as an example of a more successful solution of this double alternative. Section III presents quantitative evidence concerning the ability of the system to achieve some of the objectives that were set for it at the beginning. This evidence covers four topics: variability of nominal exchange rates, dollar policy, coordination of monetary policy, and 'real' convergence. Statistical evidence, however, is only one of the tools that need to be used for a thorough assessment of the EMS. Section IV presents some of the 'non-quantitative' elements that throw light on the working of the system. This shows how the system has combined the necessary degree of discretion with the implementation of institutionalized cooperation.

2. Systemic issues

A. Rules versus discretion

In the last 15 years the conduct of macroeconomic policy has moved in opposite directions in the international and domestic spheres. Domestically, there has been a movement towards greater reliance on rules, as can be seen in the adoption of quantitative targeting and the abandonment of fine-tuning in monetary policy, and in the proposals in several countries for constitutional amendments requiring a balance budget.

By contrast, there has been a major shift from rules to discretion in the international sphere, and in the conduct of exchange rate policy in particular. In the early 1970s the increasing rigidity of the Bretton Woods system, combined with the influence of academic thinking, induced policy-makers to adopt floating exchange rates in an attempt to free domestic policy from the external constraint. Major countries failed to agree on an alternative set of rules or guidelines for the management of international monetary relationships. In particular, no rules were established for intervening in the foreign exchange markets and the only check to purely discretionary action by individual governments was the judgmental surveillance of the IMF.

There are several factors at work in these contrasting developments. At the national level stronger rules have been seen as a way of shielding policy authorities from the pressures of political constituencies. In addition, in the early 1970s the domestic sphere was marked by greater discretion than the international one. Finally, the complexity of economic interactions combined with the degree of integration that had developed among countries contributed to the abandonment of the fixed exchange rate rule.

In general, discretion should be exerted whenever there are conflicting objectives, while fixed rules are preferable when conflicts between objectives are only apparent, or when the costs – in terms of uncertainty – associated with greater discretion exceed the benefits deriving from improved achievement of final objectives. This general principle underlies the various reasons for the movement towards greater discretion in the management of the world economy.

The nature of the present exchange rate system is the first of these reasons. A return to a fixed parity system is at present inconceivable, but the rule of pure floating has also been severely criticized. What lies between these extremes, however, is the discretionary management of a floating system by policy-oriented institutions that interact with private profit-oriented agents.

A second reason is the increased complexity of coordinating the macroeconomic policies of a group of sovereign countries. This, in turn, is due to the emergence of several centres of economic power, all of which are on a par and tied together by highly integrated financial markets under a system of floating exchange rates that appears to reinforce rather than attenuate the transmission of disturbances. In these circumstances, cooperation requires coordinated action involving a wide range of instruments and policies, something that can only be achieved through judgmental decisions.

A third reason is the increasing frequency of exogenous shocks and disturbances, such as oil embargos, economic sanctions and sudden financial crises, that require many countries to respond consistently and effectively.

Finally, discretion may be necessary to avoid the 'moral hazard' created by knowledge of government behavioural rules. A case in point is the function of lender of last resort, which should operate without a predetermined set of rules in order to discourage excessive risk-taking by private agents; another, with an adjustable peg system, is the need to avoid setting rules for currency realignment in order to avoid speculation.

In conclusion, an increasingly complex and integrated world requires that discretionary decisions should play a greater role in the solution of multi-country cooperation problems. This does not imply a loosening of the government function at either the global or the national level. Firstly, in some cases discretion should actually replace rules, but more generally it should be complementary to existing rules. Moreover, discretion should be implemented in order to increase the area of government's responsibilities and increase its effectiveness and adaptability in the face of unexpected events.

B. Institutions and cooperation

Discretion needs to be increased, but it should be exercised jointly by the agents operating in the international sphere so that action is taken at the system level. This raises the question of the role institutions should play in the management of multi-country economies.

A crucial destinction must be drawn between 'institutionalized' and *'ad hoc'* cooperation.

Ad hoc cooperation is based on discussions among the interested parties, but joint action is taken only if agreement is reached. In the last 10 years this type of cooperation has prevailed and in many cases – probably the majority – no common action was taken as a result of failure to reach agreement. There was, therefore, a usually uncoordinated response at the level of individual countries.

Institutionalized cooperation, by contrast, ensures that decisions and actions are taken at the multi-country level even when parties fail to agree; therefore institutional responsiveness is more permanent and more certain in character. Within an institution the need for action to achieve public goals is established *a priori,* whereas with the cooperative approach this need has to be established each time. For institutionalized cooperation to work effectively, some national powers must be transferred to the supranational sphere. However, this does not necessarily imply a reduction in national governments' control nor an increase in overall public intervention in the economic sphere; on the contrary, it makes it possible to regain control over phenomena that would otherwise escape any form of management and possibly to avoid the distortive actions often taken at the national level in an attempt to reconcile conflicting domestic objectives.

The difference in the nature of the two approaches indicates several reasons why improving multi-country coordination requires a strengthening of institutions.

First of all, even when cooperative methods work at their best, they are generally too slow, a feature that conflicts with the increasing need for discretionary decisions in the management of a multi-country economy. Failure to produce timely responses may even exacerbate existing problems by inducing action at the lower, national, level and thus causing welfare losses and unnecessary friction.

A second reason is that cooperative methods rarely work at their best since they are subject to greater constraints associated with the pressure exerted by local constituencies and public opinion on the officials and politicians who run the cooperative process. Especially in periods of recession it is not unusual for the electorate to be more prone to selfish and inward-looking measures than either ministers of officials. Thus *ad hoc* cooperation in less ready to compromise or to give general goals priority over particular interests.

A third reason is that political instability in the 1970s considerably increased the turnover of governments and officials in many countries. Consequently negotiators did not have time to complete the learning process or develop the personal relationships and goodwill that are indispensable to the success of *ad hoc* cooperation.

Fourth, the growth in the number of negotiating parties makes the cooperative process exceedingly difficult. Consensus becomes harder to obtain, and even if decisions were taken by a select group, it might be difficult to implement them or have them accepted by those excluded from the negotiations.

Fifth, the growing complexity of the information base leads to a dilemma that is well known to those who have been involved in international cooperation. Officials with a broader perspective and the authority to make decisions often fail to master the many intricacies of the problems: they 'see the forest but fail to see the trees'. By contrast, those who master the details, often do not appropriately perceive the relevant priorities or the correct perspective of the issues and tend to consider relatively small points of controversy as sufficient reason for delaying or even preventing agreements.

Finally, an increasing number of problems are at the intersections of different domains: exchange rates and trade, trade and financial markets, exchange rates and the EC common agricultural policy, etc. The interdisciplinary approach required to tackle such problems effectively is at odds with the highly specialized nature of the existing fora. This information base dilemma makes 'package deals' very difficult to achieve.

C. The basic proposition

To improve the management of multi-country economies will require coordinated steps to increase the role of discretionary decisions and strengthen the institutional framework. The basic proposition then reads: the scope for discretionary decisions in the government of multi-country economies will have to be greater than in the 1950s and 1960s but international institutions will have to be strengthened if such decisions are to be taken at the appropriate level.

The experience of the last 15 years in the field of international monetary relationships, among large currencies and at the European level respectively, clarify the importance of this basic proposition. A brief reference is made in this section to the international monetary system while the two that follow focus on the EMS.

In the pre-1971 monetary world the emphasis was on rules: exchange rates were fixed and parity changes, a discretionary decision almost by definition, were considered an exception to be avoided whenever possible. Moreover, discretion tended to be exercised at the national rather than at the international level, since parity changes were essentially unilateral decisions. It can be argued that the Bretton Woods system would have functioned more efficiently, and perhaps lasted longer, if the right to make parity changes had been exercised in a more timely and multilateral fashion. The combination of a weak institutional framework for the discretionary part of the system, and the bias in favour of exchange rate rigidity contributed to the final collapse.

Under the floating exchange rate regime introduced in 1973 monetary and trade relationships have again suffered from persistent misalignments of real exchange rates, thus reproducing the negative features of the previous regime. The rule of fixed parities has been replaced by the rule of exchange rate variability, but the object of discretion, the 'disciplinary element', has again been confined to unilateral decisions. Viewed in the light of the two issues of 'rules versus discretion' and 'institutional versus *ad hoc* cooperation' the two systems are very much alike: 'in both cases what was missing was the exercise of the required discretion, and this was due, in both cases, to a fundamental weakness of the institution which should have practised this discretionality' (Padoa-Schioppa, 1983)

We turn now to the case of monetary cooperation in Europe.

3. The EMS: quantitative evidence

Compared to the developments at the international level, the EMS can be regarded, five years after its creation, as a successful example of institutionalized cooperation. The objectives of the system – as defind in the Bremen annex to the conclusions of the European Council of July 1978 and in the Brussels resolution of the European Council of December 1978 – can be summed up in two points. First, to create a 'zone of monetary stability in Europe', to be understood as 'internal and external stability'. This meant a reduction in the overall inflation level and in the differentials between member countries, coupled with more stable and less volatile exchange rates. Second, 'to coordinate members' policies *vis-à-vis* third countries', i.e. to increase the cohesiveness of European currencies in the face of dollar instability and to offer a 'European' instrument to the growing reserve currency status of the mark.

The best way to assess the EMS performance would be to compare it with the estimated development of monetary conditions in member countries in its absence. Such an analysis, however, is impossible. Not only do we lack a sufficiently complete model to simulate a non-EMS path of the European economies in the 1979-84 period; but our knowledge of the behaviour of policy-makers is too anecdotal to construct a realistic hypothesis of the interactions between economic events and policy decisions in a non-EMS environment over the last five years. Thus we have chosen to identify four key elements on the basis of the above objectives and to compare their behaviour before and after the inception of the EMS in participating and non-participating countries in an attempt to identify the effects of the system. The four elements are: (i) nominal exchange rates; (ii) dollar policy; (iii) monetary policy; (iv) 'real' convergence. It is clear, however, that the methodology we propose would be equivalent to the appropriate method only if the EMS was the unique innovation between the two periods; although this assumption is unwarranted in principle, in practice the EMS was such a major change that our exercise is a good approximation of the one comparing an EMS versus a non-EMS world.

A. Nominal exchange rates

We shall start by evaluating the impact of the system in terms of exchange rate stability.

Empirical studies on the effect of the EMS on exchange rates have been carried out at the Commission of the EC and the IMF. The analysis of the Commission[1] utilizes general standard indicators of variability. This contribution is useful for the large number of currencies considered and for the emphasis given to the variability of the mark with respect to EMS and non-EMS currencies. The overall conclusion is that 'the system has made a positive contribution to exchange rate stability'.

1 See: Commission of the European Communities, 1982, and 1984.

The IMF official position can be found in the 1983 annual report which states that '. . . the EMS has not yet achieved its intended goal of fostering the emergence of a zone of greater monetary stability in Europe. In fact, the cumulative changes in nominal exchange rates that have taken place over the past four years have been larger than those during the previous four years'. However, an IMF analysis of the EMS performance[1] concludes with regard to variability that '. . . it appears that the exchange rate variability of the EMS currencies has diminished since the introduction of the system. . .'.

Compared with these studies, the original contribution of this section lies in the express consideration given to separate measures of total variability and variability around trend, and in the use of daily observations for the entire period of floating and for all the effective exchange rates considered. As will be shown, this provides strong evidence that in the first five EMS years member currencies behaved in a way that was substantially different both from that of the same currencies in previous years, and from that of non-EMS currencies throughout the 1973-84 period.

Recent academic literature on exchange rate variability has not analysed the EMS, but rather the dollar and other reserve currencies. To do this, it has used several measures, such as averages of absolute changes, standard deviations and deviations from long-term trends.[2] As Kenen (1979) has demonstrated, most measures show the same basic patterns over time and across countries. Three such standard indicators have been used here: MAP, which measures total movements of the exchange rate along trend as well as aroung trend;[3] VEER, which measures movements around trend;[4] EV, defined as the weighted average of standard deviations of bilateral exchange rate percentage changes.[5]

---

1 *The European Monetary System: The Experience, 1979-1982,* IMF Occasional Paper No 19, May 1983.

2 For examples and comparisons between different measures see: Hooper and Kohlhagen (1978), Kenen (1979), Frenkel and Mussa (1980), Levich (1981), Lanyi and Suss (1982), Bergstrand (1983).

3 This indicator is defined as the mean absolute percentage change of the effective exchange rate. It would be equal to zero if the exchange rate was constant over time, greater than zero otherwise.

4 This indicator is defined as the standard deviation of the percentage changes in the effective exchange rate. The reason for considering only the variability around trend is that costs for traders and investors derive not so much from exchange rate variations or their size as from the uncertainty and unpredictability of such changes (see: Bergstrand (1983), Lanyi and Suss (1982)). VEER would be equal to zero if the exchange rate was a constant or, unlike MAP, if it was changing at a constant rate; it would be greater than zero if the exchange rate oscillated around a constant or a trend. This indicator focuses on variability as it influences the competitiveness of domestic firms and the levels of domestic prices, wages and activity.

5 The reason for using EV is that it captures a variability that is likely to entail costs to economic agents but that is not reflected in VEER, which is defined as the standard deviation of a linear combination of random variables (the bilateral exchange rates composing the effective exchange rate) that are likely to be negatively correlated. For example, importers or exporters of a country whose currency is simultaneously appreciating against one currency and depreciating against another are facing a costly variability which causes changes in foreign expenditures and receipts, yet the VEER index remains stable. Being a measure of variability around trend, EV has the same properties as VEER.
In calculating VEER and EV we have utilized percentage changes in exchange rates rather than deviations from a moving average or a trend, because the latter induce an element of arbitrariness and distortions in the measures. The reasons are indicated by Lanyi and Suss (1982): calculating a moving average implies an arbitrary decision on the number of elements to be utilized; in addition a moving average may understate actual exchange rate changes by smoothing movements too much. Therefore the first order percentage change has been utilized to remove the trend in the exchange rate series.

Considering nominal exchange rate behaviour these three measures have been applied to monthly and daily data of two sets of three respectively non-EMS and EMS currencies. The non-EMS currencies considered were the dollar, the yen and the pound sterling, which does not participate in the European exchange rate agreement; the EMS ones were the German mark, the French franc and the lira. These are the three 'major' EMS currencies and those which had been unable to stay together for long in the previous 'snake' arrangements. The DM represents the lower inflation currencies in the system as well as the group of 'minor' currencies that belong to the 'snake'; the lira and the French franc, the higher inflation ones.

Comparison of the chosen indicators before and after the inception of the system (Table 1) shows that total (MAP) and around trend (EV, VEER) variability of the three EMS currencies fell substantially both on a monthly and on a daily basis. The variability of the DM, the lira and the French franc against the aggregate of the EMS currencies also decreased. By contrast, the variability of the non-EMS currencies increased in every case except for a (negligible) fall in the monthly MAP measure for the pound sterling.

When the currencies inside and outside the system are compared, all three measures of daily and monthly variability indicate that the three currencies belonging to the European exchange agreement were more stable than the freely floating currencies during the EMS period. Moreover, some of these currencies had shown greater variability than the dollar and the pound sterling in the pre-EMS period of floating, thus confirming that participation increased their exchange rate stability.

In summary, the variability of the EMS currencies in the EMS years was significantly less than in previous years and approximately half that recorded by non-EMS currencies.

B. Dollar policy

The need for, and lack of, a 'common dollar policy' has been and still is one of the main sources of controversy and complaint about the EMS. Undeniably, the aim of the system 'to coordinate members' policies *vis-à-vis* third countries' is difficult to formulate both conceptually and operationally.

It might be argued that a bloc of currencies tied together by fixed parities and floating *vis-à-vis* the outside should not require any such coordination. In the EMS, however, one of these currencies has a special position in two respects: first, it is the only one that plays the role of an international reserve currency and, second, having a superior price performance, it normally tends to appreciate within the system. The impact on the DM of dollar movements is thus generally greater than the DM's share of the ECU, so that the German currency tends to rise or fall *vis-à-vis* EMS currencies when it rises or falls *vis-à-vis* the dollar.

In this situation, and given that the floating of the EMS bloc *vis-à-vis* the outside is managed, coordination may range from an attempt to avoid inconsistent actions and objectives to a search for an 'optimum' ECU/dollar exchange rate. This would presumably correspond to an agreed-upon compination of the objective of minimizing intra-EMS tensions with other objectives, such as price stability and employment.

In reality what has emerged as a 'common dollar policy', is more a coordination of other member countries monetary policy with that of Germany, which, in turn, has increasingly become the monetary 'centre of gravity' of the EMS (Micossi and Padoa-Schioppa, 1984). Hence, the fact that the exchange rate, especially *vis-à-vis* the DM, has become a key indicator of national monetary conditions and of their consistency within the system, in conjunction with the increased attractiveness of the DM in international portfolios as a substitute for the dollar, implies that Germany's monetary policy has also come to play a significant role in determining the external value of the EMS currencies.

In conclusion, to the extent that the EMS has added to the attractiveness of the DM by making it the reference standard of a large and increasingly 'harmonized' area and that the exchange rate agreement has forced countries to adopt domestic policies consistent with Germany's monetary developments it can be argued that the system has been able to implement a common policy *vis-à-vis* third currencies.

In practice, movements in the dollar/mark exchange rate have still been matched by movements in the DM against the EMS currencies, but at least the frequency of such simultaneous movements has been reduced. In Table 2 we report the correlation coefficients of the dollar/mark exchange rate against the mark's exchange rate in terms of all the EMS currencies. In the EMS period the correlation with the dollar has decreased, which constitutes indirect evidence of the ability of the system to shield the DM rates of other EMS currencies from dollar movements. The same correlation coefficients calculated for the periods in which the dollar was depreciating and in which strains within the EMS tended to be greater, have also been lower since March 1979 (figures in parentheses in Table 2).

C. Monetary policy

At the inception of the system it was feared that the constraint imposed by a fixed rate regime would undermine countries' ability to pursue domestic monetary targets in their anti-inflationary strategies. The evidence, however, suggests that the EMS has not prevented a general slowdown in the growth of monetary aggregates. Today nobody, in any EMS country, seriously claims that the system has encouraged inflationary policies.

Analysis of member countries' monetary aggregates before and after the creation of the EMS shows a significant drop in growth rates compared with the years of floating rates. The growth rates of M1 and M2 have fallen from 12.4% and 15.2% to 9.0% and 12.6% respectively, with an even greater slowdown in 'real' M1 and M2 growth. Furthermore, dispersion around average, as measured by standard deviation, has also been reduced (Table 3).

Indirect evidence on the degree of monetary policy coordination is provided by the correlation coefficients of monetary indicators (Table 4).

Nominal as well as real interest rates have shown a marked increase in correlation among the EMS countries (Table 5). In part this can be attributed to the response to interest rate developments in the United States (IMF, 1983) but it also reflects the need to equalize interest rate developments among member countries in order to maintain exchange rate stability. It should be noted that correlation has increased more among long-term than short-term rates, especially for real rates. This development reflects the need, with a system of limited floating exchange rates, to manage short-term interest rates with the aim of influencing capital flows and correcting for fundamental disequilibria in exchange rates. This applies particularly to Italy's and France's real short-term rate movements *vis-à-vis* Germany's and is consistent with the changes in their relative prices and exchange rates. Indirect evidence of the leading role played by Germany's monetary policy can be detected in the fact that the correlation of its interest rates with all the countries considered has increased during the EMS period in almost all cases.

Nominal money growth rates provide only scanty evidence of increased correlation after March 1979. But if one looks at real money aggregates, often considered a more reliable indicator of the 'tightness' of monetary policy, a stronger correlation can be detected, especially for M1.

Finally, it can be noted that since the start of the EMS the number of cases in which the correlation has increased for UK monetary aggregates is smaller than for other countries; the fact that sterling does not participate in the exchange rate agreement may partly explain such difference.

D. 'Real' convergence

The most radical criticisms heard in 1978 and 1979 against the EMS can be summarized as follows: 'The system cannot by itself enforce convergence of costs and prices. The artificial exchange rate stabilization of widely diverging currencies will generate increasing misalignments of real exchange rates, trade distortions and protectionist pressures. Worse, it may force stable members to inflate. If, on the other hand, high inflation countries were to adopt a more stability-oriented policy, the fruits of it could be reaped even without the EMS'.

Preliminary quantitative evidence on some of the relevant variables suggests that the system has indeed been less than successful in taming inflation, but that the too pessimistic expectations have not been borne out.

As regards real exchange rates (Table 6a), monthly observations show all the EMS currencies, as well as the pound sterling, as having reduced their total (MAP) variability since March 1979, while the dollar and the yen recorded increases. This development seems to indicate that, in spite of fixed parities and inflation differentials, exchange rates have been allowed to move enough to avoid excessive changes in relative competitiveness. Moreover, the changes have tended to foster internal adjustment, in the sense that weak currencies have shown an appreciating real exchange rate and thus a loss of competitiveness. Variability around trend (VEER) has been reduced during the EMS period for the mark, the lira and the French franc.

In terms of price stability the EMS can only claim some modest results. This is presumably due to the fact that the inception of the system was followed by the second oil shock and the rapid rise of the dollar, two external factors which caused inflation rates to accelerate and diverge in Europe.

Consumer price inflation during the five EMS years did not come down in some member countries compared with the pre-EMS period, although the average inflation rate of the member countries was reduced (Chart 1 and Table 6b). In the first two years of the EMS, inflation rates rose and the differentials between member countries widened. This was partly due to the above-mentioned external factors but also to the fact that France, Ireland and Italy had joined the system with depreciated real exchange rates that allowed inflation rates to diverge before the exchange rate constraint made itself felt.

Starting in 1980 the disciplinary effects began to exert pressure, the average inflation rate fell and the divergence of inflation rates was slowly reduced. Although the two oil shocks had a very similar effect on industrial countries, it seems that the inflationary impact was parried better by the EMS countries in the second case. After the first oil price increase, inflation rose on average from 9% in the third quarter of 1973 to a maximum of almost 16% at the end of 1974, while in 1980 it peaked at about 13.5%. On the contrary, in most of the remaining industrial countries including Canada and the US, inflation after the second oil shock peaked at a higher level than after the first. Finally, an improvement can be claimed by the system in terms of a uniform pattern of inflation rates as revealed by bilateral correlation coefficients (Table 6c). These increased significantly in every case, except one.

As for the EMS effects on economic activity, results are mixed. The aggregate growth rate of industrial production in the EMS fell considerably in the EMS period; the cross-border standard deviation of these growth rates also decreased, pointing to greater convergence of economic activity. By contrast, coordination seems to have decreased as indicated by the fall in the bilateral correlation coefficients among the major EMS countries (Table 6c).

4. The system at work

A. Early criticisms

In early 1978 the decision to set up the EMS was viewed with scepticism by many market operators, economists and experts, and even by some officials.

It was considered another invention of politicians, rather than a serious remedy to the shortcomings of the existing situation. At best the potential benefits were minimized and seen as limited to fostering intra-EEC trade, while intervention in the foreign exchange market was considered useless or even harmful.

Several arguments were used to support this attitude of scepticism. It was said that a fixed exchange rate regime would undermine national monetary targets; defence of the parity would cause strong currencies' countries domestic targets to be overshot and produce an unacceptable inflationary bias. It was argued that real exchange rate movements would be amplified by nominal exchange rate rigidity and stubborn defence of agreed parities, thus increasing protectionistic pressures. It was claimed that the asymmetry of the burden of adjustment would soon force weak currencies to abandon the exchange rate arrangements. It was also thought that the enlarged credit facilities – a key element of the system – would create a 'moral hazard' and allow diverging countries to postpone adjustment. Finally, it was suggested that the need to sustain exchange rate parities in the face of massive speculation would prove a serious threat to the stock of official reserves.

Even after five years of experience with the system the validity of these criticisms cannot be definitely upheld or refuted by quantitative analysis alone. An element of judgment, based on *a priori* arguments and a subjective reading of events, is still necessary. As we said earlier, we believe that the system has had a significant influence on the formulation of policy objectives, particularly in certain countries and at certain critical junctures, and that it has modified the nature of the 'cooperative game' between member countries in areas that go well beyond exchange rates.

To support this view, a careful examination of the actual working of the system at both the Community and the national levels would be necessary. Policy decisions, their chronology and their determinants would have to be assessed to detect the role played by the EMS. Since such an analysis would go beyond the scope of this paper, we shall only present some anecdotal evidence of the way the system has actually worked, drawn largely from direct personal experience.

B. Institutional aspects

To understand the way the system has actually functioned, it is not enough to read the written provisions. It is also necessary to consider the practices and interpretations that have gradually been established in five years of sometimes turbulent operation. This has generated new, unwritten rules, that are now just as important as the original written ones. Some of them regard the fundamental, constitutional aspects of the system; others its management. Taken together they have made the European Monetary System differ from the Bretton Woods regime much more than most observers, and perhaps also the founders, originally expected.

In the first place, central rates have been realigned in a much more timely and pragmatic way than ever occurred under the Bretton Woods arrangements. The contradiction inherent in the expression 'adjustable peg' has been resolved in a fairly balanced way. Over-protracted defence of parities has not been a feature of the system. On some occasions realignments were delayed, thus giving ground to speculation, but the delay was never too long, and generally allowed conditions favourable to the adoption of adjustment measures to mature. The experience of the 'snake' has been very important in this respect, since it showed that an adjustable peg system could be managed with a fair amount of flexibility and still retain credibility.

The second and, we believe, the most important aspect of constitutional practice, is that the setting of new central rates in the EMS has become a truly collective decision. The importance of this cannot be stressed too much. A basic aim of a system like the EMS is precisely to eliminate the scope for obtaining trade advantages by unilateral exchange rate management. The past does not offer significant previous experiences of this process of collective decisions. Under the Bretton Woods system the rare changes in central rates were basically decided by the interested country, while the role of the other countries and the IMF was virtually limited to formal ratification. In the snake, the leadership of Germany was so strong that there was little room left for bargaining.

Realignments in the EMS have only gradually become collective decisions. The first, in September 1979, largely repeated the 'snake' pattern: one country, Germany, took the initiative of calling a ministerial meeting, at which it presented a complete set of new rates. It was then realized that this method could not work a second time, as the number of parties around the table and their relative importance were very different from those of the 'snake'. The following two realignments (Denmark, November 1979; Italy, March 1981) were essentially unilateral, and limited to exchange rates: no meeting was called, only one currency was involved and no policy measures were presented and discussed. The Community procedures were limited to giving a sort of 'multilatéral approval' to the decision taken by one member. After these three realignments the procedure has become one of collective decision, much closer to those of the other Community areas, such as trade and agriculture, than to those of monetary cooperation. The actual outcome of realignment sessions rarely met the requests of member countries in full; countries often emerged from negotiations with a somewhat different grid of parities from the one they were seeking at the start.

The third institutional aspect of the system that has been shaped by practice is that changes in parities have coincided with the adoption of substantial policy measures. This, of course, had always been part of the spirit of an adjustable peg system, and had been stressed many times by theorists. However, experience justified a certain degree of scepticism about the ability of member countries to follow this line. And indeed, as we have recalled, the first realignments were not satisfactory in this respect. Increasingly, however, changes in parities have been part of major policy changes, which has also meant that policies of domestic adjustment have been increasingly discussed in Community fora as a result of the working of the EMS.

C. Functional aspects

These three features are 'constitutional' aspects of the system, and they distinguish it sharply from the Bretton Woods approach to multi-country cooperation. Their nature is best clarified in terms of the systemic issues analysed in Section II above. The system has succeeded in coupling the appropriate degree of discretion with the appropriate level of decision-making. It has achieved a form of institutionalized cooperation unknown with earlier regimes.

Other aspects of the experience of the last five years do not belong to the 'unwritten constitution', but rather to the operation of the system. Nevertheless they help explain how this has actually worked and what its achievements have been.

Many observers have noted that, contrary to world exchange rates (the dollar, the yen, the German mark), EMS exchange rates have always moved 'in the right direction', which is in itself a positive result from the point of view of what could be termed the 'trade objective' of the system: i.e. to keep trade open and avoid distortions due to protracted misalignments of real exchange rates.

Less attention has been given to the fact that the timing and the size of realignments have not fully accommodated divergences in price and cost behaviour in member countries. From the point of view of the 'stability objective' of the system this is very important because it means the greater flexibility with which the system has been managed compared with the Bretton Woods regime has not been pushed to the point of losing the benefits of a disciplinary exchange rate effect. Pressure to restore cost and price competitiveness through internal adjustment has been maintained.

The third important aspect of the way the system has been managed is that, compared with the asymmetrical changes of the Bretton Woods system, parity changes have been spread more evenly between weak and strong currencies. The philosophy expressed by the European Commission concerning such decisions has been that 'strong currencies should revalue while weak currencies should adjust'. In the seven realignments that have occurred so far, the mark and the guilder have been revalued against all other currencies respectively four and three times.

Finally, in addition to the 'constitutional' and management aspects of the system, mention must be made of a third. This is the fact that the very existence of the EMS has significantly deepened the cooperative character of the policy coordination game among member countries. Procedures for such coordination that had been legislated by the Community well before 1979 were given a new life by the fact that a new commitment had been made in the field of exchange rates. The level of representation in the relevant policy committees, the quality and openness of the debates held in such fora, the readiness of the Commission to 'speak out', and of member countries to listen, improved after 1979.

5. Conclusions

The increasing complexity of the management of multi-country economies requires a greater role for discretionary decisions and a strengthening of multilateral institutions. The EMS has been fairly successful so far in striking a good balance between 'rules' and 'discretion', absorbing major external shocks without incurring a disruption in its structure or a weakening of its commitments. On decisive occasions the system has played a crucial role in catalyzing the necessary political will to take the difficult and often unpopular decisions that were required to achieve better monetary stability.

However, this relatively successful experience should not cause us to overlook the inherent vulnerability of the system in its present setting. That is the conflict between unrestrained national sovereignty in fiscal and monetary policies, on the one side, and capital mobility and supranationalism in trade and exchange rates on the other. Political and economic pressures could cause member countries to choose a non-cooperative course of action in any moment of the future. Seen in this light, the system has not yet achieved the degree of institutional strength that is necessary to bring European monetary cooperation beyond the 'point of no return'.

Rome, September 1984

Chart 1a

Consumer price inflation in selected EMS countries (quarterly averages, annual rate in %)

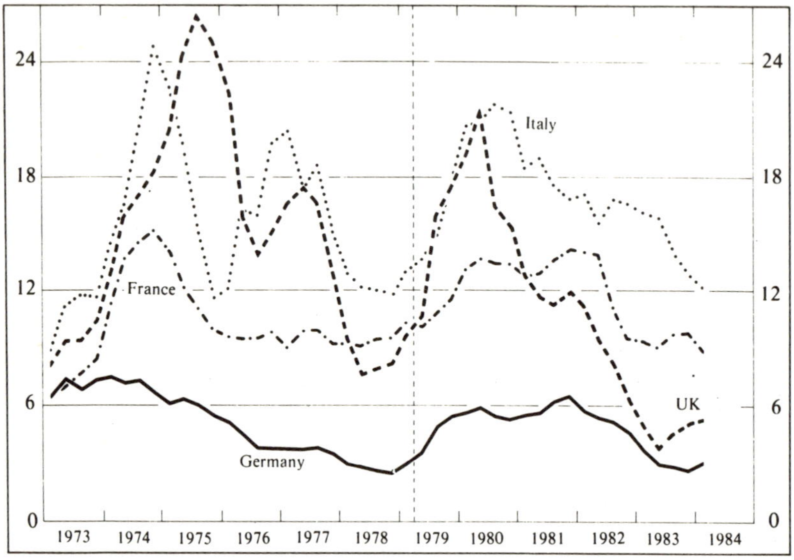

Chart 1b

Consumer price inflation rates in the EMS countries (quarterly averages, annual rate in %)

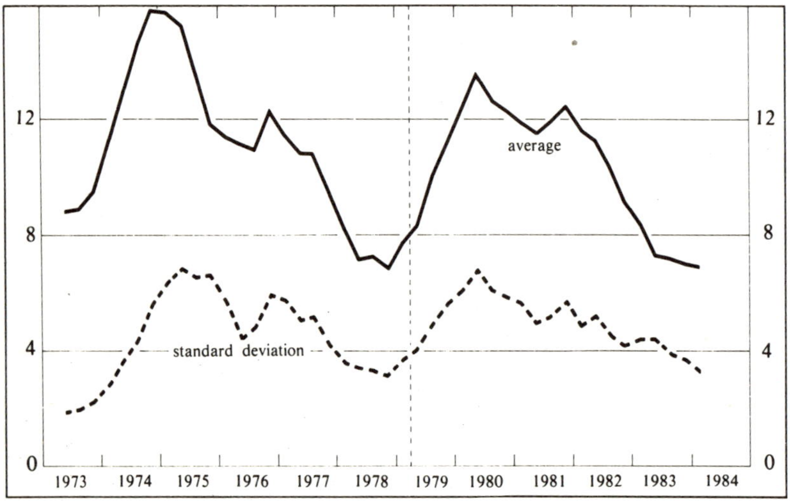

Table 1
Nominal exchange rate variability

	Mean absolute percentage change (MAP)				Effective exchange rates (VEER)[1]				Effective variation (EV)[2]			
	Before EMS[3]		After EMS[4]		Before EMS[3]		After EMS[4]		Before EMS[3]		After EMS[4]	
	daily	monthly	daily	monthly	daily	monthly	daily	monthly	daily	monthly	daily	monthly
Non-EMS currencies												
Against major currencies[5]												
US dollar	0.21	1.01	0.36	1.51	0.32	1.33	0.51	1.86	0.47	1.99	0.64	2.30
Yen	0.29	1.52	0.41	1.88	0.47	1.97	0.58	2.52	0.53	2.43	0.69	2.90
Pound sterling	0.27	1.56	0.35	1.53	0.43	1.68	0.52	2.04	0.55	2.17	0.63	2.46
EMS currencies												
Against major currencies[5]												
German mark	0.19	1.00	0.14	0.80	0.29	1.41	0.22	0.88	0.45	1.87	0.38	1.41
Lira	0.23	1.38	0.10	0.58	0.46	2.00	0.20	0.65	0.56	2.37	0.36	1.32
French franc	0.21	1.00	0.14	0.70	0.34	1.40	0.28	0.98	0.47	1.97	0.40	1.44
Against EMS currencies												
German mark	0.20	1.04	0.11	0.57	0.30	1.42	0.22	0.75	0.41	1.76	0.31	1.09
Lira	0.26	1.52	0.11	0.55	0.48	2.13	0.21	0.69	0.55	2.36	0.31	1.08
French franc	0.21	1.03	0.12	0.57	0.34	1.44	0.26	0.89	0.44	1.88	0.34	1.16

[1] Standard deviation of percentage changes of the trade weighted effective exchange rate.
[2] Measured by the weighted average of standard deviations of percentage changes of bilateral exchange rates, with weights equal to foreign trade shares.
[3] March 1973-March 1979.
[4] March 1979-March 1984.
[5] Major 14 currencies.

Table 2
Correlation coefficient of German mark exchange rate changes[1]

	Before EMS[2]	After EMS[3]
USD/DM, EMS/DM[4]	.61 (.57)	.36 (.47)
USD/DM, HFL/DM	.32 (.32)	.26 (.13)
USD/DM, LIT/DM	.59 (.50)	.50 (.57)
USD/DM, FF/DM	.44 (.42)	.16 (.42)
USD/DM, BFR/DM	.36 (.41)	.20 (.13)
USD/DM, DKR/DM	.43 (.46)	.31 (.26)
USD/DM, IRL/DM	.68 (.63)	.22 (.44)

[1] Based on weekly averages observations. Numbers in parentheses are correlation coefficients of exchange rate changes during periods of dollar depreciation.
[2] March 1973-March 1979.
[3] March 1979-March 1984.
[4] Effective exchange rate of the DM *vis-à-vis* the EMS currencies (excluding pound sterling).

Table 3
Money growth rates in the EMS countries[1]
(Quarterly data, annual change in %)

	Nominal		Real[4]	
	Before EMS[2]	After EMS[3]	Before EMS[2]	After EMS[3]
	M1		M1	
Average	12.4	9.0	1.4	-1.5
Standard deviation	6.6	6.2	7.0	5.8
	M2		M2	
Average	15.2	12.6	5.8	1.7
Standard deviation	8.9	6.8	8.7	5.8

[1] Aggregates refer to the 9 EMS countries.
[2] From 1973 II-1979 I.
[3] From 1979 II-1983 III.
[4] Deflated by consumer price changes.
Source: IMF, *International Financial Statistics.*

Table 4
Correlation between monetary aggregates in the EMS countries

Countries	Nominal growth rate						Real growth rate[1]					
	D		I		UK		D		I		UK	
	Before EMS[2]	After EMS[3]	Before EMS[2]	After EMS[3]	Before EMS[2]	After EMS[3]	Before EMS[2]	After EMS[3]	Before EMS[2]	After EMS[3]	Before EMS[2]	After EMS[3]
			M1						M1			
F	.24	-.70	.17	-.40	.07	.36	.19	.45	.57	.32	.34	.79
D	–	–	-.36	.46	.69	.58	–	–	-.06	.60	.47	.69
I	–	–	–	–	.08	.24	–	–	–	–	.68	.25
			M2						M2			
F	.27	-.05	-.25	-.30	.12	-.17	.05	.12	.18	.09	.50	-.84
D	–	–	-.44	.06	.11	-.20	–	–	-.30	.66	.10	-.21
I	–	–	–	–	.05	-.79	–	–	–	–	-.37	-.30

[1] Real growth rates are calculated on the basis of consumer price changes.
[2] Correlation before the EMS: 1973 II-1979 I.
[3] Correlation after the EMS: 1979 II-1983 III.

Table 5
Correlation between interest rates in the EMS countries

Countries	Nominal interest rate						Real interest rate[1]					
	D		I		UK		D		I		UK	
	Before EMS[2]	After EMS[3]	Before EMS[2]	After EMS[3]	Before EMS[2]	After EMS[3]	Before EMS[2]	After EMS[3]	Before EMS[2]	After EMS[3]	Before EMS[2]	After EMS[3]
			Short term						Short term			
F	.56	.62	.37	.79	.29	.11	.69	.08	.19	.65	.54	.67
D	–	–	–.33	.38	.24	.57	–	–	–.11	–.03	.65	–.27
I	–	–	–	–	.23	–.15	–	–	–	–	.42	.75
			Long term						Long term			
F	.32	.73	.14	.94	.59	.31	–.33	.55	.60		.30	.82
D	–	–	–.79	.68	.28	.69	–	–	–.05		.37	.70
I	–	–	–	–	.25	.24	–	–	–		.31	.80

[1] Nominal interest rates deflated by changes in the consumer price index.
[2] Correlation before the EMS: March 1973-March 1979.
[3] Correlation after the EMS: April 1979-February 1984.

Table 6a
Real exchange rate variability[1]
Monthly observations

	MAP[2]		VEER[3]	
	Before EMS[4]	After EMS[5]	Before EMS[4]	After EMS[5]
Non-EMS currencies				
Against major currencies[6]				
US dollar	1.00	1.60	1.32	1.98
Yen	1.58	2.01	2.07	2.67
Pound sterling	1.78	1.61	1.69	2.12
EMS currencies				
Against major currencies[6]				
German mark	1.01	0.69	1.45	0.86
Lira	1.23	0.62	1.90	0.83
French franc	0.97	0.83	1.30	1.09
Against EMS currencies				
German mark	1.02	0.54	1.42	0.75
Lira	1.38	0.60	2.04	0.82
French franc	1.04	0.80	1.38	1.08

1 Real exchange rates are calculated on the basis of wholesale prices.
2 Mean of absolute percentage changes.
3 Standard deviations of percentage changes.
4 March 1973-March 1979.
5 March 1979-December 1983.
6 Major 14 currencies.

Table 6b
Consumer price changes in the EMS
(Quarterly data, annual changes in %)

	Before EMS[1]	After EMS[2]	
		1979 II-1980 IV	1981 I-1984 I
D	4.9	5.0	4.8
UK	15.1	16.6	8.1
F	10.3	12.4	11.4
I	15.7	18.7	16.0
Average EMS[3]	11.0	11.5	9.8
Standard deviation	5.1	5.6	4.8

1 From 1973 II-1979 I.
2 From 1979 II-1984 I.
3 All EMS countries.

Table 6c
Correlation between inflation rates and between industrial activity in the EMS countries

Countries	D		I		UK	
	Before EMS[1]	After EMS[2]	Before EMS[1]	After EMS[2]	Before EMS[1]	After EMS[2]
			Inflation rates[3]			
F	.35	.85	.73	.71	.47	.71
D	–	–	.15	.65	.34	.61
I	–	–	–	–	.46	.73
			Industrial activity[4]			
F	.91	.85	.94	.61	.64	.60
D	–	–	.82	.66	.71	.52
I	–	–	–	–	.54	.05

1 Correlation before the EMS: March 1973-March 1979.
2 Correlation after the EMS: April 1979-March 1984 (inflation rates), December 1983 (industrial activity).
3 Consumer price inflation rates.
4 Growth rates of industrial production.

CHAPTER VII

European capital markets between liberalization and restrictions (1982)

The last paper of this chapter on European monetary problems deals not with the EMS but with European capital markets. It was prepared in June 1982 for the 'Second symposium of European banks' organized by Credito Italiano in Milan.

The links with the issues dealt with in the previous papers on the EMS are strong. Indeed the main contention is that capital market integration, monetary union and consistent and coordinated macropolicies are alternative, and in a sense equivalent, ways to achieve effective integration of the European economies. Difficult as it may be, however, a policy of advancing simultaneously on the three fronts seems to be the only one available today.

1. Introduction

The founding fathers of the European Economic Community placed the abolition of obstacles to the free movement of capital among the main tasks of the new venture (Article 3), along with such fundamental aims as the elimination of trade restrictions, the establishment of a common customs tariff, the free movement of persons and services, the adoption of a common agricultural policy and the establishment of a European Investment Bank.

While many of these aims have been broadly attained, the creation of a genuinely integrated European capital market still remains a distant goal. After an initial spate of liberalizing activism in the early 1960s, no further progress has been recorded. On the contrary, national restrictions have been reintroduced in several countries, and there is today a marked divergence in the degree of liberalization prevailing in the Community Member States. Instead of the development of an integrated European capital market, we have witnessed the remarkable growth of a parallel and unregulated worldwide financial market, the so-called Euromarket.

This situation is usually deplored either on almost moral grounds, with much waving of fingers at those countries who have sinned, or on narrowly legal ones, with lengthy quotations from the Treaty and other Community texts. While the failure to build an integrated European capital market is certainly lamentable, it raises questions going beyond mere indignation. Why has this goal, contrary to others, not been achieved? Is it simply by accident? Or is there a basic economic or other reason explaining it? Has the goal become obsolete, being surpassed by wider developments on a world scale, and/or being undermined by continuing national desires to preserve control over domestic markets? Or was there from the very beginning some inconsistency among the various Community goals?

These are the questions I intend to address. To this end, I shall, as a first step, throw a spotlight on the period 'where it all started': the early 1960s. After that first section, the complementary second piece of analysis has to deal with the situation today, i.e. the early 1980s. The comparison should bring out the change in our environment during the past two decades: the evolution in markets, institutions, theories and (maybe) policy principles pertinent to a European capital market policy. Finally, I will attempt to look ahead and to derive some policy conclusions on capital market liberalization and restriction in the Community.

2. The early 1960s

A. Legal framework

Article 67 of the Treaty of Rome provides that '... Member States shall progressively abolish between themselves all restrictions on the movement of capital' ... 'to the extent necessary to ensure the proper fuctioning of the common market...'. And the Council was called upon, in Article 69, to '... issue the necessary directives for the progressive implementation' of this provision.

The Council was then remarkably rapid in its response: it adopted a first directive in 1960 and a second in 1962, graduating the freedom of capital movements according to the differing nature of the flows concerned, ranging from direct investments, to financial placements of various maturities, to purely short-term and potentially speculative flows, etc. Member States were thus unconditionally obliged to fully liberalize movements of capital directly connected with the flow of goods and services (e.g. for direct investments, investments in real estate, commercial credits), of personal capital, of securities quoted on the stock exchange (lists A and B). In another category, 'conditional' liberalization was envisaged for the issuing of bonds and for capital flows with purely financing purposes such as longer-term financing loans (list C). Liberalization remained non-compulsory for short-term financing loans and new foreign bank accounts (list D).[1]

The basic philosophy underlying these initial successes on the road to liberalization was clear enough. Its most comprehensive expression is to be found in the well-known report on the formation of a European capital market, drawn up in 1966 by a group of experts chaired by Professor Claudio Segré.[2] This study, which has become a Community classic in its own right, argued that a European-wide capital market would become increasingly necessary, not only to better finance economic growth, but also to stimulate the implementation of Community policies in other areas. In particular, a European capital market was considered a necessary precondition to economic and monetary union within the Community, contributing to a smooth functioning of an international monetary system based on fixed exchange rates and completely liberalized foreign exchange transactions.

These ideas, hopes and initial realizations were tacitly founded on the existence of fixed exchange rates. Such a regime, provided by the Bretton Woods arrangements after the end of the Second World War, seemed so natural a component of an envisaged common market, that nobody bothered to write it down explicitly in the Treaty. This insight is

[1] The problem of short-term capital movements and their control has occupied a central place in international economics during recent years, and has been covered extensively in economic and theoretical literature. Suffice it here to draw attention to the important distinction to be made between controls affecting long-term and short-term capital movements; this is in fact reflected in the different treatment accorded them in the first two Council directives, as well as in the IMF Articles of Agreement and in the OECD code of liberalization of capital movements.

[2] *Le développement d'un marché européen des capitaux*, European Commission, Brussels, November 1966.

important, as the presumption of fixed exchange rates has been a potential source of early inconsistencies in the overall conception of EEC stabilization policies. I shall return to this matter in more detail later.

B. Facts

To understand the force of conviction carried by arguments such as those of the Segré report and to realize why those initial successes were blocked in the late 1960s and finally reversed in the course of the 1970s, one needs to trace the factual background to those events.

The first element relates to the broad historical perspective: the lessons of the Great Depression – when many countries attempted to maintain employment through competitive devaluations and resort to exchange and trade restrictions – were deeply engraved in the minds of post-war policy-makers. The Bretton Woods agreement, the Charter of the United Nations, and especially the Rome Treaty reflect a keen awareness of interdependence, a strong political will to further integration and cooperation, and a widening acceptance of the need for an agreed code of conduct in international trade and financial matters. There was a deep recognition of the self-defeating nature of 'beggar-thy-neighbour' policies and of their contribution to lower global employment and welfare.

Secondly, the interpenetration of financial markets and the degree of openness of the industrial economies were much lower than they are today, so that policy-makers were less fearful of uncontrollable exogenous developments impinging on their domestic autonomy. As regards the financial markets, for example, longer-run net private capital flows (over one year) within the Community totalled under 1 000 million dollars in 1960, while 'classical' foreign bonds issued within the EEC amounted to only 200 million dollars (1961).[1] The Euromarkets were, for their part, just beginning to see the light of day. On the 'real' side of the picture, the major European economies were much less open than they are today: measuring openness by the ratio of total exports to GDP, in 1960 this ranged from 12% in Italy (against 25% today), 14% in France (22%) and 18% in Germany (30%).[2]

Thirdly and finally, the general economic climate of the late 1950s, and early 1960s, was also propitious to a process of relatively harmonious and shock-free integration. This was a period of steady, non-inflationary growth, of easy labour supply and mobility, of low and declining energy and raw material costs, of asynchronous and compensating cycles among the major industrial countries: all factors favouring a generally convergent economic performance and a reduction of per capita income disparities among

[1] *Source*: Segré report, op. cit., Statistical Annex, Tables 13 and 15.

[2] *Source*: Commission of the European Communities (Directorate-General for Economic and Financial Affairs): *European Economy*, No 10, November 1981, and *Economic Forecasts 1982-83*, May-June 1982.

the original six members of the Community. In this environment, the dismantling of capital controls seemed to lie in the mainstream of developments and to be in the natural order of things.

Having thus described the legal and the factual background to the events of the early 1960s, I would like to sketch out their broader implications for economic policy, having recourse to the conventional economic wisdom prevailing in those early days after the Treaty of Rome.

C. Policy analysis

Open economy macroeconomics prevailing in the early 1960s focused on 'insular', i.e. basically independent national economies and governments. Between any two countries, a real and a financial relationship was suggested to hold in the case of fixed exchange rates.

The 'real' relationship linked domestic policies to the trade balance: if a national government conducted expansive policies, the trade balance would worsen via increased domestic spending on imported goods. The 'financial' relationship maintained that international capital flows react to interest rate differentials: an increase in (nominal) interest rates in a given country would raise capital inflows, thereby improving the capital account.

The analytical combination of these two relationships demonstrated how international flows of financial capital fit into national stabilization policies. Take for example the case of a slowdown in economic activity. A policy of budgetary expansion would then stimulate the economy, while restricting monetary policy would keep domestic interest rates high enough to attract capital inflows. Overall balance of payments equilibrium would be maintained, as the trade deficit would be financed by interest-sensitive capital inflows from abroad. The result is a policy mix in which monetary policy is not directed towards domestic goals, and becomes, rather, a tool for balance of payments financing, working via the interest sensitivity of international capital flows.

Thus, the economic wisdom of the early 1960s suggested that, in a fixed exchange rate regime without capital controls, there is in principle no room for an independent national policy mix. In particular, monetary policy is constrained to be used as a tool for external stabilization. This consequence follows from the coexistence of free capital flows and fixed exchange rates.

Both these elements were, however, built into the Treaty of Rome, as mentioned before. Free capital flows were explicitly considered as an objective. Fixed exchange rates were an implicit pillar of the Treaty. It should follow that the use of monetary policy for domestic purposes is ruled out, i.e. that national monetary policies are to be constrained by balance of payments considerations. We cannot aim simultaneously at (i) free trade, (ii) capital mobility, (iii) independent domestic monetary policy and (iv) fixed exchange rates. The circle cannot be squared: one element has to be surrendered in order to avoid any inconsistency. The incompatibility between fixed exchange rates, free capital movements and independent national monetary policies has been referred to in economic literature as the 'inconsistent trinity'. To this trio we have added a fourth element, that of free trade, which is a pillar of the Rome Treaty and an aspect which cannot simply be taken for granted in our present economic environment. As Henry C. Wallich has observed, the incompatibility of these elements is 'a fact well known to economists but never recognized in our institutional arrangements or avowed principles of national policy'.[1]

Given the Treaty's explicit provision for the free flow of goods, services and capital, the choices open were to give up either the autonomy of domestic monetary policy or the system of fixed exchange rates. The latter option being hardly conceivable at the time, the Community's founding fathers made a definite choice in favour of the coordination of policies, overcoming the incompatibility of the various objectives by indicating that in the 'inconsistent quartet' it is the autonomy of national policies which will have to yield to the exigencies of coordination, so that fixed exchange rates, free capital flows and free trade may coexist. There are a number of articles in the Treaty bearing this out: Article 145, in particular, sets the task of ensuring the 'coordination of the general economic policies of the Member States' alongside 'the power to take decisions' as one of the two fundamental Council tools for the attainment of the Treaty's objectives. The fact that in a regime of fixed exchange rates and free capital movements, economic policy is necessarily constrained by external considerations is furthermore recognized in Article 104: 'Each Member State shall pursue the economic policy needed to ensure the equilibrium of its overall balance of payments and to maintain confidence in its currency. . .'.

The analytical foundations of the Treaty are therefore sound and conceptually consisten: the subsequent inconsistency and related difficulties have arisen because the principle of economic policy coordination, enounced in the Treaty, has remained precisely only a principle. Its practical implementation continues to rest on extremely loose and largely ineffective arrangements, so that coordination remains without 'bite', at times degenerating into a mere exchange of information on policy actions decided upon unilaterally. That is the main shortcoming and the root of the problem: the Treaty set coordination as a finality and an objective, but failed to provide for implemental norms and concrete instruments to render it a reality.

---

[1] Henry C. Wallich: 'The monetary crisis of 1971 – The lessons to be learned', the Per Jacobsson Foundation, 24 September 1972, Washington DC. A similar dilemma faced the Bretton Woods negotiators. They solved it by agreeing that members of the IMF should be able to control capital transfers (except for current transactions). Already in his 'Proposals for an International Clearing Union', issued in 1943, Keynes had declared that no country could safely permit unwanted movements of fugitive funds, for which reason it was 'widely held that control of capital movements, both inward and outward, should be a permanent feature of the post-war system'. See Joseph Gold: *International capital movements under the Law of the International Monetary Fund,* IMF Pamphlet Series No 21, Washington DC, 1977.

3. The early 1980s

A. Legal framework

The two Council directives of 1960 and 1962 marked the last progress so far achieved towards the liberalization of capital movements. Since then there has in fact been a retreat. A third directive, aiming at a stepwise further liberalization, was submitted by the Commission in 1967, but had to be withdrawn after 10 years of fruitless negotiations at Council level. A decision is still pending on a more recent proposal (1979) to broaden directly the scope of the first directive (inclusion of investment fund certificates). To be sure, there have been other directives with some, albeit indirect, bearing on our subject: as bankers you are all certainly familiar with the 1973 directive on financial institutions (freedom of establishment and freedom to provide services) and with the 1977 directive relating to the taking up and pursuit of the business of credit institutions. There have also been directives on insurances, and two directives (in 1979 and 1980) on the admission of securities to official stock exchange listing and stating the particulars to be published for such admission.

These measures are of undoubted indirect significance for our subject matter, insofar as capital market integration requires a harmonization of regulations and institutional structures. But as regards the main stage of direct capital movements liberalization, the account remains negative. The overall degree of liberalization is lower today than in the early 1960s, and differs widely as between Community countries.

The existing imbalance in the degree of liberalization may be briefly illustrated as follows. There are no restrictions on international flows of financial capital in the United Kingdom and (apart from marginal heritages from the past) in Germany and the Netherlands. The obstacle of additional transaction costs in the form of a two-tier foreign exchange market exists in Belgium/Luxembourg and in France. Direct restrictions on capital flows, which were formerly liberalized under the first two Community directives, have been imposed since 1968 in France, since 1974 in Italy, and since 1978 in Denmark and Ireland. These restrictive measures were authorized by the Commission, under recourse to the 'safeguard clauses' laid down in the Treaty of Rome, whereby Member States may be authorized to take protective measures when 'movements of capital lead to disturbances in the functioning of the capital market' (Article 73) or 'where a Member State is in difficulties or is seriously threatened with difficulties as regards its balance of payments' (Article 108).

The Italian requirement to deposit 50% of financial investment abroad in a non-interest bearing, domestic bank account is one example of a continuously existing long-term restriction; the French recourse to safeguard clauses to control various operations is another.

To do justice to the 'restrictive' countries, it should be added that the various obstacles are diversified in such a way that some types of capital flows are less restricted than others. In the Italian case, for example, the deposit requirement does not apply to direct investments in EEC countries. In Denmark and Ireland, the restrictions do not apply to the acquisition of securities issued by Community institutions.

This listing of details could continue, but for our present purposes, it suffices to state the fact that the degree of liberalization is markedly imbalanced across the Community and generally *less* that 20 years ago. We face the existence of protracted long-term controls on capital flows – controls which were originally authorized on a transitory, short-term basis only, consistent with the rationale of the 'safeguard clauses'.

One may finally add two critical remarks on the legal framework within which capital movement liberalization may be enacted in the Community.

Firstly, liberalization of capital flows in the Community continues to depend, from a legal point of view, solely on directives issued on the basis of Article 69 of the Treaty. This is to say that even today, after the end of a long 'transitional period' for the Community, the general principle of free capital flows (Article 67) does not constitute, by itself, directly binding law. This clarification has been given recently, and for the first time, by the European Court of Justice (*Casati* case, decision of 11 November 1981). Hence, the legal framework is one which obliges us to continue along the troublesome road of issuing directives, building European capital market integration step by step.

This approach is, secondly, troublesome in another way. There is the serious drawback of very long internal decision lags within the Community itself. The time seems to be gone when it took the Council only a few months to approve a proposal put forward by the Commission, as was the case with the first two directives in 1960 and 1962. Today, we sometimes have to wait for years until a proposal by the Commission gets Council approval, if any (as illustrated by the table on the following page).

To the lag in the internal decision-making process, one must furthermore add – once approved by the Council – the very long implementation delays and/or grace periods granted. You are undoubtedly familiar with the considerable time it took certain Member States to apply the 1973 directive on the freedom of establishment and the freedom to provide services of financial institutions, risking the initiation of formal proceedings against the countries concerned.

B. Facts

Let me now turn to the factual background of the present situation, looking in turn at the financial, real and policy phenomena of the early 1980s.

(i) The EEC-scenario of detailed regulations applied to some national capital markets contrasts sharply with the existence of international financial markets which are global and mobile in scope, not subject to official regulations and ever growing in volume.[1]

[1] See table in annex for figures on the growth of these markets.

Internal lag of Community directives on capital markets and related issues

Directive (subject)	Year of		Decision lag
	Commission proposal	Council approval	
1. First Directive on Article 67 of the Treaty	1960	1960	2 months
2. Second Directive on Article 67	1962	1962	7 months
3. Third Directive on Article 67	1967	withdrawn in 1977	(120 months)
4. Directive on financial institutions	1965	1973	95 months
5. Directive on international capital flows and domestic liquidity	1971	1972	9 months
6. Directive on conditions of stock exchange admission	1976	1979	38 months
7. Directive on contents of prospectus to be published	1972	1980	90 months
8. First coordination directive on financial services	1974	1977	36 months

Against this background the continued existence of nationally-regulated capital markets in the Community appears somewhat anachronistic. This impression is intensified, if we acknowledge that the very failure to build a European capital market was one of the reasons for Euromarkets to come into existence: the absence of a liberalized and integrated official capital market within the Community constituted a vacuum which was filled by private activities, with the informal construction of a free and integrated capital market outside the Community. There is some analogy here with the way in which US multinationals have been able to take advantage of the opportunities offered by the common market more fully and better than most European firms.

(ii) The golden period of steady, non-inflationary growth which accompanied our first liberalization successes has been followed by one of poor growth, price and employment performance throughout the industrialized world.[1]

More importantly for the subject at hand is that the structural imbalances in the balance of payments situation of the major country groupings, and particularly the persistence of a large deficit for the non-oil developing countries, continues to mean a sustained need for financing, i.e. for compensating international capital flows, giving an es-

[1] See table in annex for some indicators comparing performance in the early 1980s to that achieved in the early 1960s.

sential role to international financing markets as 'recycling vehicles'. Let me just mention that in 1981 OECD countries raised medium and long-term loans on the Euromarkets in the order of magnitude of 100 000 million dollars; adding the 35 000 million dollars raised by OECD countries in the form of international bond issues, one arrives at a total of 135 000 million dollars which surpasses by far the current account deficit of OECD countries in the same year (29 000 million dollars). This demonstrates, in general, a saving-investment dissociation at an international (global) level. Again, a large need for international capital mobility is the consequence.

To complete the list of relevant facts, let me point to a policy feature which is closely related to the financial and real features mentioned so far, and which may bring us back to a more specifically EEC dimension.

(iii) In a world of generally floating exchange rates, there exists, since March 1979, the currency area of the European Monetary System (EMS) with fixed (but adjustable) exchange rates. Obviously, there is a contrast between the EMS, which provides free convertibility of European currencies within fixed exchange rate margins, and the continued existence of nationally regulated European capital markets. In other words, while the 'short end' of financial capital transactions, the money markets are tied together and integrated by means of the EMS, the longer-term end of European capital markets, comprising long-term loans as well as the issue and circulation of securities, is still segmented. The policy dimension of the EMS relates precisely to this contrast with the existence of regulated capital markets.

C. Policy analysis

Theoretical developments as well as factual experience have modified in an important way the analysis of 'insular' economies, outlined above for the early 1960s. It is now clear that in a world of capital mobility full insulation from external influences is impossible, even with floating exchange rates.[1]

This conclusion is supported by the following line of reasoning. The main fundamental determinants of exchange rates, that is relative cost and price developments and balance of payments positions, operate consistently in the long run only. In the short run, exchange rates may be pushed in different directions, away from their fundamental equilibrium level, by rapidly changing expectations influenced by a variety of factors. Recent analysis of exchange rate determination has explained the frequent overshooting of the equilibrium level (defined by purchasing power parity or by other underlying determinants) by treating exchange rates as financial asset prices, i.e. prices which are determined in the short term by portfolio adjustments in the assets markets and are thus closely influenced by often unstable expectations.[2] Short-run changes in exchange rates are thus brought about by massive flows of short-run financial capital, generated by and transmitted via efficient international financial markets.

---

1 See, for example, J. Tobin and J. Braga de Macedo: 'The short-run macro-economics of floating exchange rates: an exposition', Cowles Foundation discussion paper No 522, New Haven, April 1979.

2 For various versions of the asset market approach to exchange rate determination, see the *Scandinavian Journal of Economics,* Vol. 38, No 2, 1976.

The deviation of exchange rates from their 'normal' level, i.e. their over- or undershooting, has important real effects on domestic economic activity – on domestic industries, on export- and import-competing sectors. It follows from this reasoning that national authorities of widely open economies cannot afford a 'benign neglect' as regards their exchange rate.

Their reaction varies according to their possibilities: returning to our 'inconsistent quartet', Community member countries have dealt with the policy dilemma it involves by adopting different combinations and yielding on one or more of the various fronts. In very general terms the situation could be described as follows: the smaller open economies, such as the Benelux countries, have sacrificed the independence of their domestic monetary policy on the altar of exchange rate stability and free capital flows. On the other hand, France and Italy have broadly aimed at insulating their domestic monetary policy and at maintaining their currencies' exchange rate via the use of capital controls (and other direct controls, such as credit ceilings). The United Kingdom did not join the EMS because, *inter alia,* it felt that an exchange-rate commitment was incompatible with the lifting of exchange controls and the pursuit of quantitative monetary targets, to which it gave priority.

One could object that Germany, at least, has in some measure succeeded in squaring the circle: to the extent that this may be true, it is obviously due to its pivotal position in determining monetary conditions in the Community as a whole. But if one enlarges one's horizon beyond the confines of the Community, one only needs to look at developments over the last decade to realize the extent to which even Germany had, firstly, recourse to capital controls (special minimum reserve requirements, cash deposit requirements, limitations on the sale of domestic fixed-interest securities to non-residents) in the early 1970s[1] and, in more recent times, has had to design its monetary policy in the light of external considerations; in the words of its own monetary authorities: 'During the year under review (1981) the Bundesbank was unable to take as much account as in previous years of domestic economic problems (which it always kept very much in mind) in its policies, which had to be oriented more towards external requirements at times'.[2] In the present international monetary system, an effectively independent monetary policy is feasible only in what could be termed the n-th currency country, i.e. the United States.

4. Looking ahead: policy approaches

In order to reassess European capital markets policy, the picture of a changed economic environment should now be completed with an attempt to look ahead. The comparison of the early 1980s with the early 1960s reveals the persistence of the old problem in a new environment: we still have to reconcile the four elements of free trade, exchange

[1] Causing the German Expert Council to remark that 'in restricting international capital movements, the Federal Republic has embarked on a path which will lead us away from a European monetary union'. Quoted in N. Walter: 'Capital controls and the autonomy of national demand management: the German case', in Alexander K. Swoboda, ed. *Capital movements and their control,* Geneva 1976, p. 170.

[2] See *Report of the Deutsche Bundesbank for the year 1981,* Frankfurt, April 1982, p. 1.

rate discipline, capital mobility and national policy autonomy. The problem, and the whole question of capital market liberalization in the Community, has to be tackled on the basis of a consistent, and Community-oriented, organization of all these four elements. We may think of trade, money, control and policy as constituting the four rings of what must be a coherent and organized chain, and we may distil three policy approaches which could alternatively bring about full consistency between the four rings of the chain. We will describe them briefly, in their pure and conceptual form, i.e. for clarity of exposition, we will intentionally ignore the existence of political difficulties and the constraints of gradualism.

A. Follow consistent macro-policies

If each member country followed a policy line consistent with that of its partners and oriented to commonly agreed objectives, no tensions would develop in the chain. Thus 'policy coordination' looks like the road of wisdom and simplicity. So much so that, starting with the Treaty, a little library of Community texts has legislated in detail the procedures by which groups, committees and councils of experts, officials, central bankers and ministers should reach *ex-ante* consistency, as if one policy were followed in the whole of the area. In the Commission in Brussels we spend the best of our skills and efforts to maximize the effectiveness of coordination. And it is perhaps just because of that, that we are very familiar with the formidable limits of this exercise: what appears to be the road of wisdom and simplicity is, in many ways, the road of simplification and deception.

Complete and systematic consistency of macro-policies conducted by a group of sovereign governments is extremely difficult for a variety of reasons. Each government ultimately responds to its own electorate: there is little probability, and we have evidence of this every year, that voters of different countries vote for the same policies at the same time. In addition, policy calendars do not coincide: budget proposals for a given year are presented at very different points of time in different countries; not even the definitions of a fiscal year coincide. For monetary policy difficulties are also great, as they concern not only calendar, but also choice of targets, choice of instruments, structures of the banking industry and financial intermediaries in general. Finally, policy mixes are shaped in very different ways according not only to choice but also to the institutional relationships between national central banks and Treasuries. And more reasons could be given.

Complete and systematic consistency of policies achieved without any institutional infrastructure is a dream, a beautiful and dangerous one like the anarchic dream of universal love and altruism. On the other hand, to create an international infrastructure that would force the dream into reality would raise enormous difficulties, much greater difficulties and objections than those raised by more limited institutional steps in the areas of capital market or monetary integration.

To the extent to which coordination does not work, or at best, in the words of J.J. Polak, is only 'a relatively weak form of international influence on national policies',[1] we have different forms of distortions in the other rings of the chain. One of them is the development of various types of controls, possibly of capital market controls, as we have already seen. Another is, of course, the widening of economic divergences that create tensions in the EMS and threaten trade and agricultural arrangements, thus endangering the very foundations of the Community. In other words, if the policy coordination ring in our chain of four elements does not hold, at least one of the other elements is bound to come under tension and perhaps break: trade, money or controls.

To prevent such negative consequences, approaches have to be implemented which tend to strengthen policy coordination either indirectly, via capital market integration, or directly, via the completion of monetary union.

B. Enforce capital market integration

The idea conforms closely to a cooperative Community spirit, and carries the logic of enforcing policy coordination in an indirect way through the institutionalization, or organization, of a European capital market. Detailed proposals to enact further liberalization directives and to revitalize the legally established supervising functions of the Commission and the Monetary Committee are its basic practical ingredients.

The proposal might however meet with the objection that the integration of European capital markets has by now become an obsolete or redundant goal: financial markets throughout the world are already linked via the Euromarkets, which have repeatedly proved their worth as efficient vehicles for international capital mobility, and have in practice raised the degree of integration between different money centres. It may be argued that there are, in this sense, 'market pressures' towards conformity and coordination, as observed by Lindbeck: 'The internationalization of credit markets and the integration of goverments in those markets as regular lenders and borrowers, as well as the increased importance of market forces for exchange rate determination, mean that the coordination of government actions is increasingly brought about by the 'invisible hand of markets', rather than by the more visible hand of government authorities'.[2]

This may be partially true, but it does not mean that the problem of government action in terms of management and surveillance can be evaded by sole reliance on market forces. This is borne out by the tendency in all major countries, over the last decade, to increase the authorities' regulatory and supervisory powers, in many cases enacting far-reaching legislation for the first time since the 1930s (another crisis period), and by the attempts to increase the transparency of the international financial markets, which have tended to grow faster than the authorities' ability to supervise them.

The fact of the matter is that money and financial markets 'do not manage themselves': to the extent to which there, therefore, is a need for control and supervision, the question

[1] See J.J. Polak: 'Coordination of national economic policies', Group of Thirty Occasional Papers, No 7, New York, 1981.

[2] See 'International coordination of national economic policies', in Samuel I. Katz, ed., *US-European monetary relations*, American Enterprise Institute for Public Policy Research, Washington DC, 1977, pp. 229-230.

arises of determining the appropriate space over which they should be exercised, and in this regard there is a solid case for operating them at a Community level: the EEC could in this regard be seen as constituting an optimum regulation area. This would be certainly preferable to a completely independent use of controls by individual member countries, which may work at cross purposes and invite retaliation and competitive restrictive measures. A rational use of controls based on Community cooperation and consultation would alleviate such difficulties: its intention would not be to extend the area of government regulations, but on the contrary to forestall conditions leading to a widespread expansion of restrictions.

The Treaty in fact advocates a Community approach of this type in Article 70, providing for 'the progressive coordination of the exchange policies of Member States in respect of the movement of capital between those States and third countries. For this purpose the Council shall issue directives, acting unanimously. It shall endeavour to attain the highest possible degree of liberalization'. This article is at the basis of the 1972 directive on regulating international capital flows and neutralizing their undesirable effects on domestic liquidity.[1]

The implementation of this strategy does however encounter the difficulty of being a very 'legislation intensive' matter. There are not only extremely long decision lags within the Community, as already mentioned. More importantly, the legislative process in the EEC is paralysed, as national governments are increasingly absorbed in the control of domestic matters. They are more and more passive and immobile in building the necessary institutional arrangements to conduct systematic, and foreseeable, Community-wide policies in monetary and financial matters. Nevertheless, stagnation might be overcome, if the political will is there. Hence, this proposal is a candidate to be considered seriously. Its realization would mean a large step towards exploiting the above-mentioned potential of the EEC as an optimum regulation area.

C. Complete monetary union

This approach is of course well-known and the one most often attempted after the end of the Bretton Woods system had deprived the common market of the vital monetary organization required for its proper functioning. It is therefore not necessary, in this paper, to expound on it further. Suffice it to say that the marked attention and many studies devoted to the question of European monetary union derive from the realization that the twin goals of free capital movements and fixed exchange rates (explicit or implicit in the Treaty) imply a single currency area and a single monetary authority. Within a single country – where there are of course free capital flows and a single exchange rate – it is clear that 'the various branches of the central bank cannot pursue independent monetary policies. The Federal Reserve, whose 12 regional banks were

[1] This directive, approved in the wake of the unsettling events following the demise of the Bretton Woods system (and to respond particularly to the formidable 1971 short-term capital inflows to Germany), provided that Member States 'adopt measures immediately in order to have available, should occasion arise, the appropriate instruments for purpose of discouraging exceptionally large capital movements, in particular to and from third countries', seen to cause 'serious disturbances in the monetary situation and in the economic trends in Member States', likely to 'hinder the establishment by stages of an economic and monetary union'.

established on the contrary assumption, learned this early in its career, and most other central banks never tried'.[1]

Fully-fledged European monetary union is thus the high road to policy coordination and economic convergence, implementing these directly by replacing a number of monetary authorities with a single, central authority. Its realization should in practice be easier than the capital market liberalization approach: it would not be necessary to overcome a multitude of intricate, difficult obstacles and regulations. It would suffice to realize one major achievement: monetary union. Here too, its realization would conform to an optimum concept, i.e. that of the Community as an optimum currency area.

5. Conclusion

In conclusion, where do we in the Community stand today as between these three approaches of: (i) directly following consistent and coordinated policies; or arriving at such policies through either (ii) capital market integration or (iii) monetary union? It would seem that on all three fronts we are, to a lesser or greater degree, at a sort of half-way house between, on the one hand, purely national policy formation and, on the other, policy-making that is entirely lodged at Community level. It is a situation in which the Community is still contending with the problem posed by the 'inconsistent quartet' of free trade, exchange rate discipline, free capital movements and autonomous domestic policies. Until a coherent, Community-oriented organization of all these four elements is found, the temptation is to yield a little on each, including even the principle of free trade, thus calling into question the very foundations of the Community. There is no point in assuming an attitude of moral or legalistic condemnation in the face of such developments and risks: the problem needs to be tackled, and in this regard there would seem to be two broad possibilities.

The first, and certainly preferable solution, would be to realize to the full any one of the three alternatives examined above: either complete coordination of policies, or full capital market integration or monetary union would 'square the circle' of our incompatibilities. There is no need to illustrate the considerable difficulties of arriving at the final destination along any one of these three roads: the experience of the Community to date is unfortunately an eloquent and sufficient testimony in this regard. But if the will to take the important qualitative leap which is involved were to materialize, it would seem that the way of monetary union is still the one likely to offer less 'mechanical' resistance and the greater chances of success.

The second, less satisfactory but in practice more probable, alternative is that of gradualism. Here the transition from purely national approaches to a Community-oriented organization is seen as a progressive shift in a spectrum, as a gradual but nevertheless on-going process. The EMS, for example, by focusing attention on convergence, may be seen as a strategic catalyst in this process of integration, enhancing the legitimacy of each participant's concern for the others' policies and inducing Member

[1] Henry C. Wallich, op. cit., p. 7.

States to discuss fundamental issues sooner in time, in greater depth and in terms of more concrete policy options than in the past. Barring the great leap forward to full Community coordination or complete capital market and monetary union, we therefore appear to have no choice but to persevere on all three fronts, taking a series of steps, lengthening our stride where possible, and gaining momentum until the leap – which will then perhaps not have to be so 'great' – to effective integration will be the natural and logical culmination of our efforts since the early 1960s.

Table 1
The early 1960s versus the early 1980s: some indicators for the Community

	1960-65	1980-82
1. GDP volume growth	5.3	0.8
2. Consumer prices	3.3	12.3
3. Unemployment rate	2.1	7.7
4. Net lending (+) or net borrowing (–) of general government (% of GDP)	in balance	–4.5
5. Real short-term interest rates	+0.4[1]	+2.1[1]
6. Share of exports in GDP (%)	18.5	29.5
7. Current account balance (% of GDP)	+0.3	–0.8
8. Cumulative change in ECU/USD rate	+1.3[2]	–28.0[2]

[1] Average 1961-65; and 1980-April 1982.
[2] For 1960-65, change between the two yearly averages; for 1980-82, change between January 1980 and May 1982 (+ sign indicates ECU appreciation).

Sources: Commission of the European Communities, Directorate-General for Economic and Financial Affairs – *European Economy* and *European Economy – Supplement A – Recent Economic Trends,* various issues; and Commission staff internal calculations.

Table 2
Growth of international financial markets, 1970-81

(USD '000 million)

	1970	1975	1981
Eurocurrency market estimated size – Gross	110	460	1 800[1]
Net	65	250	905[1]
Eurocurrency bank credits, publicly announced in period	4.7	21.0	133.4
New international bond issues	4.6	19.9	53.0

[1] Provisional.

Source: Morgan Guaranty Trust, *World Financial Markets,* various issues

PART TWO

International monetary problems

CHAPTER I

Problems of interdependence in a multipolar world (1981)

This paper was presented in June 1981 in Bruges at the conference organized by the College of Europe and the Institute of European Studies on the 'European Monetary System and international monetary reform'.

It first looks at long-term issues, such as the relative economic growth of the US, Europe and Japan and the evolution of the international monetary system, underlying trends which are still very much with us. It then considers the (then) recent developments in American monetary policy.

Re-reading the paper in December 1983, I found that the same problems are still with us: high American interest rates; high value of the dollar; and the reluctance of the US authorities to take the exchange rate into account in their monetary policy. Things have happened in the last two years: inflation has been brought down dramatically in the US, in Japan and in the UK while it has further decreased in Germany; we have witnessed the most ambitious exercise in 'negotiated econometrics' ever attempted, the so-called study on interventions on the foreign exchange market; the recession has proved longer and only now are there signs of an incipient recovery. Still I would not change much of what I wrote in June 1981.

1. Introduction

In November 1978, after a period of extremely erratic exchange rate developments, a phase of relatively smooth exchange rate developments was ushered in by the various understandings concluded with the United States authorities. A month later, with the launching of the European Monetary System, a new framework was given to intra-European monetary relations.

In October 1979, the Federal Reserve announced that it would henceforth be using new monetary control procedures. Since then the reliance on these procedures has grown stronger. As a result, United States interest rates have become extremely volatile and have imposed a similar volatility on an apparently rising trend of the dollar-ECU and dollar-DM rates.

Last May, the United States Under-Secretary for Monetary Affairs, Beryl W. Sprinkel, publicly drew the conclusions which the new monetary control procedures entail for the United States international monetary policy by stating before the Joint Economic Committee the intent 'to return to the more limited pre-1978 concept of intervention'. Both Europe and Japan are preoccupied by what some observers consider a radical version of the 'benign neglect' policy that imposes, *de facto,* free floating interest or exchange rates upon Europe.

This conference provides an excellent opportunity to detail the reactions of a European to transatlantic monetary events of the spring of 1981 and to express the concerns that may be felt in the Community: sharp fluctuations in the dollar disturb trade between the Community and the United States, may affect the price of oil and other primary commodities, aggravate tensions within the EMS, and disrupt the coordination of exchange and intervention policies.

Yet, if we were to focus entirely on today's events, we would not do justice to the complexity and to the depth of our monetary relations.

Indeed, this is not the first time that Europeans have voiced their dislike of American monetary stances. Did we not suffer from the dollar scarcity, from United States investments in Europe and from American seignorage? Later the inflationary potential of excess dollar balances left some of us aghast while others welcomed the United States dollars which – at long last – enabled them to escape the balance-of-payments financing constraints. How often have 'substitution accounts' been discussed only to be replaced by an excessively strong dollar and inflationary oil prices?

The long list of European complaints suggests that we should examine the United States-European monetary relations from a broader perspective. Money is an instrument of macro-economic management. We cannot therefore simply limit our investigations to interest rates, exchange rates and to monetary policy, but we must ask ourselves more generally how our policies have influenced trade and domestic production. Furthermore, the United States and Europe have constituted the core of the international monetary system in the past and, together with Japan, can be expected to retain primary responsibility for world macro-economic policy. Such a discussion of United States-European monetary relations thus inevitably leads us to investigate how – together – they have managed both domestic and world monetary affairs and to what extent their conceptions on how the system works have been adequate and compatible.

2. The emergence of a tripolar world

In the last 20 years the relative position of the United States in the world economy has profoundly changed. While the Community's gross domestic product was about half that of the United States in 1960, the two were roughly of the same size 20 years later (Table 1). During the same period, Japan's GDP rose from some 10% of the United States' GDP to about 40%. Owing to these developments the United States influenced less and less the other two countries through mere interplay of economic flows.

On the other hand, the United States has become more open to foreign trade and services. In the early 1960s, imports of these goods and services accounted for only 4% of United States GDP: in the late 1970s, this figure had risen to some 8-10%. Community imports of goods and services, excluding intra-Community trade and services, were about 11% at the beginning of the 1960s and 14% towards the end of the 1970s. Finally, the 'openness' of Japan rose from some 9 to 13% of gross domestic product over the same period. The figures are influenced to some extent by the rise in the price of oil which has led to an increase in the degree of dependence of the developed countries on imports.The respective shares in world trade (excluding intra-Community trade) of the United States and of the Community have remained remarkably stable during the past 20 years, hovering around 25% for the Community and 15% for the United States. However, Japan's share rose from 5 to 9%.

Towards the end of the 1970s, overall productivity as measured by per capita GDP at current prices and exchange rates, reached roughly the same level in the three areas: it stood at some 7 800 ECU in the United States as against 6 700 for the European Economic Community and 6 400 for Japan.

When we come to financial and monetary data (Table 2), the statistics become more difficult. Rough indications show that, in spite of considerable changes in exchange rate relationships, the dollar accounted for some 70% of the Eurocurrency markets in 1980 as against 80% at the beginning of the decade (Bank of International Settlements data). However, throughout the 1970s, the Eurocurrency market has grown each year faster than the domestic monetary aggregates and much faster than nominal GDP, so that the quantitative importance of the dollar in world finance has increased whilst the output of the United States has diminished relatively. The share of the German mark in official reserves has risen from some 6% in 1973 to some 12% in 1979. Comparable figures for the yen are 0.5% in 1973 and 4% in 1979. The share of the dollar fell from 85 to 78%.

What do these figures tell us?

Firstly, while the United States economic weight has decreased, its financial importance does not seem to have diminished much. On the other hand, the economic importance of the Community and of Japan has increased considerably, but this has not been paralleled in the financial and monetary field. These developments explain the difficulties encountered in managing world macro-economies as there is no absolutely dominant power as in the 1950s, while the United States nevertheless still seems to hold a preponderant position.

Secondly, world economic integration has continued to make progress and has even accelerated. Cyclical and policy interdependence is high.

The third conclusion concerns the gradually emerging European pole. This pole is obviously much less coherent than the other two: its foreign trade and GDP aggregates reflect to some extent only statistical magnitudes. However, the relative decline of the United States' economic power and especially the exchange rate regime that has prevailed since 1973 has brought about a degree of individualization of the Community in the field of macro-economic policy that did not previously exist.

The evolution which led to the present floating regime and floating itself have 'deprived' individual European countries of the organizing factor represented by the dollar. After a long period of increasing divergences and of a lack of any form of monetary organization, the coordination of monetary and exchange policies has been strengthened by the implementation of the European Monetary System which has thus resulted in an increasingly more orderly joint float against the dollar and the yen. This tends to individualize the third pole without it being possible to determine its nature exactly: for example whether it could be considered a DM zone, given the important role of Germany, or whether it could be seen as an ECU zone in which policy coordination is predominant. The third pole manifestly lacks a widely held international currency.

3. Interdependence and floating

Without taking any side in the fixed versus floating exchange rate debate, I shall try to draw from the experience of the last years to emphasize the links between policy formulation, external signals and market reactions in an interdependent world when governments take account of this interdependence in differing degrees.

The proponents of a floating exchange rate system were not only aiming at improving the technical working of the then existing system by making exchange rate changes more timely, by bringing about a more adequate exchange rate structure, or by introducing a greater degree of exchange rate or interest rate variability to take account of larger capital mobility. They were also advocating greater independence for national policies. It was claimed that exchange rate flexibility was a way to comply with what could be called the 'interdependence constraint'.

During the 1970s we have thus observed the interplay of highly independent national policies: floating has not only strengthened the technical ability of central banks to control money supply, it has also made it possible for governments to pursue for longer periods of time different national objectives. On the other hand, floating rates have also brought new problems, that were not all expected by their proponents, such as J-curve effects and destabilizing capital flows. Such problems have placed new and unexpected constraints on the elaboration of national policies.

I shall single out three types of problem that emerge when governments, encouraged by floating, follow non-coordinated policies and, to a great extent, 'let the rate find its own level'. Ranked by a decreasing time dimension they are the structural and allocation problems posed in the long run, the effects of cyclical divergences on exchange rates and trade, and the dominance of monetary policy in the short run. I will now turn to them, drawing examples respectively from Europe, Japan and the United States. I shall not, indeed, deal with exchange rate variability on a day-to-day basis as it seems to me that, within limits, it serves a useful role in inciting portfolio managers to prudence.

4. Longer-term problems

Exchange rates are most often discussed within a short-term horizon extending at most over a cycle. But there is also a very different type of long-term exchange rate problem which has not been discussed much, nor its structural impact on industry and on resource allocation fully assessed.

In the early 1970s it was widely held that a country could support expansionary policies by a depreciating exchange rate. It was thought that, despite high inflation, such a country could not only sustain its exports and hence its employment by restoring the export industries' profit margins through devaluations, but it could also improve its industrial structure as the profits earned in the export sector would lead to investment.

To some extent, Italy and the United Kingdom, at least up to 1978, followed such a policy, by compensating domestic and imported inflation by an even faster declining effective exchange rate; the real exchange rate depreciated sharply. This resulted in typical 'open scissor' type graphs, such as those presented in Chart II.

For various reasons, however, the experience of the 1970s has not supported such views with as much success as it had been predicted. Firstly, industrialists are well aware of the temporary nature of the depreciation of the real exchange rate achieved when inflation rates are high. They refrain therefore from investing their profits. Secondly, the depreciating real exchange rate grants, though only temporarily, a new lease of life to otherwise obsolescent industries; furthermore, if investments are being undertaken, they may be misallocated to industries that will turn out to be non-competitive once the exchange rate has returned to a more normal level. In any event, investments in industries whose profitability is mainly ensured by devaluation do not contribute much to the rejuvenation of a domestic industry. Thirdly, since domestic consumption is not cut back sufficiently by such a policy, there is little room for exports and investments. Finally, when inflation becomes unbearable and must be reversed, a 'stabilization crisis overshooting' occurs and false signals are once more given to the markets, though in the opposite direction (see Chart II – United Kingdom).

In the opposite sense, continuously appreciating real rates, which were celebrated a few years ago as the driving force behind virtuous circles also may give rise to problems. Such a case is well illustrated by Germany: here the 'open scissor' graph in Chart II is the inverse of the Italian case. The real exchange rate of the German mark appreciated strongly between 1968 and 1972 in response to the realization that the dollar was overvalued and the German mark was undervalued. In 1973-76 the German stabilization effort led to a further appreciation. After another bump the real rate of the German mark fell back, in 1981, to the 1970 level, i.e. to a level that used to be considered undervalued.

The appreciation of the German mark, fuelled by capital movements that were related to the emerging role of the German mark as an 'international currency', was welcomed because of its stabilizing effects on the price level, especially after the first oil shock. And for some time, Germany seemed to enjoy the best of all worlds as protracted J-curves, modernization and productivity increases in the export sector prevented the balance of payments from being hard hit by the appreciation of the currency. However, new foreign products gradually penetrated the German markets and finally the export sector also 'adjusted'. Once these long-run phenomena began to make their influences felt, in combination with those of the oil shock and cyclical factors, it became apparent that the German mark had been overvalued. It is important to note that such structural effects of an overvaluation appear with a lag that is measurable in a number of years rather than in the space of, say, 12 months.

These long term or structural overshootings in real exchange rates do not always receive all the attention they deserve given the extensive misallocations of resources and social problems that accompany them, perhaps because exchange rate regimes are discussed mainly by monetary economists who tend to follow either very short term or extremely long run equilibrium approaches. However, they are particularly important in a tripolar world because economies in such a world, being very large and having a relatively small open sector, can maintain disequilibria for a long time before they become apparent. 'Macro-dumping' is therefore a real threat to a tripolar world, because the country's expansionary monetary policy, via asset market phenomena, can 'temporarily' depress the real exchange rate below a 'long-run equilibrium' rate.

Real exchange rate movements of the dollar and the yen, as illustrated in Chart II, provide other examples of such problems.

In the United States, the combined effect of changes in the effective exchange rate and relative price performance has resulted in movements in the 'real' exchange rate which may be regarded as a measure of price and cost competitivity. After a rapid improvement between 1950 and 1952, the United States entered a decade of stability in the real exchange rate. After 1962, economic activity expanded and productivity rose, but inflation remained subdued and United States 'competitivity' increased until 1967. Between 1967 and 1971, inflation rose and bottlenecks appeared. With a stable effective exchange rate, competitiveness declined. The fall of the real exchange rate between 1971 and 1974 resulted from the combination of the depreciation of the dollar and relatively low inflation rates.

The current account developments of the United States do not support the conclusions that could be drawn from a superficial reading of these indices. Massive surpluses were recorded during the 1950s, when the United States still enjoyed a considerable technological lead, but they shrunk during the 1960s, in part because of the high level of domestic demand. In the 1970s large deficits appeared, essentially for two reasons. On the one hand, notwithstanding a strong lead in highly advanced technology, many United States products were not competitive on world markets (big automobiles are one symbol). On the other hand, the United States began to import many consumer goods with high income elasticity, and became dependent on imported oil. Thus, for a long time, the decline in the United States real exchange rate was insufficient to compensate for the structural factors which led it to become progressively less competitive.

5. Cyclical divergences

Cyclical movements have continued to distinguish economic activity in the 1970s and have led to a type of exchange rate overshooting which can be contrasted with the performance of an exchange rate system in which both national and international authorities take a stronger view on the exchange rate.

In a regime under which governments take a longer-term view of their exchange rates and act consistently with that view through intervention or other instruments, the balance-of-payments adjustment mechanism exercises self-correcting influences and the government is led, in due time, to conduct its policy in a way favourable to international equilibrium. When the rate is left to float, the signals that can be derived from the foreign sector may be alarmist and typical overshooting spirals can be observed: the current account imbalance is worsened by J-curve, or inverted J-curve, effects. The current account performance then unleashes capital flows that bring the exchange rate further away from what would be a more adequate level. Eventually, very strong policy measures must be adopted to reverse the situation. These measures may be at the origin of exaggerated movements in the opposite direction.

There are many examples of such cyclical problems, and I shall illustrate the case of Japan since the movements of the yen are both recent and of great trading interest to us. Between 1976 and 1981 we have witnessed formidable swings in the value of the yen – in both effective and real terms – that can hardly be justified in terms of either long-run competitiveness or relative inflation rates and which, although not exclusively of a cyclical nature, may usefully serve to illustrate the point. We must first remember that, until very recently, Japan has maintained strong capital controls so that the exchange rate was mostly influenced by the current account and some short term capital movements. In 1978, the Japanese authorities were forced to let their rate appreciate and took further expansionary measures, in response to the Bonn Summit. Shortly before the second oil shock unfolded, the yen had already begun to fall. This decline was accelerated by the effects of the oil shock; at the same time, the authorities adopted severely restrictive fiscal policies but maintained low interest rates. These 'measures' were strongly supportive of exports, which rose considerably.

Japan's position was obviously difficult because of its extreme dependence on oil and also because of the highly expansionary cyclical position in which it found itself and for which it was only partially responsible. It was therefore inherently difficult to determine an adequate new exchange rate, especially under conditions of genuine uncertainty.

Yet the floating exchange rate system appears to have increased rather than reduced this uncertainty. Firstly, important J-curve effects considerably magnified the swing in the exchange rate. Secondly, the absence of a strong view of the rate by the government, its foreign partners and by international authorities, increased market uncertainty. Thirdly, floating and controls helped the government to maintain artificially depressed interest rates; the huge foreign exchange intervention of the Bank of Japan had thus reduced effects. In a system of jointly managed rates, the question of the 'rate to hold' would have come up, monetary policy would have had to tighten interest rates, and interventions, if necessary supported by official borrowing, might have been more substantial.

There are consequences that cannot, in the real world, be dissociated from the enormous swings in the yen: the low level of the yen in 1979 and in early 1980 has contributed to foster Japanese market penetration in Europe to a degree that is perhaps not warranted by longer-term trends in Japanese price and cost competitivity and has nurtured protectionist feelings and reactions. This large swing has thus exerted lasting real effects that would have been avoided if the Japanese Government and the international community had taken a different view of the yen and of policy coordination.

This example illustrates the problems that emerge from the pursuit of 'an independent policy course in an interdependent world'. The rapid correction of the imbalance in Japan's current account – desirable as it may be from this nation's individual standpoint – was only a temporary benefit because it gave rise to far-reaching secondary reactions of a protectionist nature.

6. Monetary policy: today's developments

The third type of problem is illustrated best by the events of the last weeks and months and relates to the question raised by the recent course of monetary policy in the United States.

As is shown in Chart III, in the two years since the start of the European Monetary System there have been substantial fluctuations of the dollar against Community currencies. During the first few months of the European Monetary System the dollar was on a rising trend but this was soon reversed and in the second half of 1979 the dollar fell sharply, by over 5% against the ECU. In 1980 the increased volatility of United States' interest rates – associated with the change in the techniques of monetary control initiated the previous October – gave rise to more pronounced fluctuations in the dollar.

These sharp fluctuations in the dollar are a cause of concern to the Community; firstly, because of the direct – albeit lagged – effects on trade between the Community and the United States and of US competition with the Community in external markets; secondly, because of the possible effects of dollar fluctuations on the prices and cost of primary products, particularly oil; and, thirdly, because sharp external currency movements can aggravate tensions within the European Monetary System and disturb coordination of exchange rates and intervention policies.

The influence of fluctuations in the dollar-DM exchange rate on the relative position of currencies within the European Monetary System band can be seen in Chart IV. When the mark has been strong against the dollar it has often been strong against other European Monetary System currencies and when it has been weak against the dollar it has been weak within the European Monetary System band. This is due to the fact that the mark is a closer substitute for the dollar than other Community currencies, and, therefore, any 'flight' from the dollar is accompanied by a movement into the German mark and vice versa. Of course, only a part of European Monetary System tensions are due to this dollar-DM relationship and I am personally convinced that the lack of a 'dollar policy' is too often blamed for difficulties and tensions that are due to our own making. This does not reduce, however, the relevance of the phenomenon.

The same degree of volatility can be observed in United States and European nominal and real interest rates.

The extreme volatility of United States nominal interest rates in the period from the end of 1979 until now is well-known and is illustrated in Chart III. The effect on European interest rates is also shown in that chart where it can be seen that European countries have been forced somewhat to follow the American developments, although attempting to dampen them down as much as possible.

What is less widely realized is that real interest rates have fluctuated widely as well. In the United States (Chart V) *ex-post* real interest rates climbed from broadly zero at the begining of 1979 to a peak of about 4% by the end of 1980 and well in excess of 5% more recently. In Germany, taken as a representative European country, the *ex ante* real rate of interest has recently reached record levels. It is hard to reconcile such volatility of real interest rates with any clear policy objective.

In a situation of very high financial interdependence, the ups and downs in United States interest and exchange rates confront the European Community with difficult choices. It could eliminate exchange rate volatility *vis-à-vis* the dollar by pegging its interest rates to United States interest rates. In this case the Community would be guided by a variable the movements of which are explicitly disregarded as meaningless by the very authorities who determine them. Moreover, both European interest rates and money supply would be determined by short-run domestic developments in the United States and by the personalities and institutions of that country. Alternatively, the Community could itself adopt the United States procedures of giving absolute priority to quantity-oriented monetary control; exchange rate volatility could then be compounded. Imagine the extreme case in which all major countries adopted United States procedures: in these periods when short-term economic fluctuations failed to offset one another, there would be extreme exchange rate volatility. It seems highly unlikely that private speculators would even it out.Thus we seem to be left with no other choice than the one we are making in practice, and that consists of a mixture of devaluation and restrictive policies, of passivity, solidarity and expressions of concern.

We must be able to find a way to subdue these strains by an enhanced coordination of our monetary policies. We have lost, as I have illustrated above, the 'dominant country' method of organizing international monetary relationships. We have lost faith in organizing the world around perfectly flexible exchange rates. As a consequence we must be capable of finding a new solid principle around which to organize international monetary matters. Just because we have no ready solution, the problem will not go away.

The first change which is needed in this respect is one of attitudes. There was a period when 'international cooperation' was in fashion; now in some quarters, the pendulum has moved to the extreme in which the wise maxim 'put your own house in order first' is caricaturized as meaning that the external aspects of monetary policy are not merely to be ignored but are indeed irrelevant. I believe that we should be able to find a solution in which a recognition of the consequences for trade relationships of policy actions on our partners is in some way integrated in the process of policy formulation.

A change of attitude is, however, not enough. It is necessary to pursue some systematic improvement in the way monetary actions are coordinated among the three poles of which I spoke before.

7. United States monetary policy as seen from Europe

A. Objectives

From the abandonment of simple rules for international monetary coordination, such as fixed or freely floating exchange rates, one should certainly not draw the negative conclusion that coordination is unnecessary or automatically assured by ensuring 'domestic order'. Interdependence is still there and would require appropriate action even among perfectly stable and well-managed economies, as long as economic policies are actively conducted in each of them. Instead of that negative conclusion, two positive conclusions have to be drawn from the existing state of monetary relationships.

Firstly, that a much wider range of policies, objectives, instruments, etc. have to be discussed in the fora where officials discuss problems stemming from interdependence. An exchange rate rule was a simple way, perhaps too simple for our complex world, to summarize the links between partners. Today we have to engage on the much more complicated and politically-delicate exercise of discussing and comparing our policies in all their aspects including some which have a less evident relationship with the external sector, like the techniques adopted for monetary control.

Secondly, to the extent to which the recognition of interdependence involves not only an exchange of information but also leads to action or to changes that are, in substance, acts of international policy, then this is closer to the 'discretionary pole' of the rule versus discretion spectrum than it would be under the simple, objective regime of an exchange rate rule.

For both these reasons, international policy coordination has become more difficult, not less necessary, than in the past and it requires that we go rather deeply into each others' 'internal affairs'.

To do so, I shall offer a commented text-book description of the United States monetary policy since October 1979, when the Fed[1] changed its operating procedure, to see at what level a European observer may have disagreements with his transatlantic friends.

The first aspect of the new American monetary policy is the increased weight attributed to the final objective of restraining inflation.

One must always be wary of dubbing policy declarations as historical events and I could not accept that the October 1979 measures signal the final burial of Keynesian monetary policy. The great English economist has been buried so many times already in the last few years that it reminds me of the phrase that Italo Svevo attributed to one of his characters: 'to stop smoking is very easy, I have already done it several times ...'. However, even without proclaiming that a new monetary era has begun in October 1979, I think it is safe to say that a shift of emphasis took place on that date and that short-term support of economic activity lost weight, in favour of price stability, in the complex of objectives pursued by means of monetary policy.

There is little to disagree with this change of emphasis. I think it is now accepted by economists of all 'schools' that money is, so to speak, an input to the production, investment and consumption process and that its efficiency as an input depends on its stability. This means that inflation hampers growth in a basic, structural sense and that the short-term benefits to be obtained by pumping money into the economy are not worth the long-term costs of inflation.

It is with some European pride that I can point out that some European countries, Germany and the Benelux countries in the EEC and Switzerland and Austria outside it, understood this very early and their relative success is one important reason why other countries are now more convinced in their opposition to inflation.

[1] Federal Reserve Bank.

Not having found anything to disagree within the final objective of United States monetary policy, let's consider the so-called intermediate target variables.

These are expressed in the United States as rates of increase in the monetary aggregates which are set normally for the period from the last quarter of the present year to the last quarter of the year ahead. Target ranges are set for narrow and wider definitions of the money supply. The actual numbers for the lower and upper range for each aggregate are rates of increase thought compatible with, and necessary for, the achievement of the final targets.

The philosophy behind the fixing of these targets has been expressed at the highest level by the Chairman of the Board of Governors of the Federal Reserve before the Senate Banking Committee: 'Our intent is not to accommodate inflationary forces; rather we mean to exert continuing restraint on growth in money and credit to squeeze out inflationary pressures. That posture should be reflected in further deceleration in the monetary aggregates in the years ahead, and is an essential ingredient in any effective policy to restore price stability'. However, he added: 'I know that the case is sometimes made that monetary policy can alone deal with the inflation side of the equation. But not in the real world – not if other policies pull in other directions, feeding inflationary expectations, propelling the cost and wage structure upwards, and placing enormous burdens on financial markets with large budgetary deficits into the indefinite future'.

Another high exponent of the Federal Open Market Committee, Anthony Solomon, has put it in these terms: 'Gradual reduction of money and credit growth as the centrepiece of broad monetary strategy has indeed almost ceased to be a matter of controversy. In a period of prolonged and substantial inflation, virtually all schools of economic thought can accept such an approach and I certainly do myself. But I would like to suggest that it would be a mistake to assume that slowing monetary growth by itself offers a simple or painless, purely "technical", solution to our inflation problem ... . On the whole, the experience abroad tends to confirm the suspicion that slowing monetary growth by itself may not be enough to control price inflation within acceptable periods of time and without unacceptable side effects. A good record on achieving money growth targets has not necessarily ensured a good performance on the inflation front – and conversely. Over periods of up to three or four years, there seems to be at best only a rather loose relationship between the growth of the aggregates and price inflation. Over longer periods, to be sure, the relationship is closer.'

I find it very difficult to disagree with these well-balanced statements and Alexander Lamfalussy, distilling recent monetary policy experiences, especially European ones, has reached very similar conclusions.

B. Techniques

Looking for disagreements between Europe and the United States we have therefore to go further through our textbook description and examine the so-called operating target.

Under the pre-October 1979 method, the trading desk in New York operated to peg the Federal Fund's rate, i.e. the interest rate charged by banks with excess reserves for lending them to banks in need to bring their balances with the Federal Reserve Bank up to the required level. The drawback of adopting a level of interest rates as a short-term operating target was that, in order to keep this rate within its tolerance range, the manager of the open market desk had to supply any amount of reserves to the banking system which was demanded by the banks at that level of the Federal Fund's rate. Whenever the money supply was rising strongly, banks' demand for Federal Funds increased equally and open market purchases had to be stepped up to prevent the Federal Fund's rate from moving outside its tolerance range. In addition, there was some reluctance by the Federal Reserve Board to adjust, at its monthly meetings, the tolerance range speedily and by sufficient amounts to correct deviations in the money supply from its target path, partly because it was not always clear if the deviations in the money supply figures were only temporary aberrations likely to reverse themselves, or on the contrary more fundamental changes in trends, partly because the interest rate was regarded as a politically sensitive indicator. Consequently, frequent short-term deviations in the money supply led to an erosion of public confidence, especially in a period of rising inflationary pressures, in the willingness or the ability of the Federal Reserve to stick to its own targets.

The new operating target adopted on 6 October 1979 is the amount of unborrowed reserves supplied to the banking system through open market transactions. There is still a tolerance range for the upper and lower level of the Federal Fund's rate, but this range is now so wide (e.g. from 8.5 to 14% in June 1980) that the rate is largely left to find its own level. Thus, in order to gain control over reserves supplied to the banking system, the Federal Reserve has more or less abandoned discretionary control over the level of interest rates.

The Federal Reserve is careful to point out that there is nothing sacred in the new rule and it is supposed to be applied 'cum grano salis'. In front of the Senate Committee, Chairman Volcker emphasized 'that swings in the money and credit aggregates over a month, a quarter or even longer should not be disturbing, provided there is understanding and confidence in our intentions over more significant periods of time'. Anthony Solomon goes as far as commenting that the Federal Open Market Committee had exaggerated in pursuing monetary targets during the second quarter of 1980, causing unnecessary downswings of the interest rates.

Even with these qualifications, however, there is possibly a difference of emphasis between Europeans and Americans on the importance to be given to money aggregates and interest rates in conducting monetary policy. I say 'between Europeans and Americans' because this is both the subject of today's seminar and, I would say, the geographical distinction of the arguments. It is necessary, however, not to forget the existence of all those who take a radical 'quantity' view on this side of the Atlantic as well as of those who continue to advocate a more price-oriented approach in the United States.

The first reason which would justify paying greater attention to interest rates is somewhat pedestrian but, in my view, important. That is that while everybody knows what an interest rate is, the price they pay (receive) to borrow (lend) money, the issue of what is money is in contrast much more complicated, both conceptually and statistically. A casual look at the several definitions of money in a given economy (not to speak of inter-country differences) is enough to prove this statement. Some recent difficulties created by the development of new financial assets, especially in the United States (NOW accounts) or the peculiar effects created by the lifting of quantitative controls (the 'corset') in the United Kingdom, just make this eternal problem worse. A small sign of this difficulty is the fact that Paul Volcker, in front of a Senate committee, had to spend something like 3 of his total 11 pages just to show how M1A and M1B figures were altered by the growth of NOW accounts. Close to this reason is the fact that interest rates are observed continuously without delay.

A second reason is that interest rates are, so to speak, a universal variable while monetary aggregates are much more segmented. A change in the rate affects all market participants, having widespread consequences in terms of relative costs, resource allocation, and economic behaviour. This is not so for a temporary deviation of a monetary aggregate from the chosen path. If a few thousand million of whatever M you like are lying somewhere in the economy for some time, nothing happens, nobody's behaviour is really affected. To seek control of the aggregates instant by instant, dollar by dollar would be to ignore realities and to produce more shocks and uncertainties than it eliminates.

If demand curves were stable and known, there would be a known one-to-one correspondence between price and quantity and it would make no difference which of the axes one looks at. As they are not, we do not exactly know what price corresponds to what quantity and hence we have to choose what to control. Now, one has to believe that demand curves are very very thick indeed to be ready to accept a succession of swings of about 10 percentage points without suspecting that a change in monetary stance goes with them. But, if curves are so thick, why should the 'play' of a point on the curve be dramatically important for quantities and quite irrelevant for the rate?

If one believes that in the long-run the demand for money is rather stable, one would tend to avoid huge swings in interest rates also as part of a well-balanced 'aggregate-oriented' monetary policy. A look at 'real' interest rates may be a useful guidance to those who think that prices affect economic behaviour.

One could go further down to even narrower issues such as the opportunity of contemporaneous reserve accounting or the adjustment in the path for non-borrowed reserves and the like, which are actually discussed within and outside the Federal Reserve. But that would go beyond the scale of this paper and it would also implicitly suggest that the difficult problems of world economic interdependence can be solved at the lowest level of technicalities.

C. Exchange rates

A last issue is, in a sense, the corollary of the emphasis put on aggregates in performing American monetary policy: the policy of free floating on the foreign exchange market.

I think that in this domain the differences between 'Americans and Europeans', where again I use the terms as shorthand devices, are more than just a matter of emphasis.

The Under-Secretary in the Treasury, Mr. B. W. Sprinkel, has officially declared that the United States '... intend to return to the more limited pre-1978 concept of interventions by intervening only when necessary to counter conditions of disorder in the market'. In November 1978, as it will be remembered, after a dramatic run-down on the dollar, the Carter administration had announced the commitment to a more active intervention policy. The new policy is, therefore, a return to the *status quo ante.*

The position in Europe is, in this respect, traditionally different from the one described by Under-Secretary B. Sprinkel.

A first reason, peculiar to Europe, is that, as I have shown above, Europe is much more open to international trade than the United States. As a consequence of that, exchange rate changes have very large and rapid effects on inflation rates and, therefore, an 'eye' on the exchange rate is an 'eye' (possibly a very sharp one) on inflation, and avoiding excessive depreciations means subduing inflationary tensions.

There are, however, also more general reasons. Some are the same, *mutatis mutandis,* as those mentioned above as regards the relative weight of interest rates and money aggregates in conducting monetary policy. Let me just underline that the fact that you have to give a certain quantity of, say, German marks to have one dollar is much more 'solid' than the fact that *a* money aggregate has grown by X% in a given period.

There is finally, a somewhat more philosophical argument involved. Under-Secretary Sprinkel made it clear that the new administration does not favour interventions because: 'Significant and frequent interventions by governments assume that relatively few officials know better where exchange rates should (or should not) be than a large number of decision-makers in the market, and that public funds should be put at risk on the basis of that assumption'.

It is clear to me that the (price) result of a competitive market is a very weighty variable, being, indeed, the end result of a very large number of transactions. This does not imply, however, that one cannot have one's own idea on the 'right' price and bet on it. Indeed operators do this all the time; just think what would be the turnover of, say, the Chicago futures market if people did not have their own ideas and did not act on it.[1]

But if we admit that anyone can make his own idea about the appropriateness of the 'market price' without being accused of *lèse-majesté,* why should we just exclude from the game the arm of collective judgment (is not the government just this?). To admit that the game is tough and competition stiff does not mean that one should not even enter the ring.

---

[1] In theoretical terms, the same point has been made very clearly by Grossman and Stiglitz: 'If competitive equilibrium is defined as a situation in which prices are such that all arbitrage profits are eliminated, is it possible that a competitive economy always be in equilibrium? Clearly not, for then those who arbitrage make no (private) return from their (privately) costly activity. Hence the assumptions that all markets are always in equilibrium and always perfectly arbitraged are inconsistent when arbitrage is costly' (Sanford J. Grossmann and Joseph E. Stiglitz: 'On the impossibility of informationally efficient markets', *American Economic Review,* June 1980, Vol. 70, No 3, pp. 393-408.

In addition, intervention may be needed to avoid disruptions to trade and inconsistency with fundamental economic factors. Quite apart from cases of erratic movements due to disorderly market conditions, circumstances may arise where intervention designed to dampen exchange rate variations will be opportune.

Large and sudden changes in the exchange rate can disrupt trade relationships between countries by altering competitive conditions in a manner which does not reflect changes in relative costs, factor endowment and other 'fundamental' factors. In these cases, there is a danger of protectionist pressures, which can trigger a chain reaction limiting the free flow of trade, exacerbating inflation and seriously hampering growth. In such circumstances, even in the absence of evident disorderly conditions, action designed to restrain or slow down movement of the rate may be required.

However, dramatic changes in the exchange rate can spotlight, often more sharply and opportunely than other variables, deep economic changes in the country concerned as compared with others. In certain cases such exchange rate movements will be acceptable because they reflect explicit policy choices (such as a revaluation for the currency of a low inflation country). Nevertheless, if a movement is very sharp and sudden it will generally be unwelcome to country concerned. In such cirumstances, intervention aimed at damping the movement may beneficial, although it should be underlined that the border line between 'leaning against the wind' and 'manipulation' of exchange rates is very easy to trespass and therefore great care has to be put in performing this kind of intervention.

Any action aimed directly at the exchange rate will spill over into other fields, even if the authorities attempt to offset its direct effects on internal monetary conditions. In particular, conflicts may arise between the exchange rate objectives and aggregate-oriented monetary policies or interest rate policies. The existence of these spillover effects implies that, in general, a compromise will have to be found between exchange rates and other objectives of economic policy. It also implies that policy actions in other fields will influence the exchange rate. As a consequence any exchange rate policy has to be seen as a component of overall economic policy whose internal consistency has to be preserved.

8. Conclusions

I shall try to summarize my remarks in a few points.

Firstly, the world monetary and economic order that prevailed in the first two post-war decades has disappeared in the 1970s. The break of the double, fixed link between gold and the dollar, and between the dollar and the other currencies, the emergence of a multicurrency reserve system, the floating of exchange rates, the shift of the power to fix energy prices from oil companies to OPEC, are all at the same time manifestations and causes of the end of that order. They are interrelated expressions of the same historical developments.

Secondly, that order has not been replaced by a new one. Interdependence being as close as before, and probably closer, an organization to grant 'peaceful' economic and monetary relationships is as necessary as it was under the old order provided by the 'pax americana'.

Thirdly, in the existing world institutional setting, problems stemming from interdependence can only be dealt with by way of bi- and multilateral consultations, in the (perhaps too) numerous fora where officials and/or politicians meet: OECD, IMF, G-10, summits, etc. The assumption on which such consultations are made is an acceptance of the proposition that each member's policies have effects on their partners, and that it may not always be true that what is good for one is good for the others. A denial of this proposition by one of the partners is a dangerous step, particularly when none of the partners is sufficiently strong and well-behaved to impose order on the others.

Fourthly, when there are no agreed rules (like, in the past, fixed exchange rates), and severe stagflation makes policy choices politically very hard, consultations are a difficult and fragile instrument to deal with interdependence. In such circumstances, consultations have to touch upon a wide range of policy objectives, instruments, and techniques.

Fifthly, if asked to speak about US policies in a consultation round, I would say that there is little reason for a European to disagree either with the high priority given to anti-inflation policy in the US, or with the importance given to the control of monetary aggregates. However, the choice of techniques of monetary control unnecessarily increases the strains imposed by a tough monetary policy both on the economic system and on the external partners. The relief coming from improved techniques would, however, be marginal. On the other hand, an approach to exchange rate policy based on a rule of no intervention is hard to accept for European countries. As the exchange rate involves two currencies, disagreement in this area is particularly undesirable.

Sixthly, and lastly, the fact that there may be only limited desagreement on US policies means that we recognize that these policies are good for the US. It does not mean that they are good for their partners, or that they do not hurt. For several European countries, in particular, the level of real interest rates necessary to keep their currency from depreciating to a level inconsistent with economic fundamentals, is much higher than the level required for domestic reasons.

Thus, the ball comes back into our court. What can we Europeans do to get out of this impasse? Two things, I would say: to show that our approach works in practice and to be united. And, I would add, these two things largely coincide. That opens up another field, that I shall not explore here. But, to put in a nutshell what ought to be said in this respect, I could find no better words than those used by Anthony Solomon less than two years ago:

'If we can't lead the way, through meaningful policy coordination between the US and Western Europe, there is little reason to expect broader success. Understanding of each others perspectives is prerequisite to building a stronger relationship. We should acknowledge and build on our mutual successes. Close US-European cooperation dominates the post-war record. But there are also irritants and sources of tension. The United States continually hears European calls for stronger US leadership in the economic area, and specifically in the monetary area. Yet when the United States does attempt to exercise leadership, there is frequently a notable absence of European willingness to follow. This is not a recent phenomenon. It is understandable if there are differences of view over the substance of such questions. There inevitably will be.The substance can be debated. But Europe itself has and should acknowledge a growing responsibility to exercise leadership, not only in the expression of its view, but in contributing to the solution of common problems. The responsibility cannot be one-sided, and Europe collectively has major potential for leadership of its own. What is not constructive is for Europe to cloak its substantive disagreements, and avoid accepting its own responsibilities, by resting on accusations of failure of US will and leadership. Much of the problem may well relate to the particular phase of European efforts to unify through the Community, it is in a unified Europe that real and constructive leadership becomes possible. But the present decision-making processes make that possibility difficult to realize. Hopefully, this problem will evaporate as the unification process evolves – it is generally least evident in the trade area, where the European Community has formal competence – but it does represent a real impediment to meaningful policy coordination on a global scale.

TABLES AND CHARTS

Table 1

Some structural characteristics of the world economy

	1960	1965	1970	1975	1979
1. *EC and Japan GDP as % of US GDP*					
EC 9	54	62	64	90	102
Japan	n.a.	13	21	33	43
2. *Relative shares in world trade (excl. intra-EC trade)*					
EC 9	26	26	24	22	24
Japan	5	5	8	8	9
USA[1]	15	15	18	15	18
3. *Openness: imports of goods and services as % of GDP*					
EC 9[2]	12	11	11	13	14
Japan	–	9	9	12	13
USA	4	4	5	7	10
4. *Productivity (in ECU, at current prices and exchange rates)*					
– GNP per capita					
Japan	n.a.	1 853	1 937	3 631	6 367
USA	2 655	3 306	4 685	5 761	7 777
EC 9	1 105	1 627	2 438	4 290	6 735
– GNP per employed person					
Japan	n.a.	1 631	3 682	7 242	13 119[3]
USA	6 765	8 332	11 107	13 437	16 330
EC 9	2 528	3 828	5 903	10 717	16 739
– Compensation per salary earner					
Japan	n.a.	n.a.	2 434	5 702	10 172[3]
USA	4 474	5 351	7 553	8 986	11 095
EC 9	1 640	2 487	3 820	7 427	11 165

1 US: fob + 10%.
2 Excluding intra-Community trade and services (estimated).
3 1978.
Source: Eurostat. All figures are rounded.

Table 2
Currency composition of international financial assets

	1968	1970	1971	1973[2]	1974[2]	1975	1976	1977	1978	1979	1980
A. *Currency denomination of Euro-market liabilities*[1]											
US dollar											
estimate A			76	73	77	78	79	76	74	72	75
estimate B	80	78	72	68	71	73	74	70	68	65	69
German mark	9	11	15	17	15	15	15	17	18	19	16
Japanese yen								1	1	1.5	1.5
B. *Currency denomination of official reserves*[3]											
US dollar				85	84	85	87	85	82	78	
German mark				6	7	7	7	8	10	12	
Japanese yen						1	1	1	2	4	

[1] Source A: Morgan Guaranty Survey; an estimate relating to non-European as well as to European markets. All other data: BIS, Currency breakdown of external positions of banks in the reporting European countries.
[2] The figures for official reserves refer to 1973 I and 1974 II respectively.
[3] IMF, *Annual Report*, 1980.
N.B.: All figures are rounded.

Chart I: Twenty years of US-European monetary relations

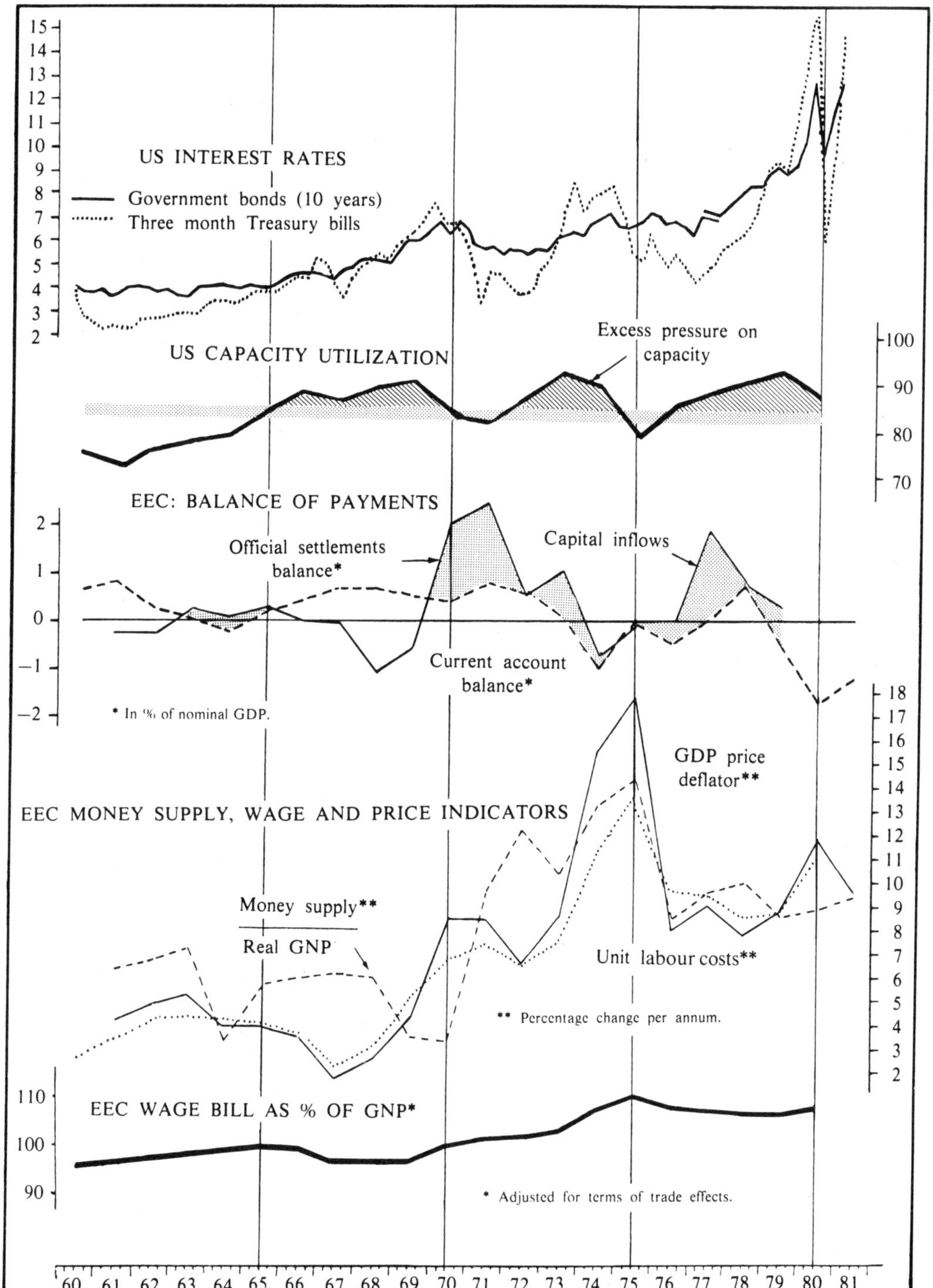

Chart II: Relative GDP price deflators, effective and real exchange rates, balances of payments

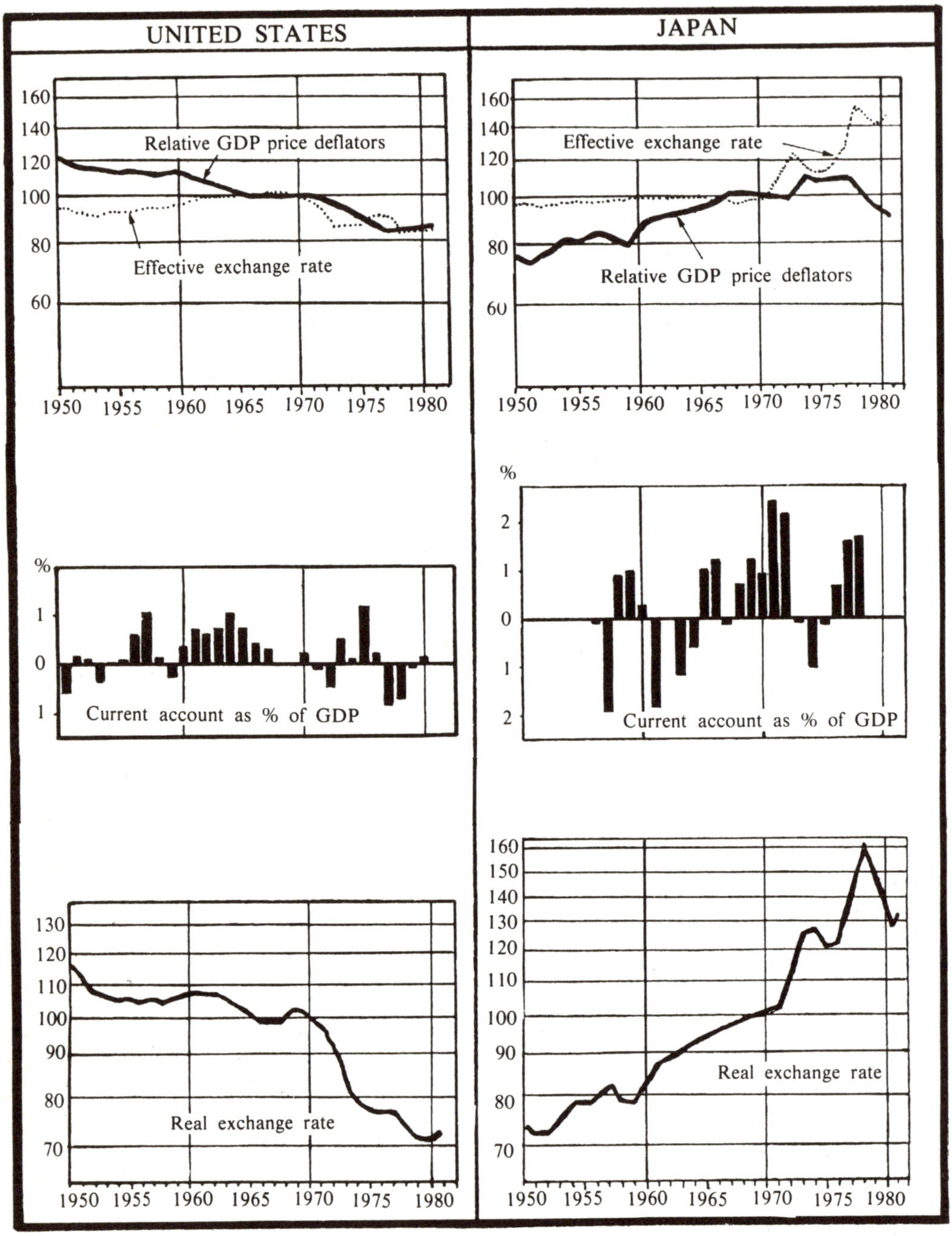

Chart II (contd)

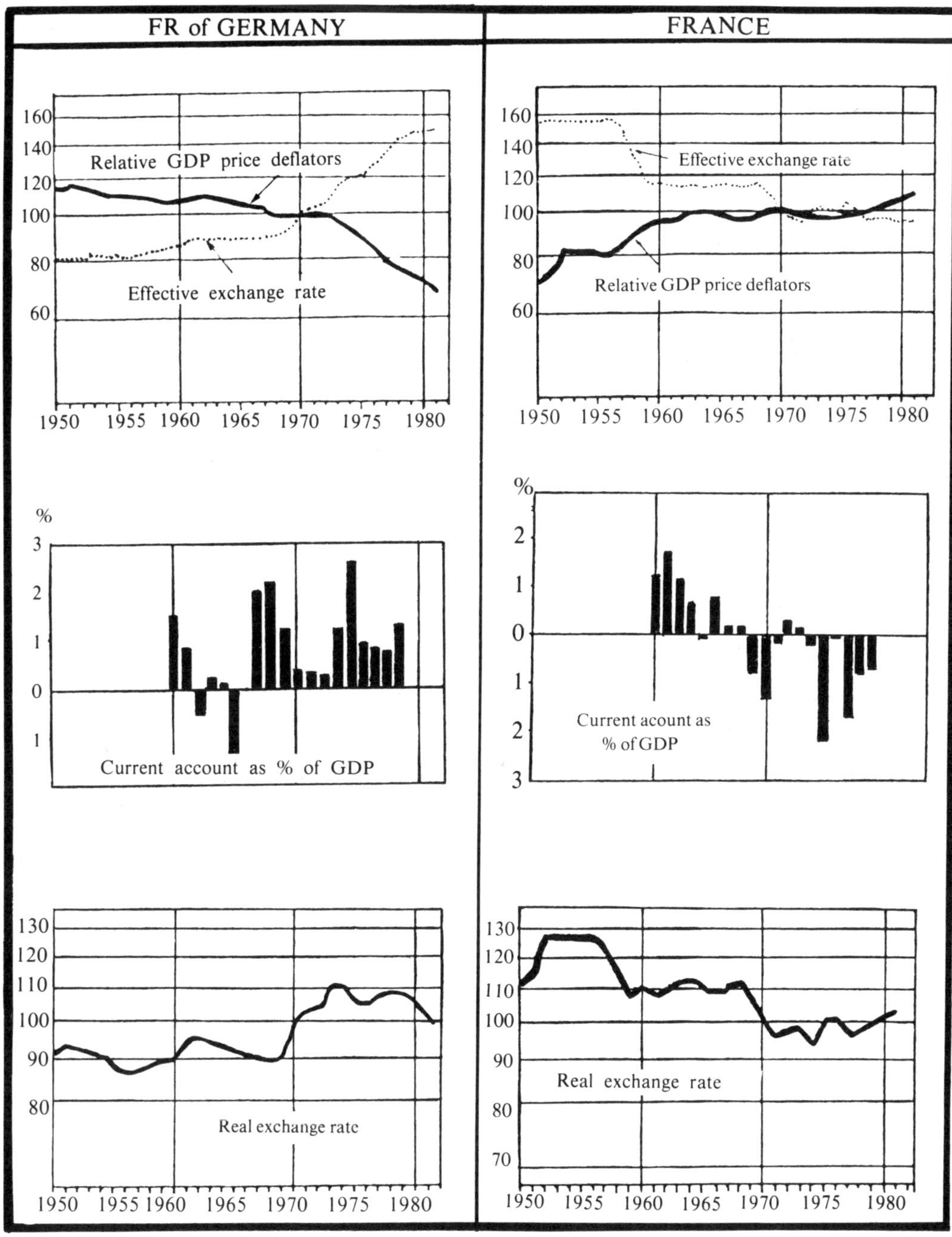

Chart II (contd)

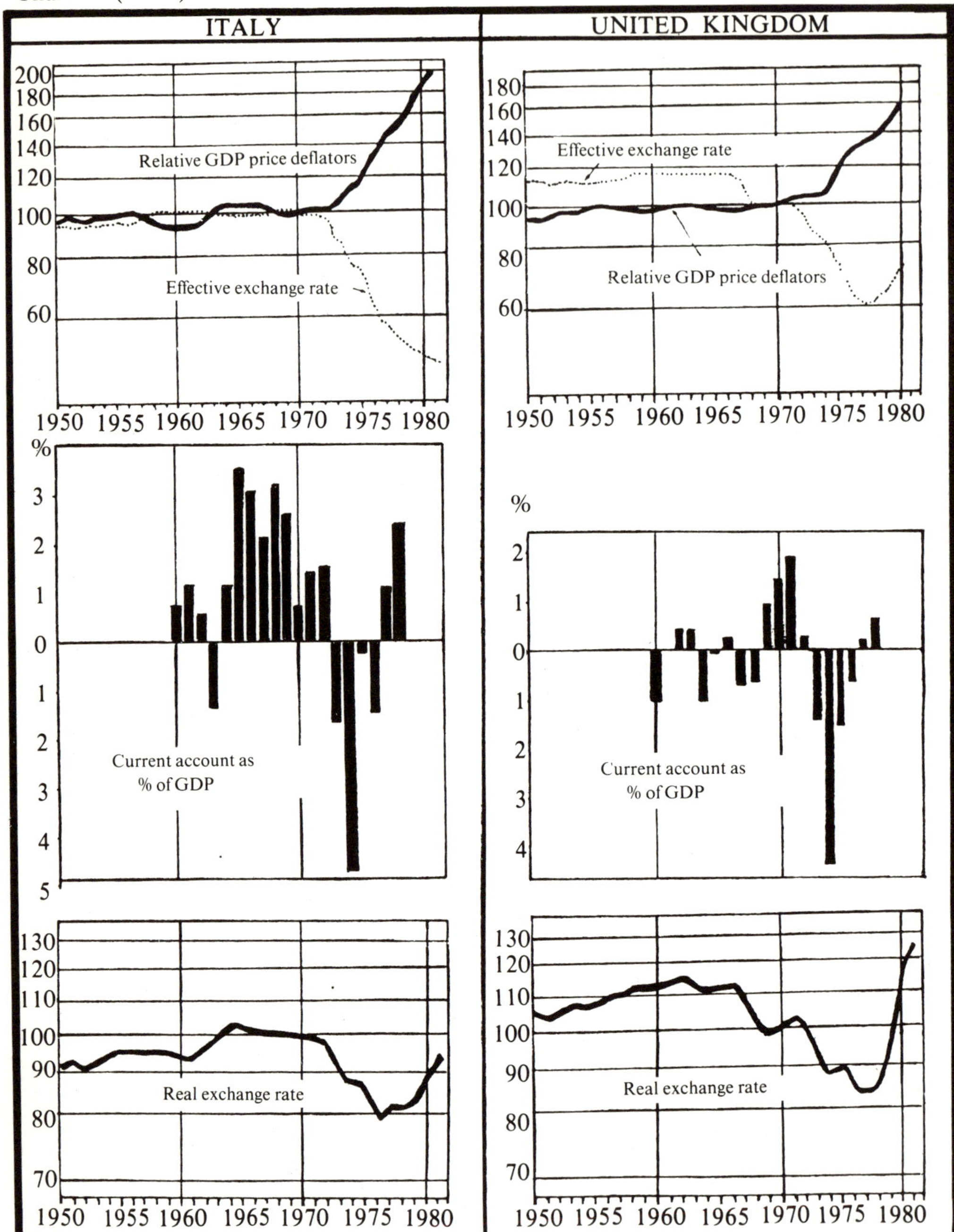

Chart III: Short-term interest rates and exchange rates, 1978-May/June 1981

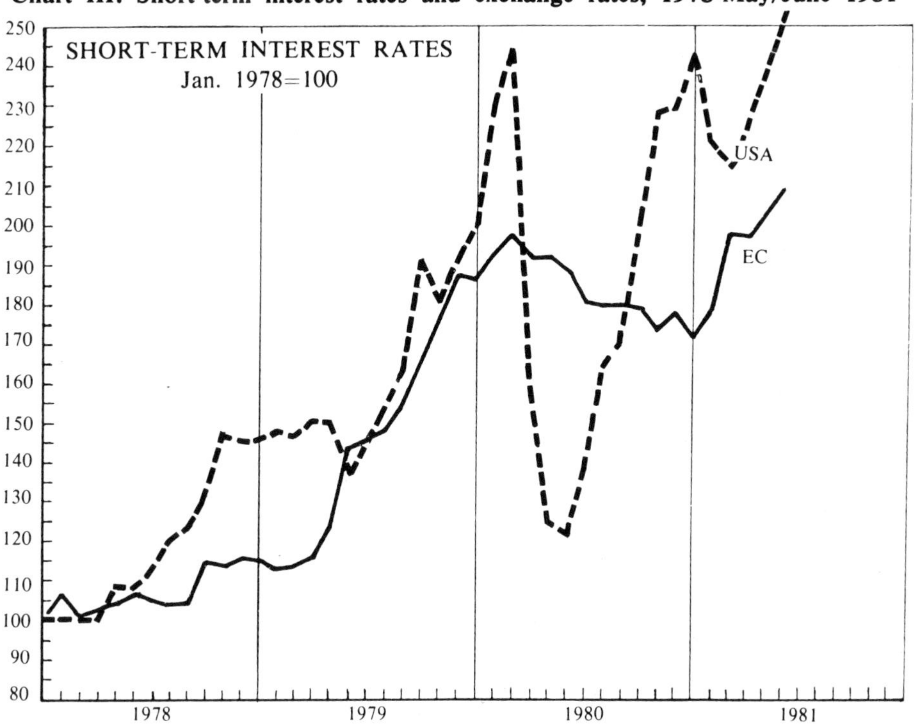

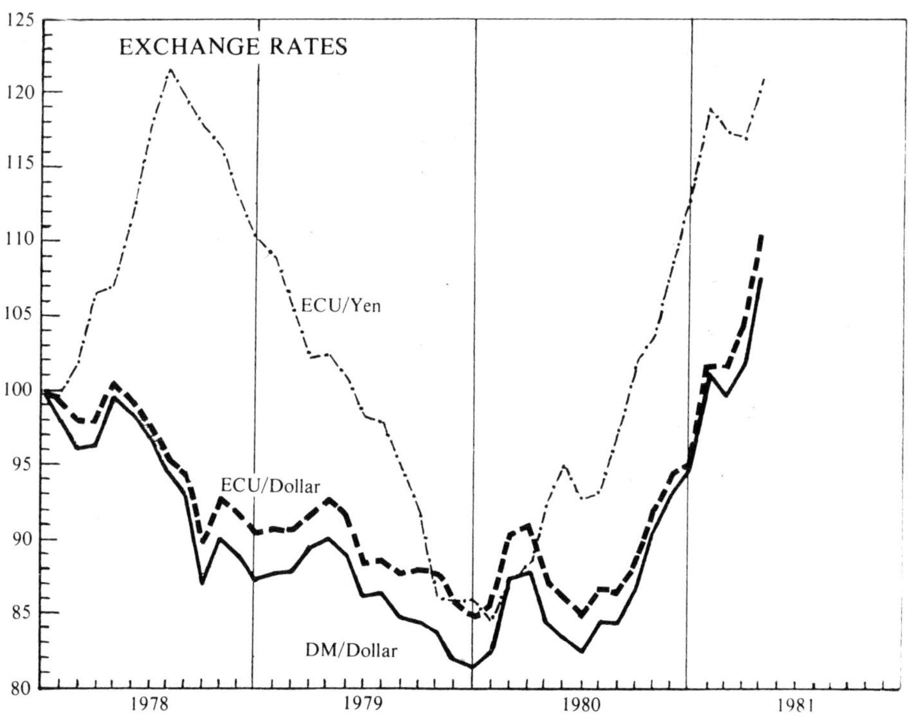

Chart IV: Fluctuations of the German mark against the dollar and in the EMS band

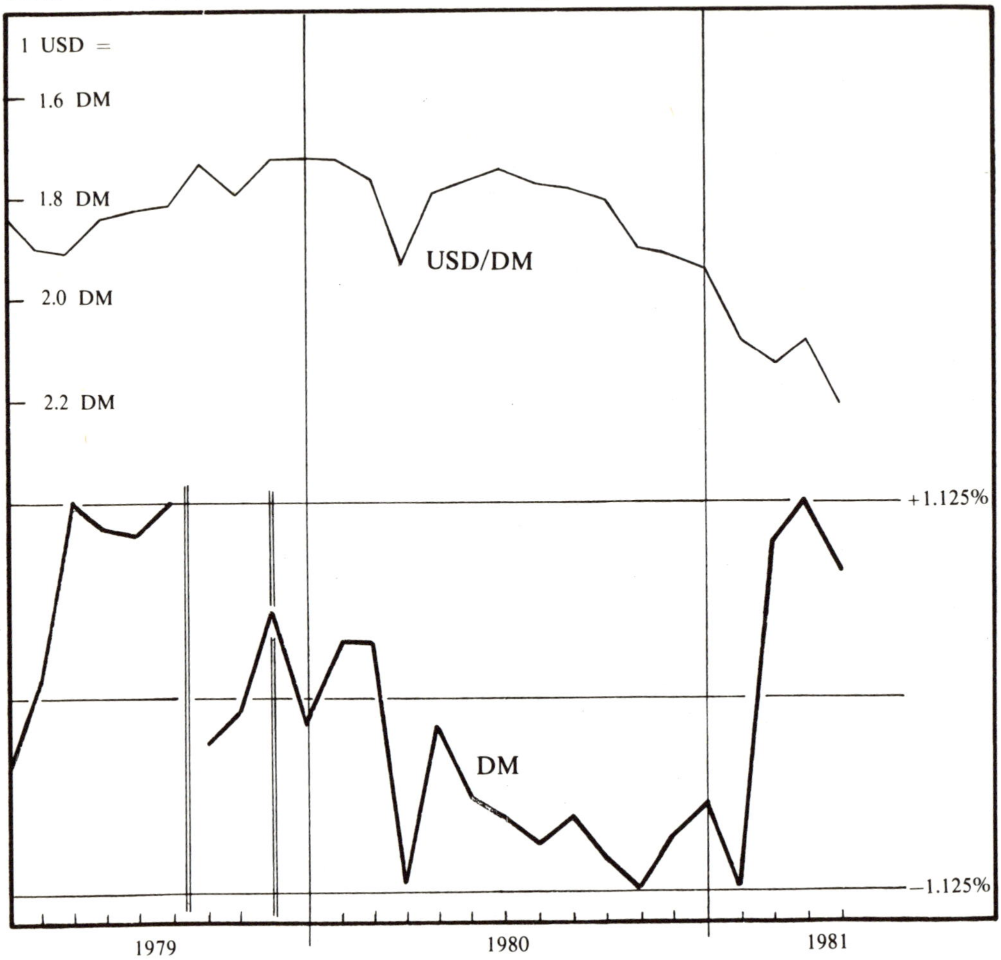

Chart V: Consumer prices and short-term real interest rates

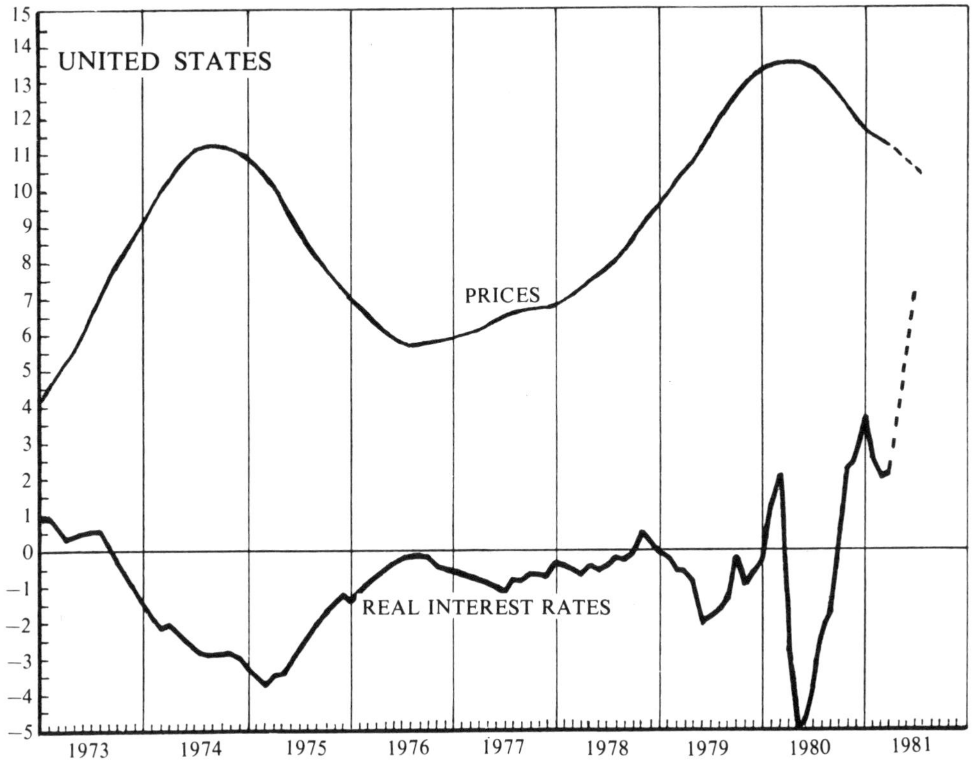

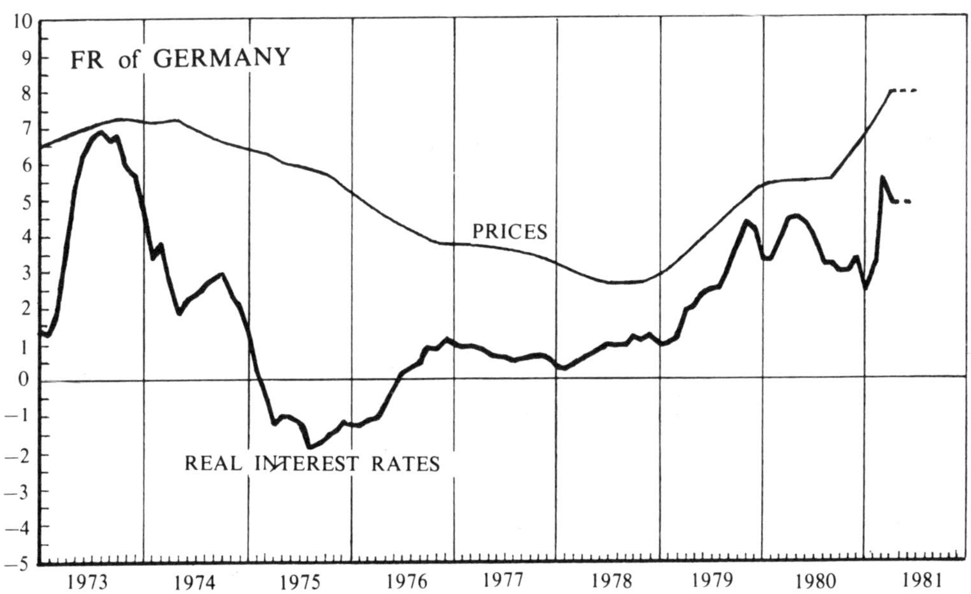

CHAPTER II

Exchange rate policy (1981)

This paper on exchange rate policy was prepared between 1980 and 1981 for the Group of Thirty. It tries to detect the changes in attitudes towards exchange rates, to give an organized description of the environment in which exchange rate policies are carried out and to draw some policy guidelines.

The central idea is, on the one hand, that exchange rates cannot be left to themselves and that explicit management is required, although it is possible that this will not be active; on the other hand, that exchange rates should be managed in the context of a stability-oriented monetary policy.

As it stands, the paper owes much to discussions that took place within the Group of Thirty and in particular with some members of it. The responsibility for what it says, however, is only mine.

1. Changing attitudes towards exchange rates

A. From the Smithsonian to the Jamaica Agreement

The Smithsonian Agreement of December 1971 constituted a final effort to infuse life into the regime of fixed but adjustable exchange rates. Following the second dollar devaluation in February 1973, there was a fairly general acceptance of floating rates, if in some cases heavily qualified and unenthusiastic. This was confirmed in practice as the currencies of the larger European Community countries, other than the German mark, dropped out of the 'snake'. By early 1974, the currencies of all the major industrial countries were floating independently.

Initially, exchange rates, both nominal and real (i.e. adjusted for inflation differentials), showed a large degree of variability, larger even than during the last turbulent years of the pegged system that included major devaluations. For the major industrial countries, the average monthly change of the exchange rate, regardless of sign, increased from 0.4% in 1967-69 to 0.6% in 1970-72 and finally to more than 2.0% in 1973-75. The real exchange rates of industrial countries (adjusted for inflation differentials using wholesale prices) showed an analogous pattern, with variability increasing from less than 1% in 1967-72 to about 2.3% in 1973-75.[1] Thus, not only did the variability of nominal exchange rates increase by a factor of two to three between the last year of the adjustable-peg regime and the first years of floating but real rates were more volatile than nominal rates contrary to what one would expect if exchange rate changes were caused mainly by inflation differentials.

As the world ecomomy was afflicted by large shocks, which exacerbated differences in monetary and business-cycle conditions among countries, the large variability of exchange rates was perhaps unavoidable. The dispersion of national inflation rates around the mean for industrial countries (measured by consumer prices) was about three times as high in 1974 and 1975 as it had been in 1971 and was several times higher than in 1967. The increase in the disparity of monetary conditions among industial countries appears even larger if measured by *ex-post* real rates of interest. As these rates became even more negative on average in 1971 and 1975, their dispersion also tended to increase substantially.

---

[1] These indicators of variability include both short-term reversible movements in the rates and longer-term swings. There is, however, no completely satisfactory way to distinguish between the two.

Finally, foreign exchange markets had not had much experience of floating rates for some 30 years, and part of the variability was attributed to the adjustment and learning process required by the new exchange rate regime. This interpretation was seemingly substantiated by the fact that the exchange rates of industrial countries, both nominal and real, tended to behave less erratically as the years of floating passed.

These developments went a long way to explain the general feeling of satisfaction with floating exchange rates that emerged in the next few years. Floating was accepted as the only answer available in a situation of large unprecedented disparities in monetary conditions, and there was some evidence that, as time passed, the system was becoming less unstable. This cautious and pragmatic optimism was reflected in the decisions taken in Jamaica in January 1976 by the IMF Interim Committee. It decided to legalize the new exchange rate system and to expel gold formally from the international monetary system. Nevertheless, due regard was paid to the issue of stability, and the responsibilities in this respect of member countries and of the International Monetary Fund (IMF) were clearly underlined.

B. New turbulences in 1976-78

Soon after the Jamaica Agreement, however, exchange rates experienced a further bout of stress and disorder, first at a regional level and then at the world level.

Within the European Community, both sterling and the lira came under heavy selling pressure early in 1976, and their subsequent depreciations were halted at the turn of the year only with the adoption of stabilization programmes under the surveillance of the IMF. Between January and December 1976, sterling depreciated by 17% on a trade-weighted basis and the lira by 21%.

At the world level, exchange rate stability persisted until the last quarter of 1977, when the dollar came under pressure. From the end of September 1977 to the end of October 1978, the dollar depreciated by 17% on a trade-weighted basis, and the decline was much greater against some individual currencies (25% against the German mark and 33% against the yen). The exchange market disturbances of 1977-78 were caused by the large and unexpected current account deficits of the US (11 000 million dollars in 1977, and 10 000 million dollars in 1978 according to IMF definitions) and the surpluses of Germany and Japan (8 and 11 000 million dollars in 1977, and 13 and 17 000 million dollars in 1978, respectively). In contrast to earlier years, interest rate and inflation differentials did not play a significant role.

After more than five years of floating, when one might have expected the learning process to be completed, and with fairly well balanced monetary conditions, exchange rate variability rose up and beyond the 1973 peaks.

C. 1978: EMS and 1 November

A year of turbulence on exchange markets produced a change of attitude on the part of monetary officialdom. This appeared in the spring of 1978 within the European Community, when the idea of setting up a new European Monetary System was first considered by the European Council at Copenhagen. The proposal constituted a move towards greater intervention and towards the fixed rate end of the spectrum of exchange rate regimes that ranges from freely floating to rigidly fixed rates. It received the seal of official approval with the creation of the EMS in December 1978 and its actual start in March 1979. In the new system, the currencies of three of the four major Community countries, together with those of all smaller members, are linked by fixed but adjustable rates. To date, the new system has shown a remarkable stability insofar as exchange rates are concerned. Among Western European countries, the pound sterling is the only major currency that is not subject to an exchange rate rule and that moves independently.

At the world level, the new attitude found expression in the package of dollar support measures announced by the US administration on 1 November 1978. The package included internal monetary measures (an increase in the discount rate and an increase of reserve requirements of large denomination time deposits) but featured a formal declaration by the US authorities that 'the speculative assault on the dollar in international currency markets had depressed its exchange value well below what could be justified on the basis of fundamental economic considerations' and it affirmed their readiness to intervene forcefully on the foreign exchange market to 'break its psychological momentum'. A total of 30 000 million dollars in key foreign currencies was mobilized for this purpose, by enlarging the swap arrangements with the German, Japanese and Swiss central banks, by issuing securities denominated in foreign currency (Carter bonds), by drawing on the IMF reserve tranche, and by selling SDRs. With these measures, the US became, at least potentially, an active participant in an exchange rate management system rather than the passive observer it had been until then.

D. After 1978: new developments and attitudes

In the two years following the 1 November measures, the dollar showed no defined trend: the measures led to a short-term recovery of the dollar but afterwards the American currency steadied around the low level reached at the end of 1978. Towards the end of 1980 the dollar began a vigorous appreciation, and it has since experienced a substantial rise: between September 1980 and July 1981, the dollar rose in effective terms by about 20%. In contrast, the German mark depreciated significantly, although remaining by and large the strongest European currency: between the end of 1979 and July 1981, it depreciated in effective terms by 12%. In conjunction with the lower German inflation rates this has meant that the German mark was in the second quarter of 1981 some 3% lower in real terms than in 1970 and about 10% lower than in 1980.

In summary, at the end of 1981 or 10 years after the Smithsonian Agreement, neither the effective nor real rates of exchange of industrial nations have managed to display any lasting tendency towards greater stability. Instability was just as great in the 1979-80 period as in the most turbulent of previous years, and there was a sharp increase in instability in 1980 as compared with 1979. The existing interplay of market and policy influences on exchange rates does not seem capable of preventing exchange rates from being for protracted periods, clearly inconsistent with the fundamental conditions of the economy. At times this is due to excessive exchange rate movements; at other times to lack of exchange rate adjustments.

The reaction to the developments that have followed the changes in attitude at the end of 1978 has been widely different as between the United States and Japan, on the one hand, and Western Europe, on the other. In fact, two and a half years after the Carter package, the Reagan administration reversed the policy stance adopted in 1978: 'In conjunction with our emphasis on the economic fundamentals, we intend to return to the more limited pre-1978 concept of intervention by intervening only when necessary to counter conditions of disorder in the market'.

The Japanese authorities, for their part, made it clearly known that they no longer regard massive intervention as an answer to exchange rate changes. The new attitude is part of a general change of policy which also includes far-reaching exchange control liberalization, willingness to accept for the yen the role of an international currency, and a more market-oriented international monetary policy. However, the Japanese monetary authorities have made clear that their policy is flexible enough to allow a certain amount of intervention.

Western Europe, for its part, with the significant exception of the United Kingdom, maintained its emphasis on intensive management of exchange rates, although it failed to meet the original two-year deadline for achieving the institutional objectives of the EMS.

In Western Europe, the move towards closer monetary integration, which remains short of any commitment to fix or maintain indefinitely particular rates, has been accompanied by some reduction in reliance on exchange rate changes to deal with balance-of-payment problems. As a consequence, more attention has been given to the external effects of domestic economic policies. This has been highlighted by the readiness to accept very high interest rates, often much in excess of the rate of inflation. In fact, the weight given to external considerations in the formulation of interest rate policy led, in some circumstances, to levels of interest rates that were regarded as being undesirable from a purely domestic point of view. There is the possibility, moreover, that wide interest rate variations that derive from a situation peculiar to a given country will cause undesired movements in the interest rates of other countries as they try to combat the exchange rate effects of such variations.

In some cases, contrasts have also arisen between quantity-oriented monetary policies, that have gained in importance and diffusion in the 1970s, and the desire to avoid fluctuations in exchange rates. No fixed, general rule has been used to determine which of the two variables should yield: in some circumstances it was decided to give more weight to the exchange rate as an intermediate objective and thus override monetary policy targets; in other circumstances greater importance was attached to money supply objectives, even though this implied acceptance of a change in the exchange rate. On the whole, the coexistence of quantity-oriented monetary policies with an exchange rate constraint, does not seem to have given rise to serious difficulties in the EMS countries.

E. Differences of attitudes among countries

As there have been differences from time to time in the overall attitude towards the appropriate amount of exchange rate flexibility, so too at given moments in time there have been systematic differences of attitude among countries.

Thus the United States, Japan and the larger EC countries had for most of the time floating rates among themselves. Even in the European Community the larger countries, other than Germany, participated only intermittently in the Community's regional par-value regime (the snake) and it was during periods when they were not participating that the most striking divergence in monetary conditions occurred among them.

In contrast, small open economies have tended to keep their exchange rates closer to the fixed end of the spectrum. With their lasting adherence to the snake, the smaller EC countries have maintained pegged rates in relation to the German mark, whilst other small European countries outside the EC, have pegged their currencies, formally or informally, to the German currency. (Ireland had an enduring monetary union with the UK which was broken only by entry into the EMS and the subsequent rise in sterling.)

Developing countries have also kept their exchange rates close to the fixed end of the spectrum, often by means of a moving peg. This system has implied two sets of choices: the currency to which to peg and the speed at which the peg should move. Freedom in the first respect has been enhanced by the fact that it is now possible to peg also to currency baskets, such as the SDR. The speed at which the peg moves depends on the frequency and size of the changes and will therefore be chosen according to the overall economic strategy of the country concerned.

The tendency for small countries to keep exchange rates stable is easily understood. Small economies (developed and developing alike) will in general be more open to international trade, and floating rates do not really offer any significant additional autonomy to a highly open economy. Furthermore, changes in the exchange rate feed back very rapidly to the domestic price level in an open economy, so that the greater freedom conferred by floating rates amounts to little more than the freedom to choose a certain rate of inflation, and the desired rate of inflation can be achieved more efficiently by pegging to a currency that displays the appropriate characteristic. This is even more true for countries which have formal or informal indexation arrangements in force. *Ex-post,* however, when imbalances have grown into the economy, changes in the exchange rate become a necessary component of economic redressment: they could have been avoided in the first place, but are inevitable once the situation has deteriorated.

2. The environment of exchange rate management

A. The problem of assuring consistency

The exchange rate regime is 'closed' in the sense that any currency's exchange rate can only be expressed in terms of another currency. When all but one (n-1) exchange rates are chosen, the last (the n-th) exchange rate is determined at the same time. This implies that only n-1 countries can pursue independent exchange rate policies, the n-th country being confined to a passive role. On top of this 'arithmetic' consistency, an economic consistency has to be preserved in the system; the exchange rates have to be consistent with other relevant variables, actual and expected. This is why close cooperation between countries has always been necessary in this area and why rules of some kind, even if only somewhat loose and informal, appear desirable.

Under the Bretton Woods regime, the role of n-th currency was assumed by the US dollar.

The problem of assuring the consistency of exchange rate policies must now be solved in an environment characterized by three fundamental factors: the gradual shift towards a multicurrency monetary system, the emergence of highly sophisticated financial markets, and the impulses generated by the attempts of opposing groups, both within and between individual nations, to influence the distribution of real income to their own advantage.

B. The shift towards a multicurrency monetary system

The shift towards a multicurrency monetary system has been a natural and inevitable consequence of the changes in the distribution of world production and trade that have occurred over the last three decades. It was possible for the dollar to perform the role of n-th currency and pivot of the exchange rate system for as long as the United States occupied an overwhelmingly predominant position in world output and trade and for as long as the role of n-th currency did not entail unacceptable costs for the US economy. These conditions were to a large extent fulfilled during the 1950s and 1960s. The United States accounted for half of the industrialized world's output and for a share of world trade substantially greater than that of any other single country; yet the US economy itself, with an external sector smaller than 5% of GNP, was little affected by the vagaries of economic activity in other parts of the world. The changes in the dollar's external value that occurred in that era had virtually no impact on prices, output, or employment in the USA.

This is no longer the case. The United States still possesses the largest economy in the world, but its margin of superiority has narrowed: national product per employed person is now about equal to the US level in the EC and Japan, while it was, respectively, only one half and one fourth of the US level in 1965.Over the years, moreover, the American economy has become more open (foreign trade now accounts for about 10%

of GNP). Furthermore, the accumulation of externally held dollars over three decades, when the dollar was virtually the world's only reserve currency, has diminished the dollar's attractiveness on the margin as a reserve asset.

Well before the erosion of the dominant position of the dollar, an attempt was made to introduce an internationally managed currency, the SDR, initially to complement the dollar and ultimately to serve as the main reserve asset. This attempt, however, fell short of expectations, largely because of the large creation of international liquidity which took place at the end of the 1960s. In fact, without any deliberate decision to the purpose, international reserves grew by something about 25%, on average, between 1969 and 1971. Attempts have been made to equip the SDR to fulfil its role in the new environment, the most recent and imporant being the proposal for a subsitution account, on which little progress has been achieved thus far. More successful have been the moves to enhance the reserve asset qualities of the SDR by simplifying its definition, increasing its return and making it more readily usable.

In the conditions of floating exchange rates, both private and official holders have had an incentive to diversify their holdings of liquid assets. Indeed the profit and loss opportunities ushered in by floating are quite enormous, while diversification of investment in a group of currencies can substantially reduce risk and hedge against sharp changes in exchange rates.

The long-term trend towards currency diversification has been hastened at some times and slowed down at others by cyclical influences, in particular by variations in interest rate differentials.

C. The growing sophistication of financial markets

The growing sophistication of financial markets and technologies has diminished the effectiveness of monetary control, and constitutes a second important element of the environment in which exchange rates consistency has to be assured today.

Domestically, financial innovation has accelerated. Innovations can be usefully identified as being either induced or autonomous. Induced innovations are those which derive directly from the fact that a particular regulatory technique is used by the central bank. The clearest case of such innovation is when financial intermediaries develop new liabilities which require lower (or no) reserve requirements than 'traditional' money liabilities. Autonomous innovations are not immediately connected to regulatory interventions and derive spontaneously from developments in technology and competition between financial intermediaries. Both types of innovation make monetary control more difficult and reinforce the suspicion that money is becoming increasingly an endogenous variable.

As regards international developments, the monetary authorities in major countries other than the United States opposed in the first years of floating the use of their currencies as international reserve assets believing that it would greatly complicate their control of internal monetary developments and distort their exchange rates. Restrictions placed on the external use of their currencies, however, could only be enforced within their own frontiers. They could not be enforced on the unregulated international or 'xeno-currency' markets. There were thus strong incentives to use these markets, which are in any case highly efficient largely because they are able to exploit fully the economies of scale available to 'wholesale' banking operations. By using these markets, private operators, as well as official agencies from some of the smaller countries, acquired new freedom in pursuing their objectives. These tendencies have been accompanied by an increase in the speed of reactions to changes in anticipated profits and risks attached to financial investments. At times, these reactions were hard to justify in terms of economic 'fundamentals.'. At other times, markets correctly perceived that existing exchange rates were inconsistent with the policies of the countries concerned, but the subsequent adjustment of market rates often appeared to be excessive.

D. Inconsistent claims over income distribution

The third element in the environment is the difficulty of achieving any kind of consensus as to the appropriate distribution of income, either nationally or internationally. On the national plane, the struggle between competing groups to increase their shares of national income at the expense of others results in the wage-price spiral. On the international plane, a similar struggle can be observed between the oil producers on the one hand and the industial countries on the other – and it results in large, sudden shifts in the terms of trade between them. In both cases, the outcome is highly inflationary, and experience has shown that, as the average world rate of inflation increases, so does the degree of dispersion around the mean, and as inflation differentials widen, exchange rate instability increases too.

3. Principles of exchange rate policy

A. The role of the exchange rate in the adjustment process

Exchange rates remained stable for long periods under the Bretton Woods regime, without excessive strains or difficulties thus showing that, under appropriate conditions, the adjustment process can function effectively without exchange rate changes. As stability is a most important requisite of money, this situation was beneficial to international trade, investment and growth. However, there have also been instances when the exchange rate was prevented from reflecting changes which had occurred in economic conditions and serious distortions ensued. In the Bretton Woods system and in the present system of floating rates the presence of large and sustained divergences in cost and price movements among countries is incompatible with fixed exchange rates, and there is no viable substitute to changes in the value of the currency to restore external equilibrium. The evidence of the last decade shows that changes in nominal exchange rates can be a powerful way to achieve changes in real rates and that these have, eventually, a balancing effect on the current account, which remains an important aspect of the external position of a country, and on some important items of the capital account, in particular direct investment.

The process which leads from changes in nominal exchange rates to the required adjustment of the balance of payments is complex and by no means uniform and equally effective in all countries and circumstances. The possibility of balancing the external position of a country by changes in the nominal exchange rate is comparatively smaller for countries with a rigid price and wage formation process. In fact, if the real wage in a country is absolutely rigid, there can be no change whatsoever in the real exchange rate, whatever happens to the nominal rate. Significant intercountry differences in this area are due, essentially, to institutional arrangements such as the duration of wage contracts and the prevalence of indexation mechanisms.

Also for countries very open to international trade, which will in general be countries of moderate size, the exchange rate is a less effective adjustment tool. In fact in their case, a change in the nominal exchange rate is reflected very rapidly and thoroughly in the internal price level thus making any sustained change in the real rate of exchange more difficult to achieve.

The limited effectiveness of exchange rate changes as adjustment tools does not imply that 'rigid' and open countries can avoid exchange rate changes. They may prefer to peg their currencies to those of larger neighbours, unilaterally or by way of regional arrangements such as the EMS, but they will then have to adopt internal policies to defend these pegged rates and to accept periodic realignments to compensate for those differential cost and price developments which may materialize. Countries with rigidities, moreover, must seek to achieve greater domestic flexibility, because rigid real wage rates interfere with those changes in the real exchange rates that are required by real disturbances. This interference occurs whether the attempt to change the real exchange rate begins with a change in the nominal exchange rate or with a change in costs and prices.

B. Exchange rates may move too far (or too little)

Necessary as they are, exchange rate changes may be accompanied by problems of a short, medium, or long run nature. In other instances exchange rates seem to be insensitive to variations occurring in the economic situation and instead of changing timely and gradually, set the ground for abrupt future variations.

It is impossible to formulate a precise definition of disorderly conditions. Yet circumstances do arise where it is apparent that exchange markets are incapable of finding a stable equilibrium and large short-run variations of exchange rates occur. In certain instances, this may be due to uncertainty relating to the policy stance of the authorities. In other cases, operators appear unable to act upon their own view of medium-term developments and very short considerations dominate the actions of the market. This can give rise to great short-run volatility which serves no useful purpose.

There are, however, also problems of a cyclical nature. Exchange rates may interact with the current account balance in such a way as to produce cyclical overshooting. Current account balances, in fact, in most cases influence exchange rates in the short run, with deficits producing depreciations and surpluses producing appreciations. However, there is also a lagged relationship between the exchange rate and the current account. When a currency depreciates, the current account can deteriorate in the short run, and this can cause the currency to depreciate further, partly because of the effects of expectations. This perverse response will amplify the medium-term cycle.

Lastly, exchange rate changes may produce long-term effects on resource allocation that may be undesirable. In particular, devaluations may grant, though only temporarily, a new lease of life to otherwise obsolescent industries and may hamper the emergence of new industries. The experience of those countries in the 1970s which thought that they could support expansionary policies by a depreciating rate are illustrative in this respect. The support of exports, and hence of employment, given by restoring the export industries' profit margins by devaluations not only proved temporary but also produced a misallocation of resources towards obsolete industries. The opposite case of chronic over-valuation should also be considered. This may result from the international role of a country's currency and the strength of its financial markets and also possibly, from a strong endowment in raw materials or energy. The consequence of such over-valuation is a squeeze of profits, reduced investment and innovation, and atrophy in the tradeable goods sector.

These problems of short-run, cyclical and long-term effects have beset particularly those currencies floating independently. The countries belonging to regional exchange rate systems, such as the EMS, have sometimes interpreted their adherence to the mechanism in the sense of a too rigid exchange rate commitment.

C. The exchange rate and economic policy

The problems of a short, cyclical and long-term nature that were identified above justify the contention that it is not possible to rely exclusively and in all circumstances on market forces to achieve efficiently the required exchange rate changes. The general source of this problem can be found in the insufficiency of stabilizing speculation. Operators do not act on a relatively long view, since fluctuations have been too heavy and too long, implying therefore the risk of incurring intolerable losses simply because of bad timing. In addition, there may be a lack of confidence in the success of monetary and fiscal policies or an overestimation of the positive result of such policies, generating unjustified expectations by market operators as to the extent of the necessary adjustment of exchange rates.

Rates have been managed since floating began. The authorities cannot dispense with an exchange rate policy, i.e., without integrating the exchange rate in the set of variables that form the system of instruments, objectives and constraints of economic policy. In many cases, this policy will be of a passive nature only, and will require no specific action directed explicity to the exchange rate since in normal conditions the market, characterized by a high number of specialized operators and by an efficient flow of information, will determine the rate consistent with actual and expected basic conditions. However, cases arise where the markets alone are incapable of finding the appropriate value for the exchange rate and in which a positive policy is therefore required. There should be no objections of principle against that. Private operators engage continuously in transactions which imply a comparison between the market rate and the rate they deem appropriate, because they do not consider the market exchange rate as an unbeatable standard. There is no reason why the government, which after all is the arm of collective judgment, should be alone in refraining as a matter of principle from forming its own idea of the appropriate exchange rate and eventually acting upon it.

Nevertheless, governments should not disregard or hide the information conveyed by changes in exchange rates and should avoid interpreting their commitment to the exchange rate as a matter of principle. In fact, some degree of commitment on the side of authorities is necessary but when such commitment exists it is likely to be misused. Large and dramatic changes in the exchange rates can signal, often more sharply and opportunely than other variables, fundamental economic changes in the country concerned relative to others. In certain cases, such exchange rate movements will be acceptable because they reflect the market's approval of explicit policy choices, such as a revaluation for the currency of a low inflation country. In other cases, a very sharp and sudden movement will be unwelcome to the country concerned. In particular, downward movements, reflecting present or expected inferior price and cost performance, may signal worrying developments and induce appropriate policy reactions.

In formulating exchange rate policies, it is of the foremost importance to be aware of the fact that any attempt to aim at a certain target for the exchange rate which is not consistent with the overall economic policy stance and with general economic conditions is not only doomed to failure but can also produce serious distortions. Exchange rate policy must be seen as an important component of an overall economic policy whose consistency has to be preserved. Actions taken in the exchange rate domain inevitably spill over into other fields, while other policy actions will have an influence on the exchange rate.

Exchange rate policies cannot be made in a vacuum. They need to be supportive of, and supported by, general economic policies. Thus, the attempt to fight inflation by pegging the rate while pursuing inflationary internal economic policies distorts the price structure, delays the adjustment process and in the end makes it all the harder. Symmetrically, an attempt to stem the rise of a currency which, according to internal conditions, should appreciate will cause trade frictions with commercial partners, will suppress the powerful anti-inflation effects given by a rising currency and will create misallocation of resources towards the export sector.

D. *The instruments of exchange rate policy*

The instruments which are directly relevant to the conduct of a given exchange rate policy are foreign exchange market intervention, officially-sponsored borrowing and monetary policy. Other instruments of economic policy will also have a bearing, albeit an indirect one, on the exchange rate. Furthermore, actions taken using the tools mentioned above and aimed at the exchange rate will also have effects in other areas.

Foreign exchange interventions are the most precise instrument of exchange rate policy. They can be either sterilized or left free to influence fully monetary conditions. In the former case, the overall monetary effects will be minimized, but will not be completely offset because the total amount of financial assets will be changed. If, for instance, it is possible to absorb the money created as the counterpart of foreign exchange interventions by issuing public paper (sterilizing), the end result will be that the money supply will be unchanged but the gross amount of public paper outstanding will be increased. In this case, intervention will still have an effect, albeit a reduced one, on the exchange rate, both because the supply and demand balance of assets denominated in the currency concerned will be changed and because the intervention will have the effect of signalling policy intentions in a concrete way.

In the case of non-sterilized interventions, of course, the effect is larger and the move, being allowed to display its full effects on the money supply, has broadly the same effect as any other action of monetary policy. In addition, however, it will also have a particular effect on the exchange rate by its signalling function.

An alternative to the type of intervention discussed so far, which is rate oriented, would be a quantity oriented approach. Such an approach would aim, not at influencing the rate, but at supplying (or withdrawing) a predetermined quantity of official exchange to the market. Instead of sporadically feeding exchange into the market (or withdrawing it) whenever instability or disorder occurred, a steady daily or weekly flow could be fed into (or withdrawn from) the market, reflecting a financing plan over several months or quarters. This would strengthen the demand (or supply) side of the market in a predictable way. The magnitude of these operations might be based on an estimate of the balance of supply and demand of exchange, i.e., the overall balance of payments. If the direction and size of capital movements is uncertain, an estimate of the current account deficit (or surplus) could be made, and some fraction could be financed (or absorbed) by intervention at a stable rate. The market would be advised of the intentions of the monetary authorities and could take them into account.

In principle, the authorities would have no exchange rate objective of a longer or shorter-term kind, nor even an objective of smoothing movements in the rate. But over the period of a surplus or deficit, the operation, by reducing imbalances in supply and demand, could be expected to reduce exchange rate fluctuations. To avoid operating in clearly unsuitable ways, the daily injections of exchange might be suspended temporarily if the intervention would push the rate in a direction in which it was already moving. In a broad sense, quantity oriented intervention resembles the financing of a current account deficit (or accumulation of reserves from a surplus) such as many governments practice today, using their reserves or by borrowing. In economic terms, this quantity-based intervention is analogous to a monetary policy based on a money-supply target instead of upon interest rate targets. A quantity-based technique foregoes the use of some of the market expertise which is the speciality of central banks and which sometimes allows them to influence the rate by influencing market psychology. Instead of seeking to influence the behaviour of market participants through sales or purchases at strategic moments, quantity-oriented intervention simply shifts the balance of supply and demand. It would not work well at times, when the balance in the market is unpredictable, either because the current account outlook is uncertain or because of rapidly changing capital movements. But in a well defined balance of payments situation, it would enable a monetary authority to plan more effectively for the use of reserves in dealing with the imbalance, while leaving rate determination to the market.

Officially sponsored borrowing is also a precise instrument. In present conditions, monetary and interest rate policy has its influence on the exchange rate mainly through its effects on international capital movements. The government can, however, also influence directly the capital movements through 'off market' borrowing or lending. By this means one can achieve a result specific to the exchange rate without having recourse to a general measure such as a change in monetary policy. In addition official borrowing may be seen by the exchange markets as a more permanent and reasonable form of financing surpluses and deficits and, if the loans are from private sources, the problem of sterilization in the lending country is much reduced.

Monetary policy is the most powerful, but rather imprecise, instrument to influence the exchange rate. In fact, any monetary action aimed at the exchange rate will have a pervasive effect on general economic conditions. Conflicts may occasionally arise between monetary measures aimed at the exchange rate and purely domestic considerations. In certain cases, this may take the form of a conflict between the level of interest rates necessary for achieving a certain exchange rate and the level which would be appropriate from a domestic point of view. In other cases, there may be a conflict between the signal given by the exchange rate and the signal given by money supply developments. For instance, a strong appreciation may signal a restrictive stance of monetary policy while the money aggregates do not show any such stringency or vice versa. No general rule can be given on the appropriate course of action when there are such conflicts. This rules out among others, the conclusion that in all cases the message sent by the exchange rate is irrelevant and only the evolution of any given monetary aggregate is to be monitored.

E. Interdependence and international cooperation

In any exchange rate system, the exchange rate policies of countries are tightly interwoven, and conflicts are bound to arise unless a coordinating device is put into effect. That is why the exchange rate area is the one which needs the greatest amount of international cooperation. This problem has acquired a new dimension in recent years, since the system is evolving, without full guidance from public authorities, into a multicurrency reserve system. Although such a system need not necessarily be less stable than one based on a single currency, it has to be recognized that it presents problems which, by their very novelty, can cause strains and difficulties.

The first requisite of such coordination is the knowledge by all participants of other participants' exchange rate policies and intentions regarding policies. However, even with complete and timely information, inconsistencies may still arise among desired exchange rate relationships or between the exchange rate situation and internal conditions. A partial remedy would be to coordinate techniques of intervention. Considerable progress has been made in this area, but there is still need for further improvements. Decisive progress, however, could only be reached by coordinating monetary policy decisions which are directly relevant for the exchange rate. As the level of coordination goes from the simple exchange of information to the actual discussion of the stance of monetary policy, its technical and political difficulty increases, but so does its benefit. In present circumstances the benefits are likely to be greater than the costs.

In the present system, where nothing equivalent to the special role of the dollar in the Bretton Woods regime exists to assure the consistency of individual countries' exchange rate policies, a special emphasis has to be put on the role of international bodies.

The Articles of Agreement and the guidelines for surveillance over exchange rate policies of the IMF contain some important rules. These state that members will 'avoid manipulating exchange rates or the international monetary system in order to prevent effective balance of payments adjustment or to gain an unfair competitive advantage over other members' and point out circumstances which might be evidence of such manipulation. By this rule, member countries are prevented from trying to shift their exchange rate from the value which would be consistent with underlying conditions and policies. Furthermore, the rules require positive action to counter 'disorderly market conditions', i.e., they require the authorities to help the market in finding the right price given the existing constellation of fundamental economic variables.

The EMS rules, as set up in the Brussels' Resolution, analogously connect exchange rate policies and other economic policies, devising methods to assure their consistency. In addition, they take into account the fact that more stringent rules can be usefully introduced at a regional level, reflecting the high degree of interdependence in terms of trade and mobility of productive factors among participating countries. The rules, in fact, tend to stress the importance of internal rather than external measures in aiming at balance of payments equilibrium. The next phase of the EMS should proceed further in this direction.

However, beyond these rules there is the need for consensus among interested parties, and international organizations should play an active role in fostering it.

CHAPTER III

International monetary arrangements (1982)

This paper shows that I am indebted to both Houses of the British Parliament for the keen interest they take in European and international monetary affairs and in the views of the EC Commission. The Treasury and Civil Service Committee of the House of Commons conducted an inquiry and issued a report on 'International monetary arrangements'. I was asked to provide written answers to a questionnaire prepared by the Committee. The pages which follow reproduce the questions and my answers. The memorandum was discussed in a hearing by the Committee in October 1982.

The exchange rate mechanism

QUESTION 1. *What criteria would you use to identify a misaligned exchange rate? Have there in your judgment been substantial misalignments of exchange rates in recent years? Please give examples, and indicate the consequences which you believe have stemmed from these misalignments.*

There are no unambiguous criteria to identify a misaligned exchange rate. It is a matter of judgment, and one can doubt that the judgment of markets is at each point in time necessarily the best. Repeated exchange rate movements in opposite directions of the order of magnitude of one percentage point or more in a period of a few days or weeks are unlikely to reflect changes in fundamental economic conditions because these do not change all that fast. The same can be said when the order of magnitude is of 10 or more percentage points, and the period over which reversal occurs is one of a few quarters. Size, reversal, and time span are three factors on the basis of which judgment can be formed.

Of course, it is relatively easy to make these assessments after the event. *Ex ante* judgment is much more difficult and it entails risks of errors, but it is not impossible.

Three examples of misalignment can be given with the benefit of hindsight. First, the 44% effective appreciation of the yen between the end of 1976 and the late summer of 1978 was excessive, and the 23% effective depreciation over the following 18 months probably went too far in the opposite direction. Second, sterling depreciated on an effective basis by 19% between the end of 1975 and the end of 1976 and it appreciated by 25% over the two years from early 1979 to early 1981. Although there were changes in the fundamentals of the British economy over this later period – development of North Sea oil and the pursuit of a more restrictive monetary policy – it is doubtful whether they justified an exchange rate shift of this scale. Third, the US dollar depreciated by 13% between the late summer of 1977 and the end of 1978 and has appreciated by 34% over the last two years. Again, the changes in US economic policy over this period, though significant, do not seem to justify such a huge swing.

The consequences of misalignment are difficult to ascertain with precision and even more difficult to measure. The most important are uncertainty, extra risk and, hence, caution in international operations, trade distortion and pressures for protectionism. For example the 16% devaluation of the Swedish krona on 8 October, which does not appear to be justified by reference to the economic fundamentals, has called forth cries for protection by the paper manufacturing industry elsewhere in Europe.

QUESTION 2. *Do you believe there to be a case for a country to try to manage its exchange rate? For what economic objectives?*

QUESTION 3. *If a government decides to manage its exchange rate, should it target on a nominal rate, a real rate or some index of competitiveness?*

QUESTION 4. *If a government has resolved to manage its exchange rate, under which circumstances should it revise its target? Would it be necessary to devise international safeguards to supervise such revisions?*

QUESTION 5. *What would you regard as the best way of managing an exchange rate – e.g. by managed floating without formal commitments, or by adoption of a reference rate, crawling peg, or adjustable peg? If the rate were to be pegged, should the exchange rate be allowed to vary within a band and if so how wide should it be? Alternatively or additionally, should corrective action be taken according to some rule, and if so what kind of rule?*

QUESTION 6. *What policy instruments should be used to manage the exchange rate? In particular, what type of monetary and fiscal policies would be consistent with a decision to manage exchange rates? Is it possible for a government to pursue separate objectives for money supply, interest rates and its exchange rate? Would it be necessary or advisable to reintroduce some form of exchange control? Would one need to coordinate policy among a group of countries that resolved to stabilize their mutual exchange rates, and what type of rules would in that event be called for? To what extent would independent national economic policy be constrained by such a situation?*

A distinction should be made between not managing the exchange rate and not paying attention to it.

As far as *'paying attention'* is concerned, in practice there are very few examples indeed of total and lasting neglect of the exchange rate. Neglect could only be justified for an economy which was almost completely closed. Open economies in which economic policy is consciously designed inevitably incorporate the exchange rate in their 'instrument panel', although they may not have an objective for it, still less a declared one. Large countries with a relatively small foreign sector may at times accept the exchange rate as a residual item, as movements in the exchange rate will have little effect on either prices or output in their economies. For small open economies exchange rate changes are more important, but for such countries lasting real exchange rate changes are also more difficult to bring about.

As far as *management* is concerned, both its purposes and its instruments have to be considered in turn.

First, *purposes:* from this point of view exchange rates are linked on the one side to trade arrangements, on the other side to stabilization policies. The link between exchange rates and trade arrangements is essential and sometimes neglected in monetary circles. It is desirable that exchange rates should not behave in ways that harm trade arrangements and create frictions. As protectionism may take not only the form of competitive devaluation but also of action (subsidies to domestic producers, quotas, so-called 'orderly marketing' arrangements, etc.) designed to artificially prevent an over-valued exchange rate from falling, excessive or insufficient mobility of the exchange rate can lead to equally damaging consequences for trade. That is why exchange rates should in any event be *adjustable*. But the most efficient way to adjust cannot be stated in terms that are valid for all countries and situations: managed floating, crawling peg, adjustable peg may in turn be 'the best way' depending on circumstances. Three examples can be given: for countries with very high inflation rates (of, or close to, three digits) a 'crawling peg' may be the most efficient formula; for large, fairly open, economies floating without formal commitments but with some kind of reference rate (e.g. *vis-à-vis* the dollar) may be preferable. For smaller, open, closely integrated economies an adjustable peg *vis-à-vis* a major currency may be the best choice.

The link between exchange rates and stabilization policies is more often emphasized in monetary and macro-policy discussions. Fundamentally, exchange rate developments cannot for long be inconsistent with the basic thrust of monetary and fiscal policy, nor with cost and price developments. However, causal relationships exist in both directions. A depreciation of the currency may passively result from a loss of cost and price competitiveness, but it may also be actively directed to an improvement of output and employment. Even though in the long run the exchange rate can only move consistently with all its determinants, in the short run the size and timing of exchange rate adjustments may be important ingredients of a policy. Resistance by the authorities to pressures on the exchange rate may help to bring about the consensus necessary for policy actions. A depreciation obtained through a discrete and sizeable change may succeed in triggering policy measures that would not be taken if the exchange rate was floating down gradually – even though the size of depreciation achieved at the end of the day may be the same in both cases. The EMS experience offers several examples of the relevance of the choice in size and timing of exchange rate adjustments.

The two links (exchange rate-trade arrangements and exchange rate-stabilization policies) have features that may suggest somewhat different arrangements and techniques. The link with trade is by nature international, and may lead to a preference for automatic rules as a way of preventing exchange rate manipulations and trade frictions. The link with stabilization policies, on the other hand, is more 'domestic', and may lead to a preference for discretionary decisions as these have the double advantage of offering greater flexibility in reacting to unforeseen developments and of allowing the authorities to adjust the rate when this fits in best with other policy actions. As always, however, the more discretion the authorities have, the more scope they have to make mistakes through faulty judgment.

Second, *instruments:* the management of exchange rates logically implies the existence of an objective, whether this is explicitly formulated or not, and whether or not it takes a quantitative form. Many instruments can be used to pursue an exchange rate objective. Central bank intervention in the foreign exchange market is only one of them. Others are: manipulation of interest rates; organized public sector borrowing designed to increase the supply of foreign exchange; controls on capital movements – either inward or outward; subsidies or aids to domestic producers; the imposition of restrictions of one kind or another on imports of goods and services. More generally, as the exchange rate can only be part of a consistent set of variables, in the long run any policy action that has an influence on the exchange rate may be considered an 'instrument' of exchange rate policy.

QUESTION 7. *If sterling as an independent currency were to be managed, how would you formulate the rule or calculate the target with reference to which it would be managed? If possible, please give an estimate of the actual rate implied by your approach at the present time, expressed in terms of whatever* numéraire *you deem most appropriate (e.g. ECU, SDR, effective exchange rate, or US dollar).*

There is no single rule which would provide a reliable guide in all circumstances. If the sterling exchange rate were to be managed, this could be done with reference to a number of economic variables such as the current account of the balance of payments, the level (and changes in the level) of reserves, and competitiveness (i.e. relative price movements expressed in terms of a common currency). The difficulty is that these various indicators will not always transmit the same message. The UK's own recent experience here is instructive. If one were to base a judgment on the behaviour of the current account one might conclude that sterling was undervalued; if one looked at an index of competitiveness one would reach exactly the opposite conclusion. The authorities have to interpret all the data available to the best of their ability and form a judgment.

QUESTION 8. *Would your suggested sterling target differ if you knew that the UK had in place an incomes policy capable of preventing wages from neutralizing the effect on competitiveness of exchange rate depreciation? Should the exchange rate be used to hold down wages and prices? Are there other policy innovations which would cause you to modify your suggested rule or target?*

Certainly, if an incomes policy capable of preventing wages from neutralizing the effect on competitiveness of exchange rate depreciation was in operation, this would make the favourable impact of a devaluation on the balance of payments, output and employment greater and more durable, while the cost in terms of higher inflation would be reduced. But the question is whether incomes policy can in fact ever be as effective as is hypothesized in this question. Past experience, in the United Kingdom and elsewhere, suggests that this may not be the case. Furthermore the depreciation of the real exchange rate (increase in competitiveness) which would result from a devaluation of the nominal exchange rate and an effective incomes policy would not be favourable or welcome in all circumstances. At an international level this could be considered as a 'competitive devaluation' and trigger protectionist measures elsewhere. At the domestic level it might not be appropriate in conditions of a cyclical upswing.

Exchange rate policy can certainly contribute to restricting nominal wage increases in an open economy. However, the exchange rate should not be used in isolation for this purpose; to do this, it would be necessary to maintain an artificially appreciated exchange rate which would entail costs of one kind or another. On the other hand the kind of internal policies that are appropriate for restricting wage increases – i.e. tight monetary and fiscal policies – are also likely to have the effect of maintaining an over-appreciated rate, thus exerting additional downward pressure on wages and prices because of the threat of competition from foreign suppliers and the deflationary effect caused by reduced import prices.

QUESTION 9. *Would it be better if discussions between governments about exchange rate targets were debated more widely? Would participation in international arrangements for managing exchange rates mean that a country was substituting government by international brokers for democratic government?*

Because of their direct impact on trade, exchange rates are by their very nature a matter for discussion between governments. In this respect, the most important feature of the EMS is not that it has made exchange rates more stable, but that it has made them a matter for collective, multilateral decision rather than for individual, unilateral action. If trade frictions between the US, Japan and the Community have been greater in recent years than those between Community countries, notwithstanding the closer intra-Community trade integration this is at least partly because exchange rate developments world-wide were less orderly than in the Community.

No country – and certainly no small or medium-sized country – enjoys total autonomy in the conduct of its economic affairs. Fundamentally, external constraints come from openness, not from formal arrangements. Refusal to participate in arrangements which entail certain obligations on all sides will not remove these constraints, although it may to some extent alter their nature. For example some people used to think that a freely floating exchange rate enabled a country to 'go for growth' unshackled by the balance of payments constraint. But the countries which tried the experiment soon suffered a violent acceleration of inflation, and in order to avoid an inexorable slide into hyperinflation they had to take the same kind of measures that they would have had to take in order to correct a payments' deficit under a fixed rate regime.

QUESTION 10. *What considerations and interests do you believe to have influenced Germany, Japan and the United States regarding negotiations on the exchange rate and the harmonization of economic policies? (These might include considerations regarding national institutions, economic structure, and the size and openness of their economies as well as current political attitudes). How far are these considerations changing or likely to change?*

The word 'negotiation' is perhaps too strong. Bilateral and multilateral discussions between countries, and particularly between the three largest industrial countries, are and will continue to be influenced by the two main and interrelated areas that are relevant for exchange rates: trade arrangements and stabilization policies.

QUESTION 11. *How would your views of the international monetary system differ if there were to be a move towards freer trade or greater protectionism? Is an open international financial system compatible with an open international trading system, or is there an incentive for countries to balance unfavourable consequences from the level of their exchange rates by restricting trade unless corrective measures are forced on creditor countries as they are on debtors?*

In a multicountry economy, whether regional like the European economy or international, trade arrangements and monetary arrangements are *complementary*. It is doubtful whether free trade can survive for very long in the absence of a suitable monetary organization, meaning by the latter arrangements that oblige countries to have at least some regard for the consequences of monetary and exchange rate developments on their trading partners. The framework of international economic cooperation that was established in the 1940s was very much inspired by this philosophy. It rested on three pillars: trade, monetary and development arrangements, respectively embodied in three institutions or groups of institutions (GATT, IMF, IBRD). The monetary pillar began to show signs of erosion in the mid-1960s and virtually crumbled away in the early 1970s partly as a result of the spectacular growth of world trade and capital mobility that had been promoted by that same 'order'. The situation which has prevailed since then is not one of long-term equilibrium. From a long-term point of view the question is whether a new monetary organization will emerge, capable of sustaining and stabilizing trade flows, or whether deficiences on the monetary side will contribute to trade and capital restrictions. Economic stagnation and mistaken national economic policies increase the danger of following the second road. In addition, there are enormous political, operational and intellectual difficulties in shaping a monetary order that meets the requirements of the 1980s and, in particular, of a world characterized by a high degree of capital mobility, close trade integration and a multiplicity of reserve currencies.

The instruments of international payment

QUESTION 12. *What advantages and disadvantages do you see in the emergence of a multiple reserve currency system?*

An international monetary system based on a single currency can be compared to a monopoly; one based on several reserve currencies to an oligopoly. Advantages and disadvantages can be related to these two types of system: a single reserve currency system has the advantage of providing greater 'order' and certainty, and the disadvantage – from the point of view of the majority of participants – of less control and the possibility of abuse. A multiple reserve currency system, on the other hand, has the advantage of exerting greater pressure on the reserve currency countries to manage their economies responsibly, but the disadvantage of presenting greater possibilities for conflict, lack of determination and hence instability.

QUESTION 13. *Do you believe that the UK should take steps to promote or restrain the expansion of the reserve role of sterling? What steps?*

It is true that in the past the existence of volatile sterling balances has contributed to the difficulties of managing the exchange rate and the economy. However, deliberately to place obstacles in the way of those who wish to hold assets in sterling would hardly be consistent with the commitment of the UK and the Community to the principle of freedom of capital movements.

QUESTION 14. *Would you favour a resumption of SDR allocations? Can you envisage alternative ways of increasing the stock of SDRs in official reserves?*

QUESTION 15. *Would you see an advantage in a situation in which the SDR was generally used for purposes such as pricing oil and primary commodites, denominating international debts, and intervention in support of exchange rates? What institutional initiatives would be needed to create the possibility of such expanded use of the SDR? Please be as specific as possible on the steps that would be necessary to create a private SDR market and trading between the official and private sectors.*

QUESTION 16. *Would it be possible to reconcile use of the SDR as an intervention medium with valuation of the SDR as a basket of the five principal currencies (US dollar, sterling, German mark, yen and French franc)?*

The decision to create the SDR was taken in 1967 when there was a widespread fear that there might be a shortage of international liquidity. Its creation was also seen as a step towards an international monetary system based on a truly *international* currency, i.e. one that was not also a *national* currency and therefore was not exposed to conflicts between domestic and international objectives. Since that time the need to reach the first objective (creation of additional international liquidity) has become much less urgent, as xeno-markets have provided abundant international means of payment, while the second objective has gained importance with the gradual emergence of a multiple reserve currency system. Things are further complicated by the fact that the growth of xeno-markets and the emergence of a multiple reserve currency system have been two interrelated manifestations of the same historical evolution..

If it was part of a movement towards a more organized monetary system, the development of the SDR would have advantages for the reasons explained in answering Question 11 above. But this may not be for the near future. The existing multi-currency reserve system seems likely to last for years.

We are still far from a situation in which the SDR performs all the functions of money. In this area behaviour evolves very slowly and somewhat unpredictably. Technically, institutional initiatives are not strictly necessary for such developments to occur; habits are more important.

The evolution of the ECU may provide useful insights, as it has gone perhaps further than that of the SDR. There are two circuits for the ECU. One, the official ECU created through the EMS, has made it possible to mobilize part of the member countries' gold reserves for intra-Community official settlements. The other, the private ECU, has developed very rapidly in the international market. Two examples can be given. In the first half of this year the share of ECU denominated bonds in total Eurobond issues was about the same as that of bonds denominated in yen and larger than that of all but two EMS currencies. During the last two years the number of banks offering the facility of ECU accounts to their depositors has risen from around 20 to over 200.

The two circuits are not connected, as 'official' ECU are not exchanged against 'private' ECU. Technically, this could happen at any time without special institutional initiatives or changes in the definition of the ECU as a basket. Nor would it in all cases be necessary to take official decisions for the ECU to be used in pricing or other monetary functions. The same is true for the SDR, although the latter lacks the support of a political and institutional infrastructure as comprehensive as that which exists in the Community.

QUESTION 17. *Would world economic conditions be materially influenced if central banks were to recognize that gold is now a speculative rather than a liquid asset and were therefore to eliminate it from their balance sheets?*

Such a development seems as unlikely as restoration of the central role of gold in the international monetary system. Moreover, as long as gold is a valuable asset and is held by central banks, elimination from the balance sheet does not seem sensible. Rather, it is a question of valuation.

Finally, it is right to point out that gold does have some practical use as a reserve asset, at least for some central banks. It can be – and has been – used as security against a loan. Within the EMS it can be swapped against ECU which in turn can be used to settle debts within the system. These arrangements would be jeopardized if gold was formally demonetized.

QUESTION 18. *Does the functioning of the Euro-currency markets constitute a problem for the control of international liquidity? What, if anything, do you believe should be done to control them?*

Domestic procedures and institutions for monetary control do not add up to control of international liquidity because of the existence of loopholes of various kinds, in particular the fact that national controls frequently do not extend to deposits held by non-residents or denominated in foreign currency. Even to the extent to which they come close to it, they provide control in a slow, inefficient and uncoordinated way, much as if several central banks were simultaneously operating within a domestic economy. This does not mean that xeno-markets have not performed, and are still not performing, a most useful function for the international economy. Yet their contribution to the working of the international monetary system could be much improved if the authorities' traditional bank supervisory function over financial markets were more fully extended to the xeno-markets, especially in times when the solidity of the international banking system appears doubtful to many observers. The balance sheet consolidation of branches and parents should be relentlessly pursued; the capital base of banks should be strengthened and statistical knowledge of international lending markedly improved. It might also prove worthwhile to take another look at the possibility of imposing uniform minimum reserve requirements.

QUESTION 19. *Do you regard the sum total of your answers so far as consistent with adequate global control of international liquidity?*

No. They answer different questions concerning different segments of an international monetary picture which is not really a 'system'. The various reserve currencies, the SDR, gold, and xeno-currencies created by international banks are such segments. The establishment of a more structured international monetary system could be achieved through formal international agreements, or the spontaneous play of market forces, or a combination of both. It could take various alternative shapes, affecting any or all of the segments I have referred to, but increasing the possibility of monetary disorder and of the eventual breakdown of the existing free trade system. Global control of international liquidity is most difficult in the present, highly diversified situation.

Institutions

QUESTION 20. *Are the mechanisms for the international coordination of economic policy through the IMF, OECD, EC, BIS and summit meetings adequate?*

Would there be advantage in more explicit rules for policy coordination especially if a more structured system were to be adopted? For which economic variables should the international community seek to establish internationally-agreed national targets and why?

Where you see a case for international coordination, please indicate the institution(s) that you believe should take primary responsibility, and sketch the principles that should govern the determination of targets.

In answering this question a distinction should be made between a short-term and a long-term, or systematic perspective. In a short-term perspective, the existing arrangements seem unlikely to undergo substantial changes or improvements, and the main objective is to get out of them the best of what they can give. In this sense, it may be said that such arrangements on the whole do not work unsatisfactorily.

From a longer term point of view, however, the existing arrangements do not seem to offer a solution to the problem of governing a multi-country economy, whether regional or world-wide. This is because they lack the necessary authority or instruments to enforce or take action when action is required.

It is not lack of procedural rules that makes the exercise of policy coordination so difficult. Difficulties arise from the fact that national authorities have to respond to electorates who do not express the same priorities at the same time, nor always advocate objectives that are mutually consistent internationally. Moreover, the complexities of the policy process, and of its widely differing institutional frameworks, make coordination quite difficult even when broad policy orientations are compatible.

QUESTION 21. *Do you see a serious danger of debt default leading to an international financial crisis? Do you believe there are institutional reforms or new policy initiatives that could reduce the danger of such a crisis materializing?*

The danger exists. But it is possible to avoid it through firm and, if necessary, quick coordinated action by public authorities. The problem is essentially one of identifying and enforcing the proper mix of financing and adjustment in deficit countries. The present predominance of market financing has led to a financing-adjustment mix in which the adjustment component is often insufficient.

QUESTION 22. *In what institutional context would you see any reforms requiring international agreement which you might have advocated being negotiated?*

For world monetary problems, the IMF. In Europe, the Community and the EMS.

PART THREE

Economic policy and institutions

CHAPTER I

The crisis of exogeneity (1981)

The paper that follows was presented in October 1981 at a conference on 'Managing international risk' organized by the Global Interdependence Center and by the Group of Thirty in Philadelphia.

Among the risks economic agents are likely to face in the 1980s there is that of an increasing inability on the part of public authorities, whether national or international, to deal with problems and events requiring policy action. The paper suggests that such 'policy failures' are due to the progressive erosion of the features underlying the unique role of government as an economic agent, features that enable it to pursue 'policies'.

1. Introduction

I would wish to concentrate my attention not on the old problem of how best use a given set of instruments, but on the new problem of understanding why those instruments seem to have lost part of their effectiveness.

In these circumstances risk is not just an unexpected event to which we have to adapt our response, manipulating the tools of economic policy. It is also a state of uncertainty as to the possibility and effect of our own manipulation. In both respects risk is higher now than it has been for many years after World War II. And the two types of risk are multiplicative rather than additive: an external shock is made more threatening if we are uncertain as to the response we can give it. In turn, precisely because of poor control over our economic policy machinery, we might provoke damage to the economic system over and above the effects of external shocks.

2. Why are we so dissatisfied with our economic performance?

As economists we are exposed to an ever-increasing number of learned articles which use data relating to a few years of economic history of a particular country to proclaim as proven, or refuted, fundamental economic hypotheses. As officials and citizens, we are exposed, in newspapers, to even shorter perspectives. The predominant message, in both cases, is 'the poor state of our economies' which confirms how much economics deserves the name of 'the dismal science' that was given to it from its very beginnings. However, if we look at things from a broader historical perspective, the situation does not seem so unequivocally bad.

First of all the amount of goods and services with which the economies are capable of providing us is higher than in any previous period of human history.

If goods and services can be disputed as indicators of welfare, health and education cannot: life expectancy at birth in industrial countries is now 74 years relative to 67 in 1950. The literacy rate is 99% and was 95% in 1950.[1]

Finally, even if we take a more stringent performance criterion and look at rates of growth instead of income levels the situation does not seem bad.

Figures collected by the Italian economist Giorgio Fuà[2] suggest that the average per capita growth rate of a selected group of seven industrial countries (Italy, France, Germany, Japan, United Kingdom, United States, Sweden) from the beginning of their in-

---

[1] Figures from the World Bank's *World Development Report 1981.*

[2] G. Fua: *Occupazione e capacità produttive: la realtà italiana,* Universal Paperbacks, il Mulino, Bologna, 1976.

dustrial revolution (middle of the eighteenth century for the UK and various dates in the nineteenth for the others) up to 1913, has been between 1.1% (United Kingdom) and 3.1% (Sweden). In the following quarter of a century (1913-38) the figures range from a minimum of 0.5% (Germany) to a maximum of 2.9% (Japan). The 1938-70 period shows a minimum growth of 1.8% (United Kingdom) and a maximum of 4.3% (Japan); the overall country average in these 30 odd years is less than 3%. If we consider that in the 1970s the per capita growth rate of all industrial countries was around 2.5% per annum, we can conclude that our recent economic performance is not significantly lower than in the period of fastest growth in the whole of the industrial era.

For the future, Lawrence Klein in his Nobel lecture forecasts that the flow of goods and services in 13 major OECD countries will in 1990 be about one third higher than in 1981, which means that the average growth rate in the decade will be equal to 3.2%. A slightly lower rate of growth (always per capita) is given by the World Bank in its 1981 *World Development Report.* Again these figures compare well with our historical performance.

Thus, it is only looking at the 'golden' and limited period of the 1960s (growth in industrial countries equalled a 4.1% average annual rate in that decade) that the outlook for the 1980s and the experience of the 1970s may appear dismal. And the question is, then, why we take that exceptional decade as a standard, rather than the longer perspective I have just illustrated.

In my view we do so because the experience of the 1960s had persuaded many that our societies could add to their collection of technological trophies the capacity to substantially improve, through policy, the performance of the economy. That bold conviction is now put in doubt not only by the slowdown in growth, but even more by the marked, almost universal, worsening of the performance in the two areas, inflation and unemployment, that have been highly 'policy intensive' since even before the beginning of the industrial era.

Figures are eloquent. In the seven largest OECD countries inflation fluctuated in the 2-6% range until 1973 while unemployment was around 3%. From 1974 to 1981 inflation has fluctuated around a 10% trend while unemployment has shifted up to a plateau of about 6-7%. Again Klein, our guide to the 1980s does not forecast any marked improvement.

Our developed welfare systems have certainly made unemployment much less costly in social terms than used to be the case before World War II, but 25 million unemployed in the OECD area[1] are nevertheless a dramatic social problem. As regards inflation, economists are not very clear about its welfare cost over and above its negative effect on output, but I certainly agree that persistent two-digit inflation indicates a failure of economic policy.

The crucial question, therefore, is: what happened to economic policy? If we were to consider the experience of the 1960s merely an historical accident, then the wise atti-

[1] OECD: *Economic Outlook,* July 1981.

tude would be to accept the end of that fortunate period. If, however, we were to conclude that in the 1960s our positive experience was due to our improved economic policy, then we would have to find out why we no longer seem to be capable of the same achievements.

For these reasons, an analysis of the poor state of the art of *economic policy* is perhaps a more urgent task than an analysis of the poor state of the *economy*. And as in a democracy unfavourable events are more easily accepted when they can be attributed to external factors than when they are due to our own reduced ability to govern, there is the danger of looking for 'authoritarian' measures that promise to recover lost efficiency. The risk of 'policy failures' is thus both economic and political.

3. The crisis of economic policy

We were taught at university that, given an economic model, there are certain variables, called 'instrumental variables', which are exogenous to the model itself, and which may be manipulated to obtain the desired values for the target variables. Modern Western societies have developed a complex machinery to perform this regulatory function for the macro system. On one end we find popular will, as expressed in free elections, which ultimately dictates the instructions for the steering of the economy. At the opposite end we find 'policy-makers', holding the steering wheel to transform the general mandate given to them into day to day actions. They also have the duty to organize, interpret and clarify the economic developments and the economic options among which the strategic choices have to be made. Unfortunately, and increasingly often, the knobs of the choice variables are stuck and refuse to move into the desired position; or they move according to desiderata but give results, in terms of endogenous variables, far removed from the ones desired; or, still, they seem to be moving on their own, completely outside the driver's will.

We have a variety of examples of these 'policy failures', i.e. of circumstances in which the model which for years described economic policy satisfactorily has apparently ceased to function. One common element of these examples is the freedom private operators have acquired to 'avoid' undesired policies. The result is the substantial reduction of the effectiveness of such policy measures.

A first and perhaps the clearest evidence in this direction is the growth of xeno-markets, i.e. of financial markets basically free from control or regulation. Domestic financial markets have grown in the USA and Germany at around 10% per annun between 1973 and 1980. International markets have grown, in the same period, by about 20% per annum. These markets are evidence of a massive 'avoidance' of monetary and financial policies by operators which have preferred the unregulated, international habitat to the controlled, domestic one. The establishment of international banking facilities in New York is the last, important development in this direction and, in a sense, the seal of official approval on the phenomenon.

Domestically, an important area of avoidance of policies is the informal economy. A survey of the growing though still imprecise evidence has been recently carried out in the EC Commission[1]. Estimates of the 'underground' economy in the US range from 3% of GDP, as measured revising national accounts, to 27%, as measured from monetary statistics. For European countries, the estimates range from 2% of GDP in the UK, to 35% of the labour force in Italy. Even if not conclusive, these figures are sufficiently large and, what is more important, rising to give some plausibility to E. Feige's suggestion that the only serious productivity slowdown which has occurred in our economies is the one of the statistical offices which leave larger and larger portions of economic activity unrecorded.[2] Also in this case we have had a massive avoidance of economic policies: workers and employers have decided to participate in a black market just to avoid the effects of the action of the authorities.

Another source of policy failure is a concentration of economic power inside the economy so great that policy-makers are decisively conditioned in their action. In a sense, the cost of stabilization policy is raised to such a level that the government gives up. Decades ago, the foremost examples of this phenomenon were provided by concentration of capital. Today, in many countries, labour is often the conditioning variable.

Thus, money creation, instead of driving, is driven by wage negotiations. More generally, the monetary area is one in which policy failures have been very visible. The changes which intervened at the beginning of the 1970s were supposed to give one further 'choice variable', the exchange rate, to pursue macroeconomic goals and it was widely expected that it would have been easier to manage the economy through the monetary levers. Now, after 10 years, there are reasons to fear that we have lost rather than gained monetary control. Not only the 'real' effect of a given manoeuvre of monetary variables is much more uncertain, but also the assumed power of central banks to control nominal variables seems often to be put into question.

Richard Cooper pointed out, in his *Economics of interdependence* nearly 15 years ago, another example represented by the imbalance which has grown between the *decision-making domain* of a business enterprise and the *jurisdiction* of governments. He defined the former as '... the geographical area over which its activities range. Obviously the domain of a firm will vary according to activity, and it is useful to distinguish a firm's domain with respect to: (a) sales; (b) sources of capital; (c) sources of management personnel, and (d) location of production facilities'. He defined further: 'a jurisdiction is the geographical area over which a given governmental unit governs or could govern in the various dimensions of economic policy' (pp. 91-92). And he noted that the former had grown relative to the latter. Since 1968 the internationalization of business has continued, while only very timid steps forward have been made in the enlargement of jurisdictions. The imbalance has thus increased further.

The appearance of new actors on the international scene, such as oil-producing countries or newly industrialized ones, is of course another important aspect. Since Cooper has dwelt on this topic, I will not elaborate.

---

[1] A. Smith: 'A Review of the Informal Economy in the EC', EP No 3, July 1981.

[2] E.L.Feige: 'A new perspective on macroeconomic phenomena', mimeo, August 1980.

Finally, a particular way to evade policies is to anticipate them. Fully discounted policies become ineffective. The wider and more rapid disclosure of statistical evidence, the greater transparency of the analytical framework supporting decisions, the establishment of a language common to policy and market operators have made it possible to anticipate policy actions to an extent that would have been inconceivable a generation ago.

If all these phenomena are undoubtedly causes (and sometimes effects) of policy failures, one should, in no way, infer that they are running *against* the general interest. Xeno-markets, the black economy, multinational corporations, trade unions, OPEC, etc. all perform useful functions. Indeed, they contribute to satisfy needs which are of great concern to the authorities themselves; needs such as providing financial intermediation at the world level, assuring a degree of wage flexibility sufficient to somewhat reduce unemployment, achieving a more efficient international division of labour, etc. But if it is true that these phenomena are useful, it is no less true that they escape economic policies as they are organized today. In a sense, they run ahead of the present institutional setting of policies.

How has it become increasingly possible to refuse policies? How can it happen that the textbook model more and more often fails to work?

Of the many answers that can be suggested to this question, I want to stress one that, for lack of a better expression, I would call a 'crisis of exogeneity', to stress the fact that all the policy failures of which I have given examples above have in common a weakening or disappearance of that very special link between exogenous and endogenous variables of the model on which the very essence of economic policy rests. To be sure, there is nothing in the formal presentation of our models that tells us what is the essence of that crucial economic operator that we call government. We have, of course, symbols: T, for taxation; G, for government expenditure; M, for the quantity of money. And we assume, somewhere in the background, that these symbols are moved by the government, an economic agent for which we do not specify the systematic behavioural relationship. But what is 'government'?

Exclusivity and *purpose* are two crucial features of the action of government in the field of economic policy. I use the term exclusivity to indicate the variety of factors that includes size, lack of substitutes, monopoly, etc. I use the word purpose to indicate that the action of government has objectives that are different in nature from those that are pursued by economic agents inside the economy. Now, I think, one can visualize the crisis of exogeneity as a decline or weakening of these two peculiar elements.

Exclusivity has been gradually eroded. The government used to have superior information, it has now largely lost this advantage. It used to be bigger and stronger than individual economic agents, it is now often smaller than the markets on which the corporations that are supposed to be influenced by its decisions operate. It used to 'surprise' economic agents by action often secret, unpredictable, perhaps capricious; it is now more and more rational, more easily understood, predictable. It used to produce goods and services that had no substitutes in the economy and that were, so to say, complementary in production and consumption by the private sector. Now, while the government has extended its intervention, at least in some countries, to the production of goods and services which are in no way of a public nature, we see true public goods, such as security, justice, mail delivery, medium of exchange to be produced inside the economy, providing firms and households with substitutes for what used to be a monopoly production by the public sector. True, this vision may be influenced by the experience of countries where a special ingenuity has traditionally been developed in crossing the border between public and private in either direction. But what I am referring to is a general phenomenon, of which we have visible and very important traces in all our countries.

Now, it is clear that if the government offers goods and services that are also offered, sometimes at better conditions, by other agents in the economy, it has lost the main lever by which it could drive the economy to its policy goal.

If exclusivity has to do with instruments, purpose has to do with objectives. Government is there to address itself to the pursuit of objectives of a different nature from those that individual agents inside the economy set themselves. Individual agents are not supposed, indeed they are not asked to seek price stability, or full employment, or fast growth, or balance of payments equilibrium. The economy would not work properly if those were their objectives. Those are objectives for the system, not for individuals. When the price index swells, private operators are expected to want more money to finance an increased volume of nominal transactions. It is up to the government to reduce the volume, or the rate of growth, of money in order to stop the inflationary process. Similarly, if the wage rate is too high to make it profitable for the private sector to employ the whole of the labour force, firms are not supposed to suddenly become charity institutions and to offer unprofitable jobs with the result of going into the red and eventually into bankruptcy. It is the government who should, by various actions going from improvement of the functioning of the labour market to the stimulation of private investment, recreate conditions in which it again becomes profitable for firms to hire workers. Without a clear distinction in the very nature of the respective purposes of the economic behaviour of government and of private agents, who act on the *same* markets, policy is not possible.

Now I am inclined to think that the purpose of government action in economic policy has undergone an evolution which is even more subtle and, in a sense, insidious for the functioning of policies, than the evolution we have seen in the feature of exclusivity. This evolution has to do with the functioning of our democratic system.

Governments are elected. Today they are almost continuously campaigning to defend their position in the media, in polls, in by-elections, etc. Economic and monetary matters have become, for many reasons, matters in which a very large part of the strength and popularity of governments is at stake. In these conditions, the exogeneity of economic policy becomes a slippery concept. When there is a sharp distinction between the 'authority' of the public operator and the will of 'the people', then there is no doubt about the exogeneity of the purpose, although we have the strongest doubts about the desirability and the efficiency of an authoritarian basis for the public intervention in the economy. However, in a democratic system, the will of the public authorities is ultimately the will of the people. If this is so, is there not a contradiction between democracy and economic policy, a contradiction which becomes more and more visible as gaps of information, attention, control, knowledge, are closed? If the government wants exactly what its constituency wants, it has exactly the same preference as we have between unemployment and inflation, between guns and butter, between more social security and more equilibrium in the budget: how can its purpose then maintain the degree of peculiarity which is necessary for effective government action?

The answer rests on three different but interrelated arguments.

The first is quite technical and has to do with public goods. Even the staunchest supporters of private enterprise will admit, if you really force them, that it is more efficient to have public armies instead of private ones, a public judiciary instead of a private one and so on. The real argument starts when the area of public goods has to be defined. Some will give a very restrictive definition, others a wider one and there is really no *a priori* way to settle the issue; a case by case empirical examination is the only way to deal with it.

The second argument is that the process by which 'popular will' is expressed is by no means perfect, even, or maybe more so, in our electronic democracies. The policy-maker, the public administrator is not, and should not be, a robot simply performing the tasks that a somewhat mythical democratic power dictates. He is a necessary filter between the constituency and the economy and must filter both ways. On the one hand, he has to interpret and understand the message contained in the general choices made by the electorate and transform it into concrete, often highly technical policy actions. On the other hand, he has to interpret and clarify the message which the economy itself is sending, to make it understandable to the electorate. He has to make it clear, for instance, that if certain objectives are to be pursued certain instruments will have to be used and that there is no democratic sovereign power that can reconcile conflicting objectives. In short, he has an educational duty.

The third argument is that, in practice, it is often very difficult to separate the genuine general public will from sectoral pressure groups given the natural tendencies these have to present their interests as general ones.

However, even if in principle there is scope and need in a democratic system for some margin of autonomy by public authorities, still our societies have developed in a way which tends to reduce this independence and make the public intervention in the economy dependent on some very arguable expressions of general will.

In the field of money we often say (and I strongly share this view) that a certain degree of independence of the central bank is necessary to make the pursuit of monetary stability institutionally possible. Independence means independence from the government. Some think that is independence from demagogy, from constituencies of governments, and fear that if the printing press was directly in the hands of such constituencies, too much money would be printed. But what does that mean, if not that monetary stability is too important a principle to be left exposed to the pressures of sectoral interests and to the short term meanderings of public opinion? In our days, this independence has been eroded in many ways. The Fed may increasingly have the impression of being the prisoner of 'Fed watchers', of being increasingly dependent on a system of conventional signals which may have little relationship with the hard facts of economic behaviour, but which still conditions its choices in a decisive way. They are still called 'watchers' but they could soon be called 'drivers'. A degree of separation, of independence, of educational relationship, is necessary between monetary authorities and the public if monetary policy is to perform its function. One could characterize this delicate balance by saying that money is exogenous, but central bank governors are not. If central bank governors had to fight for their position every Friday when the money supply figures are published, money too would become endogenous and monetary policy would disappear.

4. Answers to the 'exogeneity crisis'

Various answers have been proposed, and tried, to deal with the exogeneity crisis. Some are activist in nature, others are more passive. None of them, I think, provides the decisive answer to the problem.

In the activist domain responses have been looked for in the two directions of policy coordination and of direct controls.

Policy coordination can be seen as an attempt to regain exclusivity by reassembling the pieces of policy power scattered in many different hands throughout the economy. I have recalled above the phenomenon of fragmentation of the monopolistic power that governments used to have. It is quite natural to try a reconstitution of the 'monopolistic' position through what we could call, furthering the analogy, a 'cartel'. To expand the domain of policy in line with the enlarged decision-making domain of private operators, authorities in charge of only segments of each market now coordinate their interventions.

Compared with the past, the institutional embodiments of international coordination, such as the IMF, GATT, OECD, EC and other similar organizations have grown in importance and relevance. Some of the visions of their founding fathers have vanished but, in terms of hard facts, it is fair to say that there is, by and large, more genuine coordination now than in the 1950s. However, even so a very partial answer to the exogeneity crisis was provided by improved coordination.

What is interesting in this respect is that coordination is not only the most common answer at the international level. It has increasingly been used also *inside* countries to cope with the difficulties of managing the economy.

In many countries public authorities have proved unable, or unwilling, to impose the desired economic policy and have looked for various forms of voluntary incomes policies, social contracts and so on to achieve non-inflationary and investment-fostering wage/profits/prices configurations. Price controls of the voluntary kind are just another example in this direction.

A general assessment of these experiences is hard to give. It seems that they have some effectiveness in situations where the competing claims on national product are not too inconsistent. In certain countries flexible forms of income/price policies seem to have given a long-term contribution to favourable economic developments. However, when the task was more challenging these instruments proved to be simply ineffective.

Coordination among sovereign powers (whether inside one country, or at the international level) has inherent limitations that prevent it from being an adequate answer to the crisis of exogeneity. One could say that the main problem is precisely the one confronting participants in a cartel: while everybody gains from cooperation, anyone can gain even more by cheating, but generalized cheating would destroy the agreement and its benefits. In other words, if the essence of policy is the provision of public goods that transcend individual cost-benefit analysis, then the method of seeking unanimous consensus anew for each policy decision is as inefficient and doomed to failure as would be a political system without laws or constitution, i.e. without an agreed and generally non-renegotiable set of rules that organize the process of collective decisions. In short, while coordination may well restore exclusivity, it seldom generates purpose. Purpose needs to be embodied in institutions.

The other activist answer to the exogeneity crisis has been *direct controls* or more generally an escalation of authoritarian public interventions in the economy. This has taken the form of more frequent controls, more severe sanctions for transgressors and an increasing number of variables subject to control. One can say that, when it becomes incapable to conduct policies in the physiological way described by the relationship between exogenous and target variables, the government bypasses this relationship and uses its general (non-economic) power to directly impose (by decree) the desired value of the target variable. Price and wage controls, credit ceilings, foreign exchange controls are examples of this type of response.

As with coordination, so with direct controls one should avoid being dogmatic and condemning them in all circumstances, regardless of the available alternatives. I am not sure that such measures only produce negative results and that their dismantling will always be immediately beneficial. Cutting the throat of a patient is not generally regarded as a wise medical practice, but tracheotomy is sometimes necessary to save a life.

However, while recognizing their marginal merits and occasional inevitability, it must be firmly said that direct controls, a latent sign of economic weakness on the side of governments, are both an inadequate answer to the crisis of exogeneity and a disruptive factor of the desirable order of economic and political relationships.

The essence of direct controls is the recourse to force, an 'instrument' of which the government has the ultimate monopoly, to compensate for the lack or insufficiency of normal instruments of economic policy. The police replace the trading desk. But in doing so the government crosses the line that must separate the function of managing the economy from other public functions and their corresponding instruments. In this intrusion I see a danger potentially as serious as, say, a contamination between the executive and the judiciary power.

Besides being inappropriate, direct controls are in the end ineffective. For while apparently strengthening the grasp of government over final economic variables, they further entrench the very same phenomena that originally caused the inability of the government to manage the economy by normal procedures. More financial intermediation goes through xeno-currency markets, as credit controls are applied. More production and distribution goes into the black market as wages and prices are frozen. Statistics become less and less reliable, as they are transformed from sources of information into instruments of control. And so on. From an economic point of view one could say that direct controls replace exclusivity with purpose; but by doing so they set the process of economic policy into a gear that imposes further substitutions of the same kind, with the final result of further aggravating the crisis of exogeneity.

The most pervasive and fashionable answer to the exogeneity crisis, however, is today in the passive domain and takes form of a regained strength of *laisser faire.*

According to the supporters of the new *laisser faire* the right answer to the economic policy crisis is a downgrading of the objectives which were nonsensically high anyway. In their view, any tampering by the public authorities with the market mechanism (except for some well-defined cases such as defence, justice and so on) is either ineffective or harmful, and therefore a reduction in their 'tampering ability' (what I called more respectfully exogeneity crisis) is either immaterial or even welcome.

It is now clear to both supporters and opponents of public intervention in the economy, and I limit myself to economic considerations, that its utility depends on an assessment of the efficiency of the public sector relative to that of the private sector.

And this general argument is presented today in terms that can be usefully split into two main components: the rationality, or information, issue and the flexibility issue. Let us examine them in turn.

Supporters of the futility, and potential danger, of public intervention have always been aware that their case rested on the assumption that public operators had no informational advantage over private ones. For instance Friedman founded his case on the historically accidental ignorance of the economic model.[1]

Rational expectation theories, instead, underline an economic mechanism which rules out the possibility of any informational advantage public operators may have: maximizing private operators will outguess any systematic behaviour of the public authorities and pre-empt it. The futility of macroeconomic stabilization policy is no historical accident but a result of the maximizing behaviour of economic agents and as such a permanent feature.

[1] He wrote: 'So I am led to suggest as a rule the simple rule of a steady rate of growth in the stock of money. ... while this is by no means necessarily an ideal gadget, it seems, in looking at the record, that it would work pretty well. ... I think we do not really know enough under present circumstances to do much better – and this has nothing to do with the particular people who are in control. I do not believe anybody here, including myself knows enough to do any better. 'A programme for monetary stability', Proceedings of the fifth annual conference, 1962, p. 209.

Friedman's argument is turned upside down: it is not the ignorance of the public sector but rather the wisdom of the private one which makes active stabilization policies undesirable; the practical result, however, is not reversed, rather it is reinforced.

The 'flexibility' issue can be developed along similar lines. Opponents of public intervention maintain that there exists an 'optimal' degree of flexibility and that private operators are perfectly capable of producing this optimal amount. According to this analysis, for instance, the duration of wage contracts will be no historical or institutional accident, but rather the outcome of an optimization process. In theory it could not be excluded that the optimal duration of a wage contract is five minutes and that recontracting should go on 12 times per hour.

In my view there is a basic contradiction in the argument of the extreme supporters of the *laisser faire* idea. In fact, many of them also maintain that institutions are 'endogenous' to the economic system and they are what they should be, given the economic opportunities and tastes. In a sense institutions, which of course should include public ones, are optimal. However, if this were strictly the case, there would be no need for anyone waving the *laisser faire* flag: if the 'non-tampering' option were 'optimal' then public authorities would spontaneously not tamper and the issue would not even be raised.

The actual situation is slightly different from this. The Thatcher experiment in the United Kingdom and the Reagan one in the United States suggest that the most forceful political will has to be applied to put in practice the *laisser faire* recipe, or even to marginally reduce the amount of public intervention in the economy.

Of course, one could maintain that only 'private' institutions are endogenous and optimal while public ones are not necessarily so. However, to reach the conclusion that public intervention is always inopportune we should implicitly pass a very negative judgment on our political systems. We should, in fact, conclude that our democratic process systematically produces non-satisfactory outcomes. In purely economic terms this could perhaps be a legitimate position. But who could accept it as the basis of his political philosophy?

5. Conclusions

This paper began with the consideration that, looking at it in an historical perspective, our economic performance is not that worrying. It then put forward the suggestion that our preoccupation does not really depend on the actual state of our economies but rather on the ominous feeling of having lost control of economic developments. Several cases of policy failures have been illustrated and summarized in a concept of 'exogeneity crisis'. Finally, it gave some reasons for doubting the adequacy of the answers tried so far to the crisis of economic policy.

The optimistic note of the beginning has thus been dissipated and reasons have been supplied to be more preoccupied than if the problem was just one of economic difficulties.

The excuse could be that the assignment of this paper was to raise rather than to solve problems. But the true reason is that I do not see a ready-made solution for the problems and difficulties that our policies face. And since we all have a tendency to forget the problems for which we have no solution, I think it is necessary to pay attention to the risks that may follow from such a disregard or from excessive reliance on inadequate, though popular solutions.

First of all we have to be aware of the danger in acritically transferring the gospel of 'new *laisser faire*' to the international sphere, forgetting that such a sphere is already, almost by definition, one in which there is a lack of policies and a lack of policy institutions. This lack is even more acute now that some of the few instruments of government, which had worked for decades, such as the gold standard or the Bretton-Woods system, have been dismantled. An attempt to restore these instruments as they were would be impractical. But there is an even greater and more insidious lack of realism in believing that no act of international government is necessary to help organizing extremely complex monetary, financial and trade relationships among 130 countries in the world.

On the other hand, for reasons that I have tried to explain, one should not be unduly optimistic about what can be achieved through policy coordination. It is our daily task to help get the best out of this rather weak instrument of policy, and all possible efforts should continue to be made in this direction. But those who are engaged in it are also well-placed to see the limits of the exercise.

Finally, direct controls are not available at the international level. We may be satisfied with that, because misuses of intrinsically inappropriate instruments are thus impossible. But we also have to be aware that this may entail a greater use of direct controls domestically, and particularly a use of domestic direct controls for objectives related to the external sector of the economy. The various forms of creeping protectionism that we see proliferating are an example.

If awareness of dangers is the first condition for safety, then some of these remarks may not be totally unconstructive for those who are involved in managing international risks.

CHAPTER II

Rules and institutions in the government of multi-country economies (1983)[1]

The previous paper analysed some fundamental inadequacies of economic policy at both the national and the international level without undertaking the constructive task of proposing remedies.

The one that follows tries to identify the lines along which the policy process should evolve in order to increase the effectiveness of the 'government of multi-country economies'. Only stronger international institutions permit policy decisions to be taken both with the necessary discretion and at the appropriate level (i.e. the international rather than the national level).

The paper that closes this collection is also an attempt to set out some of the reflections of a systemic nature that four years in the service of European economic cooperation have suggested to the author.

---

1 F. Saccomani, A. Steinherr and L. Tsoukalis have contributed to this paper with helpful comments. The views expressed here, however, are the sole responsibility of the author.

1. Introduction

A. Multi-country economies at a crossroads

If we abstract from the presence of actual governments and States, and define an economy as 'a set of economic agents who are engaged in various forms of exchange and interdependencies among themselves, and share a certain number of common interests', it is clear that many economies are 'multi-country' in the sense that their geographic area falls under the jurisdiction of more than one sovereign State.[1]

The rules, arrangements, and institutions for multi-country economic cooperation that were created in the 1940s and 1950s at both the world and regional level have developed the movement across borders of raw materials, manufactured goods, capital and labour to a degree never reached before, thus enormously contributing to the increase in welfare and the preservation of peace in the last decades. They have brought the process of integration to such an advanced stage that in our days not only economic well-being, but also economic disturbances and potential crises are often international by nature.

Also in the 1930s, the system of fixed exchange rates acted as a powerful transmission mechanism of crisis from one country to another, and when it collapsed competitive devaluations and trade restrictions aggravated the world depression. Yet, at the root, the problem was one of domestic economic management while international economic integration was still virtually negligible. In the 1970s and 1980s, on the contrary, an important part of the problem is not just reflected in the international economy, it is in-

[1] The world itself is a multi-country economy, as common interests are embodied in the existence of world trade and of world-wide financial relationships. 'Tighter' multi-country economies can be identified at lower levels, by considering dimensions of common interest such as geographical proximity, similarity of political and economic institutions, complementarity in natural endowments, common history, etc. Canada and the United States, Luxembourg and Belgium, OPEC, Scandinavia are thus more integrated multi-country economies than the world, or the American, or the European continent. Largely non-integrated areas may gradually give rise to an 'economy' following political and institutional events, as happened for Sicily and Piedmont after the unification of Italy. Alternatively, an economy may exist and function, albeit in a precarious way, without the benefit of political institutions, as happened for Alsace-Lorraine-Saar-Luxembourg-Wallonia. Indeed, the relationship between economic and political-institutional integration is a two-way relationship. International arrangements and rules (IMF, GATT, etc.) may initially only reflect the existence of multi-country economies, but they help in providing additional coherence, integration and common interests. The example of a multi-country economy which has developed its organization almost to the point of giving rise to a fully-fledged institutional system is the European Community.

deed rooted in it. This is the case for natural resources, borrowing and lending, exchange rates, trade and even for unemployment.

This evolution has profound consequences for the conduct of economic policy. As long as the policy-maker concentrates on the national economy, a growing share of his problems appears to escape control because it is determined by exogenous events: changes in oil prices, world interest rates, imported inflation, payments crises, etc. However, what is given at a national level becomes a variable in the wider context, and if the focus shifts all the way to the world economy, very little is exogenous.

In a rational decision-making process the international repercussions of national decisions should not be neglected. First, the instrument-target approach of Meade and Tinbergen shows that it is necessary to have at least as many independent instruments as policy targets to ensure that the latter are met. Since, however, what appears to be an independent instrument in a national setting may cease to be such in an international context, coordination is necessary. Second, the impact of a national instrument may in some cases be stronger on a partner country than on the domestic economy. The only way to match domestic instruments with foreign objectives, again is cooperation. Third, as was shown by Cooper (1969), uncoordinated policies even when eventually capable of achieving their targets, may entail longer adjustments and sometimes oscillatory paths. Coordination can help in shortening the adjustment period and dampen oscillations. In short, a multi-country economy can hardly operate in an efficient manner if the range of action of policy does not encompass the sovereign nations of which such an economy is made up. In fact no government can keep the economic promises for which it has been elected in the absence of a favourable international environment, i.e. unless compatible and, if possible, complementary promises have been made by other governments in other countries, and there is willingness to play a cooperative game.

The trouble is that international economic cooperation today is not only more necessary, it is also more difficult because, with growing interdependence, the existing 'instruments' for economic cooperation have become increasingly inadequate to avoid, and to solve international conflicts. In the monetary area, there was universal acceptance of fixed rates and of the dollar as the international currency; both have been abandoned, and nothing has really taken their place. In the commercial field, the geographic area which would be significant for GATT has grown wider than the geographic sphere of influence of that institution, which is, in addition, almost powerless to deal with cases of trade conflicts. In the area of macro-policies even the weak infrastructure represented by the common acceptance of the (Keynesian) paradigm as a basis for cooperative efforts has been lost and not replaced, so that today not only policy objectives, but also doctrines and ideologies tend to conflict. In a fourth important area, that of capital movements, a fully fledged, largely uncontrolled, international financial system has superseded segmented national markets.

Multi-country economies have thus reached a state of contradiction: on the one side, national sovereignty is formally indisputable and undisputed, and it is even 'aggravated' by deeper involvement of both governments and public opinions in economic matters; on the other side, national sovereignty is increasingly eroded by growing economic interdependence. Such a contradiction can not, and will not, last for very long. Either the necessary improvements and adjustments will be made in the system of international economic cooperation, or there will be a severe deterioration of commercial and financial relations. Of course neither the strengthening nor the disintegration of the existing system of multi-country cooperation need occur in a dramatic way. Historic dates such as 9 May 1950 or 15 August 1971 are rather the exception than the rule.

The search for the paths along which international economic relationships could evolve towards a better order usually takes one of the two following approaches. Either specific problems are singled out, such as sovereign debt or exchange rates, in order to identify technical solutions. Or an effort is made to devise comprehensive new arrangements (a 'new Bretton Woods', global negotiations, etc.). Neither of these approaches is followed here. Instead, we will analyse the methods of international cooperation and focus the attention on two limited and yet general issues that are rarely discussed explicitly, and that are nevertheless at the heart of the problem of international cooperation both in the partial and in the systematic approach: the role to be played by rules, and the importance to be attached to the evolution of institutions. The experience of the writer of these pages is that, more often than is said or thought, failures in international cooperation depend not so much on conflicts of interests, but on conceptions and misconceptions concerning the two key policy 'ingredients' of rules and institutions.

2. Rules

A. Opposite trends nationally and internationally

It may be useful to start by commenting briefly on the concepts of rules and discretion.

In a fundamental sense, whenever a choice has to be made between conflicting objectives, judgment and discretion are necessary. From this point of view all policies are discretionary and what is called a preference for rules simply reflects a belief that conflicts between objectives are apparent but not real (e.g. that there is no trade-off between inflation and unemployment) and that, even when such conflicts do exist, frequent twists in preferences have greater costs, in terms of uncertainty and risks of mistakes, than benefits in terms of superior achievement of final objectives. In a more operational sense, a rules approach is one in which the responsible agency (the central bank, the budgetary authority, etc.) acts to stay on a predetermined path of so-called intermediate targets, giving to these a sort of priority over final policy objectives.

In no way can it be said that a rule has a stronger legal basis than discretion. For not only rules are often self-imposed but, more importantly, discretion exercised within the law is as lawful as the mere execution of a stringent norm. On the other hand, it is obvious that a rules approach is only meaningful if the interpretation of the rule is straightforward, as the grey area where interpretation is needed is in practice left to discretion.

In the last 15 years the place of rules in economic policy has undergone an evolution which seems at first sight surprising.

In domestic policies the view has gained ground that the area of discretion had grown too wide and that more rules were needed. In monetary matters, this change has taken the form of at least partial abandonment of fine-tuning and adoption of commitments to quantitative targets. Another example was the creation in 1981 of the Gold Commission in the United States, with the purpose of examining the possibility of reintroducing a gold standard to stabilize inflation and exchange rates. In budgetary matters, the drift away from discretion has emerged in a revival, as constitutional requirement, of the classical prescription of balancing the budget. Legislation along such lines has been proposed, for example in the United States and Italy. In both these areas of policy, replacement of discretionary power by rules is deemed necessary to limit both realized and potential mismanagement by the executive power.

In the international sphere both opinions and facts have, on the contrary, moved from rules to discretion. This is one of the most significant aspects of the abandonment of fixed exchange rates in 1973.

In the early 1970s, under the joint influence of theoretical thinking and difficulties in macroeconomic management, policy-makers came to consider flexible exchange rates as a way to free domestic choices from international constraints. Since it was recognized from the start that pure floating represented an academic abstraction and that some management would always be necessary, a cooperative effort was undertaken to establish the rules of a new international monetary system. In the Committee of Twenty, however, it soon became apparent that no simple set of rules could be defined for a system somewhere in between the extremes of freely flexible and of fixed exchange rates. Eventually, the only feasible solution was to forego the establishment of rules and to ask the IMF to carry out surveillance of each country's policies and their impact on exchange markets. Earlier attempts at defining statistical indicators and precise rules to govern intervention in exchange markets had to be abandoned. As stated in the 1980 annual report of the IMF: 'Surveillance must be judgmental'.

Several explanations can be suggested for the paradox of these opposing trends in the 'rules versus discretion' issue.

Firstly while in the national sphere the need may be felt to shelter policy decisions from the pressures of political constituencies and a reduction in discretion can be seen as a means to this end, in the international sphere such a need does not arise or at least is not apparent. Thus, it could be argued that the reduced involvement of national interest groups in the international sphere is both an advantage and a disadvantage: it facilitates efficient and rational decision-making in the pursuit of global welfare, but it may be felt as an element of weakness in the process of democratic control.

Secondly in the early 1970s, there were almost opposite situations in the domestic and in the international spheres respectively: much discretion in the former, many rules in the lattter. It was natural, and perhaps appropriate, to interpret the increasing problems of the time as the result of misuse of domestic discretion and excessive rigidity of international rules.

Finally, the complexity reached by the international economy, the decline of a dominant power accompanied by a much increased number of actors and a fully-integrated international capital market all contributed to the demise of the fixed-parity system. These same factors also made it exceedingly difficult, both technically and politically, to formulate a new alternative rule. *Ad hoc* arrangements and largely discretionary interpretation of loose policy prescriptions came to be regarded as the road to wisdom.

Beyond these special circumstances, there is the more general fact that the government function is perceived in very different ways in a national and in an international framework. In the former, a shift from discretion to rule appears as a way to less government; in the latter as a way to more of it.

B. Why more discretion is needed

Various arguments suggest that in our days the government of multi-country economies requires a widening of the room for discretionary decisions and a more efficient method of taking such decisions, in some instances replacing rules, but more generally as a complement to rules.

The first consideration refers to the crucial area of exchange rates. It is widely agreed that neither fixed nor perfectly floating rates are viable solutions for the years to come. Unfortunately these two regimes happen to be the only simple and unambiguous rules that can be conceived. What lies between them is an interplay between private, profit-oriented agents and public, policy-oriented institutions, with discretionary management as the critical factor. The essential point is that in an interdependent world, floating must be managed jointly and discretion has therefore to be joint discretion. There is no practical possibility of framing and disciplining managed floating in such a way that, by complying with a certain number of simple rules, careful and judgmental consideration of the interest of the partners on a case-by-case basis becomes unnecessary.

A second, related point concerns the coordination of macroeconomic policies. In its days of glory, the rule of fixed rates was largely sufficient, with the help of a stable, dominant and scarcely open US economy, to enforce an acceptable degree of *de facto* policy coordination. In a polycentric world of managed floating, the process is much more complex and requires the discussion of a wide range of instruments and policies, one that includes the balance of payments, interest rates, and budgetary and incomes policies. Each of these variables has a place in the deliberation of national policy-makers; each has direct or indirect influence on other countries. In a multi-country economy they form a matrix much too complex to be governed by a simple rule. Setting priorities, weighing the relative importance of different variables, making inter-temporal choices, and deciding which countries should act, are problems that only judgment can solve.

The increased probability of unexpected events and disturbances of world-wide magnitude requiring a prompt policy reaction is a third reason. Here economic actions are often instruments of foreign policy, when they are not substitutes for military intervention: oil embargos, assets freezes, economic sanctions, etc. In a world that is politically and strategically more divided than it is economically, this is perhaps inevitable. And since the opposing camps are themselves conglomerates of sovereign countries, often without clearly established internal leadership (the Arab League, NATO countries, non-aligned countries, etc.), the possibility of taking discretionary decisions at a national level does not automatically produce consistent action by any group of countries.

A fourth and last consideration is that in certain areas an integral part of a policy may consist in leaving economic agents in the uncertainty whether public authorities will intervene or not. A major example, one that international conditions today and in the foreseeable future render particularly important, concerns the function of lender of last resort. There must be one, but its interventions should not be taken for granted; that is, they must be discretionary.

In conclusion, a movement from rules to discretion in the government of multi-country economies is in many ways necessary, because it corresponds to the nature of the problems which have to be dealt with in the present situation. Seen from this point of view, developments that have taken place in more recent years point in the right direction. But greater reliance on discretion does not mean that the government function in a multi-country economy has to be weakened or softened. On the contrary, it means that it has to be made stronger, more effective and more adaptable to complex and unforeseen situations. In this sense, there are good reasons to question whether the evolution that we have witnessed has really entailed a sharpening of multi-country government actions or, on the contrary, a loosening of the already too loose arrangements we had. This leads to the problem of institutions.

3. Institutions

A. Institutions and cooperation

The Concise Oxford Dictionary defines an institution as follows: 'established law, custom, or practice; organization for promotion of some public object; buildings used by this'. This suggests the possibility of a great variety of organizational forms, the solemnity of a comprehensive and written constitution being not indispensable. To be sure, the 'promotion of the public object' can occur in an efficient and systematic way through uncodified cooperation, and this 'practice' may become sufficiently 'established ' to deserve the name of institution. In the international sphere, such an informal approach was the pre-1914 gold standard; an example of a formal institution, based on an international treaty, is the Bretton Woods system. It is the difference between these two approaches to monetary organization that Keynes was implicitly stressing at the end of the Bretton Woods conference, in his amused remarks about the American habit of always negotiating with the help of an army of lawyers.

True, institutions are instruments of organized cooperation; and well established cooperation can be seen as a kind of institution. However, such common elements should not generate misunderstandings. Indeed, it is essential to be fully aware of the sharp borderline between an 'institutional' and an *ad hoc* approach to cooperation.

Ad hoc cooperation is a method by which partners meet, discuss, and, if they agree, act together. If they do not agree, they will skillfully draft a press communiqué to present to the public opinion the sense of a joint commitment to general values and goals, and then return to their capitals to conduct, within the limits of their national autonomy and strength, mutually inconsistent and possibly conflicting policies. The history of the last 10 years provides numerous examples for both these possible outcomes, perhaps more numerous for the latter than for the former.[1]

Institutionalized cooperation starts where the *ad hoc* approach ends. It ensures that decisions and actions will be taken at the system level even if the parties fail to agree. In other words, it guarantees not that the right decisions will be taken, but that decisions will be taken at the right level: in our case, this means the level of the multi-country economy, as defined above, whose contribution to the 'public good' is sought.

The distinction between institutionalized and *ad hoc* cooperation is particularly important in the international sphere, where failure to agree on a common course of action means unilateral, uncoordinated, and probably conflicting actions by the individual parties. The danger of confusion is specially great today, that the practice of international consultations (in committees, councils, conferences, summits, etc) has been largely 'institutionalized', giving to the public the impression that a form of international government does exist.

It is worth noting that the institutional approach is superior not only to unsuccessful but also to successful *ad hoc* cooperation, because it is more permanent and more certain in character. The institutional approach is defined by the rules on which it is based, e.g. allowing decisions to be taken by majority rather than by the unanimity which so often hampers the effectiveness of cooperation. With cooperation the existence of a public good has to be recognized anew every time, so that realization of it is difficult. With an institution this existence is assumed.

To be effective, an international institution requires the transfer of some power from the national to the international level. This, however, does not mean that nations have

---

[1] Kenneth Dam (1976) has strongly argued in favour of what he calls the cooperative approach based on an analysis of the reform of the international monetary system after the disintegration of the Bretton Woods system. He points out that the divergence of interests and of views between the United States and the major European countries was too pronounced for agreement on a new set of rules of general and durable applicability. He argues that, in addition, the complexity of the negotiation was such that the constitution-drafting-approach would have taken much too long. In his view 'cooperation' was not simply the only feasible approach but also one with a degree of flexibility absent in the constitution-drafting-approach. Dam concludes by theorizing 'Group of Five' type of meeting as the appropriate post-Bretton Woods 'system'. To clarify the terminology: Dam's 'cooperation' is our *'ad hoc* cooperation'; and his 'constitution-drafting approach' is our 'rule'. 'Discretion plus institutions' is not considered.
For the depth and quality of his analysis Dam is the oustanding example of the common failure to distinguish between the two issues of 'rules versus discretion' and *'ad hoc* versus institutionalized cooperation'. The result is that a single line of reasoning is used to reach what seems to us a desirable conclusion on the first issue and an undesirable conclusion on the second.

to surrender control of the area of competence concerned. They will continue to exercise this control at a different level, that is within the multi-country institutions. It does not imply either that control is a zero-sum game, so that what is gained at one level is lost at another. On the contrary if the principle of establishing government at the lowest possible level is observed, the very purpose of an international institution is to regain control over phenomena which, due to increasing interdependence, would otherwise escape what is deemed to be a necessary government function.

B. Why institutions should be strengthened

The simple reason why, at the present stage of the evolution of multi-country economies, a satisfactory performance of the minimum functions of government requires a strengthening of institutions, is that the alternative method, i.e. *ad hoc* cooperation, is bound to fail in too high a proportion of cases. This is due to many causes.

In the first place, as has been argued above, the areas involving a genuine common interest of the multi-country economy which require discretionary acts of policy rather than the mechanical application of a rule, have become wider. Even at their best, cooperative methods are in general too slow to produce the necessary decisions at the right time. Notwithstanding the good intentions of the partners, the process of defining a course of collective action rarely meets the deadlines set by the pace of economic reality. As a consequence, action is taken at the lower, sub-optimal level of the nation-State thus creating welfare losses and unnecessary frictions. In recent months, for example, the difficulty of launching important economic negotiations among large countries has been explained by saying: 'Nothing can be started for the moment: 1983 is the year of the missiles'. Cooperation fails because the machine of high level diplomacy in nation-States is congested.

Furthermore, cooperative methods rarely work at their best. Their performance lies in the hands of two professions, officials and politicians, who are submitted to the very severe constraints of local constituencies even when they personally have a highly cosmopolitan spirit and a genuine willingness to cooperate. The electorate, particularly in periods of recession is generally more favourable to selfish inward-looking measures than either ministers or officials. Officials at the top are mostly engaged on the domestic front and sometimes regard activity on the international side as a waste of time, and consider those who are in charge of it as too prone to make compromises and grant concessions.

The educational process of officials involved in international negotiation requires time. Indeed, the success of a cooperative approach very much depends on the personal relationships between those who are involved in the process and on their familiarity with the values and tradition of this particular 'branch of government'. Today, however, political instability has so accelerated the turnover of goverments and high ranking officials, that the training process often fails even to maintain the existing degree of know-how and willingness to cooperate. The result is an erosion of the capital of international goodwill that is necessary to efficient *ad hoc* cooperation.

Compromises in the *ad hoc* cooperative framework are becoming more difficult also because the number of negotiating parties grows with the number of nation-States and the wider participation in the international bodies. It has been said that the Bretton Woods conference was a meeting of 'one and a half' countries; the IMF gathers now close to 150 nations. The difficulty of large group negotiation is compounded by the increasing spread of interest positions among countries, particularly during periods of economic recession. Economic summit meetings among the heads of governments of the seven major countries illustrate the difficulty of reaching decisions even among a small number of countries. When such decisions are announced their interpretation immediately becomes controversial and their acceptance by excluded countries remains a problem.

Also, the information base for decision-making is becoming so complex and controversial that cooperation is increasingly suffering from a well-known dilemma: those who have authority and vision to judge and decide, do not sufficiently master the details of the problem, while those who 'studied the dossier' often have a too weak and narrow perception of the need and urgency to reach an agreement. This is particularly so when economic problems are strongly connected. The recent years show examples both of how it is virtually impossible to arrive at a synthesis of the issues in meetings where specialists assemble and of summits where heads of States willing to compromise get lost in the details.

Finally, what policy-makers have increasingly to face are international problems at the intersection of different areas rather than problems pertaining to one area alone: trade and exchange rates, exchange rate and financing, financing and aid, etc. Yet, both *ad hoc* cooperation and the existing map of international institutions are highly specialized and offer very few possibilities of negotiating 'packages' involving different areas. The summits of the seven industrial countries are a notable exception, with the interdepartmental cooperation they promote nationally as well as internationally. Unfortunately, however, they suffer from other evils: congestion of problems relative to the time available for solving them, lack of a 'central' independent body entitled to speak for the common interest, absence of essential partners like LDCs or OPEC, preference for publicity to substance.

Even if the above seem rather compelling arguments, it is nevertheless worth considering the popular objections to the main contention that international institutions should be strengthened. Though phrased in many ways, they all boil down to questioning either the need for or the possibility of building stronger institutions.

As to need, the argument is usually formulated by saying that if every country keeps its own house in order, international order will automatically follow. In a weaker form, the priority of domestic order is advocated. In either form, these objections ignore not only interdependence, but the fact that 'order', far from being a single valued variable, is the very object of political choice in a democratic society. The flaw in the 'house in order' argument is that it presents a necessary condition as a sufficient one. Its practical strength lies in the fact that it is generally used by large and strong economies to justify a certain disregard for the consequences that their policies may have on other countries.

As to possibility, it is of course an open question whether it is realistic to pursue the objective of strengthening international institutions in a period in which so many wise men have relegated supranationalism to the attic of postwar dreams. One should not forget, however, that institutions also change without requiring dramatic moves nor even new legislation. In many instances institutions are simply reshaped by the changing nature of the problems confronting them. Some claim that a recent example of such a change is the new role played by the BIS in arranging bridging operations for debtor countries in liquidity difficulties. Since such systemic changes can take place independently of each nation's will, it would certainly be preferable to control them rationally rather than accept to be driven by events. Nor should it be feared that changing an institution takes too much time. Even if that were the case, it would be better to advance late than never. But, more importantly, this is not the case. What takes time is negotiation on details. Historical experience shows that systemic changes are negotiated quickly because what makes them possible are special political, or crisis, circumstances which usually do not remain for long. The Bretton Woods Conference lasted a few weeks. The EMS was made in about six months. On the contrary, an EC negotiation to harmonize technical norms on rear reflectors of automobiles may take years.

One final word is perhaps in order to counter what is a common criticism raised as regards the performance of existing international institutions, namely that they are not, after all, so much better nor so much more efficient than the gatherings of nation-State leaders practicing *ad hoc* cooperation. The answer to that criticism is simply that it is true. Indeed present day institutions, in as much as they are not really given the charters, the powers and the instruments to follow a genuine institutional approach are bound to fall back into the *ad hoc* pattern and to act as an additional partner in an exercise of *ad hoc* cooperation. Thus, the ultimate sense of the prescription to strengthen international institutions is that of setting in motion a process whereby these are given the means to play their proper, institutional role.

4. Examples

The questions examined above are particularly relevant in the field of international money and finance for several reasons. Money and financial intermediation are areas where governments and public authorities have always played an important role and interdependence, particularly in exchange rates, is there by definition. Also, in the last two decades the process of internationalization has been particularly rapid in financial matters. Moreover, the evolution of financial markets, institutions, and instruments has been extremely rapid and has posed new problems to the role of governments. Finally, the dissociation between savings and investments has come so much to involve countries as well as individual economic agents that the process of financial intermediation has become genuinely international.

A. Exchange rates among large currencies

Exchange rate relationships among large currencies in the last 20 years are perhaps the outstanding example of the difficult search for the right balance between rules and discretion on the one side, and between the cooperative and the institutional approach on the other side.

In the pre-1971 system, the borderline between rules and discretion was drawn in such a way as to leave a large role to the rule of fixed rates and a small one to the discretion of changes in parities, a discretion that tended to be exercised at the national rather than the international level. The consequence was that rules have tended first to be too rigidly followed and then to be broken. In that regime real exchange rates moved far from plausible equilibrium levels because of insufficient, rather than excessive, mobility of nominal exchange rates. When par values were changed, as happened for the pound sterling, the German mark, and the French franc, they tended to move too late. More importantly, those changes were essentially the result of unilateral decisions taken by the countries concerned, with the IMF providing little more than a formal ratification.

The Bretton Woods system would have functioned more efficiently, and perhaps would have not collapsed, if parity changes had been more timely and multilateral in nature. Ideally, multilateralism and the central institutions should have exerted greater pressure to enforce changes in parity, and in the price of gold, on countries which were reluctant to undertake them. But the system had been created out of the experience of the 1930s, in which exchange rate mobility had been abused, and it had an implicit bias in favour of fixed rates. The area of discretion was embodied in the rather loose concept of 'fundamental disequilibrium'. Thus, the combination of a weak institutional framework and the stigma associated with the condition of fundamental disequilibrium, particularly for deficit, high inflation countries produced the excessive rigidity that eventually led to the breakdown of the system.

August 1971 was followed by the attempt to establish new parities and to reform the international monetary system. Both failed on the critical front on which the pre-1971 system had also failed, that is the establishment of an efficient mix of rules and discretion on the one side, and of *ad hoc* and institutional cooperation on the other.

As to the Smithsonian parities, they came under increasing pressure, and when the pressure became unbearable the outcome was a regime of floating rates rather than a realignment.

As to the reform of the international monetary system, the long and difficult work of the Committee of Twenty produced a regime which can be seen as the 'negative' of the pre-1971 situation: discretion and rule have, so to speak, inverted their roles. In the post-1973 situation the variability of exchange rates has become the multilateral rule, while 'discipline' has become the object of unilateral discretion. In other words, the lesson drawn from the period up to 1973 has been that the multi-country economy should not aim at any form of declared, negotiated, and defended parities. Rather, it had to accept 'realistically' the impossibility of returning to a par-value system and try to avoid exchange rate manipulation for trade purposes by the members of the system. The avoidance of such dangers was entrusted formally to IMF surveillance, and in practice to what came to be called the Library Group and later the Group of Five.

Ten years of experience with these arrangements have convinced both economists and policy-makers that the new 'order' is not satisfactory. Inflation, protectionist pressures, uncertainties and inefficiencies in the allocative process are among the consequences of the long and profound cycles in real exchange rates that have been experienced in recent years. Between minimum and maximum levels real exchange rates have moved by 60% for the British pound, 40% for the dollar and the yen and 20% for the German mark. One could almost say that the pre-1971 and the post-1973 systems have paradoxically produced the same consequence of protracted misalignments of real exchange rates. This paradox ceases to be one if it is recognized that, seen from the points of view of the 'rules versus discretion' and of the 'institutional versus *ad hoc* cooperation' approach, they largely belong to the same category. They both fail to offer a satisfactory solution to the problem of multilateral discretionality. One could almost go as far as to say that if this central problem had been fully resolved, the functioning of the two systems would have produced essentially the same results. In one case discretion would be used to reduce exchange rate rigidities associated with a fixed parity system; in the other, it would have been used to reduce excessive movements associated with a floating system.

Historical events can be read in several ways, not necessarily mutually exclusive. The reading suggested here for the experience of the last 15 years of monetary cooperation is not that the Bretton Woods rule has at some point become inappropriate and that the Committee of Twenty later failed to invent a new, more appropriate one. The movement from rule to discretion was unavoidable, and it could have taken place even under the old Articles of Agreement of the IMF. Similarly, the new, looser rule incorporated in the amended Articles of Agreement was, again, probably appropriate insofar as it recognized, at the normative level, the need for greater discretion. In both cases what was missing is the exercise of the required discretion, and this was due, in both cases, to a fundamental weakness of the institution which should have practised this discretionality. This does not mean that the decisions taken would have always been the right ones, just as policy decisions taken at the national level are not always the right ones. Nor does it mean that the institution had necessarily to be a formal one, working on the basis of formal legislation.

The outcome of the 1973-76 reform negotiations is not the technical failure of the Committee of Twenty in devising a new rule. It is the political failure of the major countries in devising efficient institutions. The talents and powers of the great men of the 1970s were deployed to manage skillfully an unviable system, rather than to create a better system. And one cannot help feeling a sense of lost opportunities both in seeing the state of cooperation among large world currencies today and in reading the reassessment of the past and the proposals for the future that are now offered by those men. The wisdom of the saying 'do not bequeath ideals, bequeath institutions' has been lost in a crucial time.

B. European monetary cooperation

The evolution of European monetary cooperation over the same period has followed a somewhat different pattern and is, on the whole, more like a success story.

Compared to the world system, the European system presents perhaps more differences than analogies. Most of these differences turned out to have a favourable influence on the process of monetary cooperation. Firstly, Community institutions are equipped to take decisions, and to introduce important institutional innovations, by means of procedures which are much simpler than those required at the world level. For example, the snake, the European Monetary Cooperation Fund, and the EMS were all created by a decision taken at the level of Community ministers and central bank governors, without any process of parliamentary ratification. This is due to the large legislative powers that the Treaty of Rome grants to the Community institutions and to the Council of Ministers in particular. Moreover, there is no country in the Community where the parliament limits the negotiating ability of the executive as much as the Congress does with the Administration in the United States.

Secondly, economic integration between Community countries is both wider and deeper than economic integration world-wide. The interdependence between monetary, trade, financial and macroeconomic cooperation is much more evident. Policy conflicts and inconsistencies emerge and develop their negative consequences faster in the tight Community system than in the rather loose international context. Thus, the Community has perceived the danger that its trade relationships were running because of the lack of a commonly agreed monetary order some years before this same danger became evident at the world level.

Thirdly, the problem of leadership manifests itself in rather different terms at the Community and at the world level. In the latter, after a long period of almost unquestioned domination, the United States have reached a position in which they do not have the power to impose their solution to problems, but they have enough power to prevent solutions they dislike. In Europe there is greater balance, so that the need for compromise is fully recognized.

If these three elements tend to give the Community a certain advantage over the world system, a fourth one, more specific to the monetary field, tends to be a source of complications. This is the fact that European monetary integration around one of the member currencies is far more difficult than an equivalent aggregation around the dollar. The German mark, which could be regarded as the natural candidate, dominates the European monetary scene much less than the dollar does in the world context. Moreover, the German authorities have long been reluctant to let their currency play a major international role. And other large European countries would be unwilling to accept a DM-based system.

For Europe, as for the world, the problem of monetary cooperation is essentially one involving the leading currencies of the area. Small countries, which are in general relatively more open, tend to peg to leading currencies anyway. Indeed, more than 50 countries are currently pegging their currencies formally to a major currency; two-thirds of them are pegged to the dollar.

In the period up to 1978 European countries, taken as a group, pursued two inconsistent paths: full independence in macroeconomic policies, and the creation of a system of stable intra-Community exchange rates. The first path prevailed over the second.

While Germany and some small countries like Austria, the Netherlands, Belgium, and Switzerland, were successful in keeping inflation under control, France, the United Kingdom and Italy experienced long periods of double digit inflation (reaching for these last two countries levels of more than 20%), made periodic attempts to stabilize prices, and never succeeded in participating in an exchange rate system for more than relatively short periods. Moreover, an exchange rate 'system' was probably conceived too much in a 'Bretton Woods way' to be realistic. The idea of a rigid rule was implicitly dominant. That of an institution capable of discretionary decisions did not emerge.

From March 1976 to March 1979 the snake became a system of small currencies pegged to the German mark. The snake had thus failed to link together the major European currencies, but played an essential role in preparing for the EMS. Not only did it show that a regional system of declared and defended parities could function even in the post-Bretton Woods era, but, more importantly, it provided a first test of the special blend of rules and multilateral discretion that was later, and in more difficult circumstances, going to characterize the EMS.

The EMS is too recent history to require more than a brief mention. The analogy of its provisions with the Bretton Woods arrangements, and the wide divergence of inflation rates in Europe, explain the scepticism with which the EMS was hailed in some quarters. And had it been known in 1978 that the following years were going to be troubled by a second oil shock, a dollar shock, the longest recession of the postwar period, continuous trade frictions and a debt crisis, not only the scepticism would have been much greater, but perhaps the founding fathers would not have had the courage to undertake what was considered a bold initiative even with the expectation of a more stable environment.

The EMS has succeeded in supporting intra-Community trade with a sufficient degree of monetary order, in reducing exchange rate variability, and in exerting a reasonable, though not decisive, pressure on national governments to orient macro-policies towards monetary stability and coordination. In all the EMS countries growth rates in monetary aggregates were lower in 1978-82 than in 1974-78. Moreover, since the inception of the EMS there has been a significant increase in the correlation between interest rate movements of the participating countries. In the EMS central rate decisions have become truly collective decisions, rather than multilateral ratifications of unilateral decisions: the system has achieved here something that Bretton Woods probably never achieved. Moreover, it has become increasingly the case that parity changes are accompanied by important changes in other aspects of economic policy. Realignments have not been unduly delayed, and when they were delayed, this was basically justified by the need to reach the point in which the domestic situation in a country made it politically possible to accompany a realignment with a meaningful policy change.

The EMS has obtained these results by combining rules and discretion, by distributing decision-making powers between the national and the supranational level, and by linking trade, macroeconomic and monetary considerations in a way that can be, *ex post,* recognized as more balanced and more efficient than perhaps any of the other experiences in multi-country economies over the last 15 years.

Of course the fundamental incompatibility between unrestrained national sovereignty in fiscal and monetary policy and *de facto* capital mobility and supranationalism in trade and exchange rates remains. From this point of view the EMS has not fundamentally corrected the precarious nature of the government of a multi-country economy. This also suggests that it is not realistic to blame the EMS for the still insufficient degree of economic convergence among Community countries. But the fact remains that the EMS has been quite successful in coupling discretion with institutionalized cooperation in a world in which discretion tends to go with unilateralism and cooperation tends to be sought by way of rules.

5. Conclusions

For more than 20 years multi-country economies, as measured by world trade and international financial intermediation, have grown at about twice the speed of national economies, as measured by GDP and 'domestic' financial assets.

This extraordinary dynamism has enabled multi-country economies to grow out of the systemic problems arising from the coexistence of sovereign powers. It has reduced conflicts. It has enlarged vested interest in the maintenance of open trade. It has fully developed not only the potential of the arrangements and institutions created in the 1940s and in the 1950s, but also the opportunities offered by a certain lack of arrangements and institutions. It has concealed the shortcomings and the lacunae of the instruments available for the government of multi-country economies.

The wide divergence between these two speeds of growth can not but be a transitory phenomenon, one that lasts the time necessary to fill the gaps due to pre-existing trade and financial barriers. As long as it is underway, the process of removing barriers which has been initiated at some point in the past continues to play the role of an act of government, replacing in some way active management of the multi-country economy. When this function is exhausted and the multi-country economy's growth rate tends to slow down to that of national economies, it becomes clear that while national economies often have an excess of government, multi-country economies have too little of it.

In difficult times, when risks, uncertainties, and conflicts are experienced in trade and financial relationships, the same economic agents which benefited so much from the removal of barriers and from international economic integration, themselves turn to 'governmental' powers for support and protection. Today, governmental powers are only national. With the exception of the European Communities, there is no multi-country economic power to which an individual economic agent can address itself directly. The almost inevitable consequence is that government interventions in support of the economy tend to have a protectionist character and to erode the capital of international cooperation and goodwill. Here is where the process of multi-country economic integration could reverse: in the 1930s it took only four years for world trade to shrink from three to one million gold dollars.

This paper suggests that an important condition to avoid the danger of disintegration is to accept the movement from rules to discretion that has characterized the evolution of international economic relationships in the last decade, but to firmly establish the exercise of discretion at the level of the multi-country economy concerned, rather than letting it fall to the lower level of national economies.

As an official, the author of these reflections is acutely aware of the enormous, almost unsurmountable difficulty of progressing in the direction suggested here. Caution, realism, awareness of the narrow limits of what is concretely possible, are indispensable instruments of any successful action. However, they do not replace the sense of what is the necessary direction. This paper was concerned with the latter.

Brussels, Rome – July 1983.

References

BERGSTRAND J.: 'Is Exchange Rate Variability "Excessive"?', *New England Economic Review*, September/October 1983.

CAMPS, Miriam: *Collective Management*, New York: McGraw Hill, 1980s Project, Council on Foreign Relations, 1981.

COMMISSION OF THE EUROPEAN COMMUNITIES: *Exchange Rate Variability and Interventions within the European Monetary System*, mimeo, August 1982.

COMMISSION OF THE EUROPEAN COMMUNITES: *Five Years of Monetary Cooperation in Europe (March 1979 – March 1984)*, 11/74/84-E, 23.2.1984.

COOPER, Richard N.: *The Economics of Interdependence: Economic Policy in the Atlantic Community*, New York: McGraw Hill, 1968.

COOPER, Richard N.: 'Macroeconomic Policy Adjustment in Interdependent Economies', *The Quarterly Journal of Economics*, February 1969, 1-24.

DAM, Kenneth W.: 'The Role of Rules in the International Monetary System', Law and Economics Center Monograph, Miami, 1976.

DAM, Kenneth W.: *The Rules of the Game*, Chicago, 1982.

FRENKEL J.: 'Flexible Exchange Rates, Prices and the Role of News', *Journal of Political Economy*, August 1981.

FRENKEL J., MUSSA M.: 'The Efficiency of Foreign Exchange Markets and Measures of Turbulence', *American Economic Review*, May 1980.

HOOPER P., KOHLHAGEN S.: 'The Effect of Exchange Rate Uncertainty on the Prices and Volume of International Trade', *Journal of International Economics*, November 1978.

IMF: *The European Monetary System*, IMF Occasional Paper No 19, May 1983.

INTERNATIONAL MONETARY FUND: *Annual Report 1980*, Washington, 1980.

KENEN P.: *Exchange Rate Instability: Measurement and Implications*, International Finance Section, Research Memorandum, Princeton University, June 1979.

KENEN P.: *A Note on the Volatility of Floating Exchange Rates*, mimeo, Princeton University, April 1983.

LANYI A., SUSS E.: *Exchange Rate Variability: Alternative Measures and Interpretation*, IMF Staff Papers, December 1982.

LEVICH R.: *Overshooting in the Foreign Exchange Market*, Group of Thirty Occasional Paper No 5, 1981.

MICOSSI S., PADOA-SCHIOPPA T.: *Short-term Interest Rates Linkages Between the United States and Europe*, Banca d'Italia, *Temi di Discussione* No 33, August 1984.